THE LAUGHTER C

LIVERPOOL ENGLISH TEXTS AND STUDIES
General editors: JONATHAN BATE and BERNARD BEATTY

This long-established series has a primary emphasis on close reading, critical exegesis and textual scholarship. Studies of a wide range of works are included, although the list has particular strengths in the Renaissance, and in Romanticism and its continuations.

THE LAUGHTER
OF FOXES

A Study of Ted Hughes

KEITH SAGAR

LIVERPOOL UNIVERSITY PRESS

First published 2000 by
LIVERPOOL UNIVERSITY PRESS
4 Cambridge Street, Liverpool L69 7ZU

British Library Cataloguing-in-Publication Data
A British Library CIP Record is available for this book

ISBN 0-85323-565-1 cased
     0-85323-575-9 paper

Typeset by Northern Phototypesetting Co. Ltd, Bolton
Printed in Great Britain by
Redwood Books, Trowbridge, Wilts.

Contents

THE HEALER

by Mark Hinchliffe

For Ted Hughes – A Thanksgiving

1. Hearing your voice
   awakened me,
   unblocked my ears,
   as if I had been underwater
   up to that moment,
   and suddenly surfaced
   to an island of
   wonderful sounds,

   and now the fox
   keeps walking out of
   the darkness into my head.

2. A class of children,
   held by *The Iron Man*,
   acted the story.
   One barely able to read,
   who hardly spoke,
   jumped on the desk
   and switched the blackboard
   light on and off
   to be the Iron Man's eyes.

   He held chalk between his fingers,
   and crawled around the floor
   as he pieced himself together.

   Later he wrote:
   'I aket as the Iron Man we had
   the lit on and off then I fell off

the besg I had chars on top of
me it look riyel then I got
togeser a gen.
I lad in the fiver three tames
and the jogen lad in the sun
three tames he give in I wan.
I was singing in the sky'.

And Ariel sang to me,
Crouched on his shoulders.

3. At Lumb Bank
   you read your journal poems
   about sheep, lambs, cows,
   ravens, death, births.
   Persephone walked
   across the room,
   and sang into
   my ear
   of Spring's return.

4. You stand over the pool,
   draw pictures
   with your staff.

   you lift them out,
   shimmering rainbows, mirrors
   they are food and drink,
   they are our parents,
   our children.

   the pictures change,
   and we are changed.

   A caged jaguar sends
   his spirit into

a dancing boy
who seeds the wasteland.
A burning fox melts
into the laughter of foxes.

You stand over the pool,
and every third thought
is healing
how to heal,

every third thought
is living,
how to live.

And you bury your books
deep into the body of England,
where they are carried
by rivers,

emerging again,
looking all around,
rubbing their eyes,

looking for places
to sink their roots,
like the piper's lost children,

like leaves stretching
from a green head.

PREFACE

Ted Hughes is, I believe, the greatest British writer of the second half of the twentieth century, and the latest addition to the great tradition of Western Literature which includes, among many others, Homer, the Greek tragic poets, Shakespeare, Blake, Wordsworth, Coleridge, Keats, Whitman, Hopkins, Yeats, Lawrence, Eliot and the post-war East European poets. In accordance with Eliot's dictum that every new great writer added to the tradition changes the tradition, Hughes has changed the way we read all these writers, not only those on whom he has actually written.

In the first chapter I try to describe the mythic nature of Hughes' imagination, and to claim great importance for the healing power of such imagination at the threshold of a new and dark millennium. This seems to me necessary because criticism, before it can undertake anything else (if there is anything else it is qualified to undertake), must first reach the point of being able to actually read the work – read it, that is, not in terms of some prior expectations or critical theory, but in terms of what we can divine of the author's own inner idea of what he or she is after. Every creative writer has a unique imaginative context, a matrix of psychologically or spiritually active imagery, for example, and can write living poems only out of it. To become an adequate reader one must approach the work, in Hughes' words, 'with the cooperative, imaginative attitude of a co-author', enter as deeply as one can the writer's imaginative world. Otherwise it is time wasted to read that author at all. Hughes' imaginative world was deeply mythic, in the sense of both drawing on the body of myth we have inherited and spontaneously creating new myths, or new expressions of the primal myths. This is the theme of my first chapter.

Hughes began to receive in the last year of his life some long overdue recognition, in the form of glowing reviews, awards and massive sales. Nevertheless, even in the obituaries, the media kept to their own agenda, in which sex, suicide and guilt are far more interesting than poetry, so that the general impression built up by the media over many years remained intact, that Hughes' greatest claim to fame was as the husband of Sylvia Plath. And the enormous amount of attention given to *Birthday Letters* showed little interest in what was at the heart of that relationship, the deep commitment of both Hughes and Plath to poetry: 'we only did what poetry told us to do'. This is the theme of the second chapter.

Like many other poets before him, Hughes fostered the half-truth that great poems write themselves in a single draft, which cannot be bettered. Though no doubt this does occasionally happen, and certainly happened occasionally for Hughes, the great majority of his poems had to be worked at over many drafts, as his manuscripts reveal, before he discovered what wanted to get itself expressed. In the third chapter I try to show how this process worked with a fairly typical Hughes poem, 'The Dove Came', from *Adam and the Sacred Nine*.

Ironically, the two works that received most of the belated acclaim, *Birthday Letters* and *Tales from Ovid*, are not part of the main body of Hughes' achievement, since, splendid as they are of their kind, neither allowed Hughes the total imaginative freedom his greatest work needed, each being Hughes' treatment of already existing material, whether Ovid's tales or the already well-documented factual record of his relationship with Sylvia Plath. In both works the plot was predetermined.

And by identifying the characters in *Birthday Letters* specifically as Hughes and Plath, the poems inevitably cast the reader in the role of voyeur, however deeply our sympathies might be engaged. *Birthday Letters* sold ten times more copies than any other Hughes book in its first year, not because it is ten times better as poetry but because there are ten times as many voyeurs as poetry-lovers among book-buyers, and a hundred times as many among newspaper editors.

Though Hughes, having begun by despising the confessional mode in poetry, came to see it as of great value, particularly as autotherapy, the claim that *Birthday Letters* is the summit of his achievement is as absurd as it would be to claim that the sonnets (revelatory as they are) are the pinnacle of Shakespeare's. As Hughes said in the *Paris Review* interview in 1995:

Once you've contracted to write only the truth about yourself
– as in some respected kinds of modern verse, or as in Shakespeare's sonnets – then you can too easily limit yourself to what
you imagine are the truths of the ego that claims your conscious
biography. Your own equivalent of what Shakespeare got into
his plays is simply foregone. (69–70)

Though there are wonderful poems from both before and after,
the body of work on which Hughes' reputation should stand (his
equivalent of what Shakespeare got into his plays) is almost everything he wrote in the seventies and very early eighties – the poems
collected in *Season Songs* (1974), *Cave Birds* (1975), *Gaudete* (1977),
Remains of Elmet (1979), *Moortown* (1979) and *River* (1983). These
books contain the inestimable healing gifts which are Hughes' legacy
to us all.

In a 1996 interview (Negev) Hughes said:

Every work of art stems from a wound in the soul of the artist.
When a person is hurt, his immune system comes into opera-
tion and the self-healing process takes place, mental and physical. Art is a psychological component of the auto-immune
system that gives expression to the healing process. That is why
great works of art make us feel good.

There are artists who concentrate on expressing the damage,
the blood, the mangled bones, the explosion of pain, in order
to rouse and shock the reader. And there are those who hardly
mention the circumstances of the wound, they are concerned
with the cure.

There are also artists who begin in the first group and painfully, mar-
vellously, drag themselves into the second (though perhaps to discover, at the end, that some damage is incurable). In doing so they
are enacting, in their work, the classic quest myth. What Hughes said
of Plath's work is equally true of his own: 'The poems are chapters in
a mythology where the plot, seen as a whole and in retrospect, is
strong and clear' (Faas 180). Nearly every poem from *The Hawk in
the Rain* to *River* is a station on the spiritual and poetic journey by
which Hughes, with many set-backs, many cul-de-sacs, arrived at last

full circle from a world made of blood back to that same world now seen, as a result of the journey with all its transfiguring pain, to be a world made of light. This is the theme of the fourth chapter. The journey ends with *River*. Though there are fine poems from the remaining years, they are few in comparison with the outpouring of the seventies, and to one side of the driving quest. After *River* Hughes lapsed largely into prose and translations, putting his own imagination at the service of the imaginations of others – of Aeschylus and Euripides, Ovid, Shakespeare, Racine, Coleridge, Pushkin, Wedekind, Lorca, Eliot, Keith Douglas, William Golding, Leonard Baskin and Marin Sorescu. *Birthday Letters* also stands apart. Hughes came to feel that they were the poems he should perhaps have written, or tried to write, in the three-year silence after 1963. That they took over 30 years to force themselves into utterance is its own tragedy.

The Life and Songs of the Crow would undoubtedly have been one of Hughes' greatest works had that vast project not been aborted in 1969 following the second paralysing 'explosion of pain' in Hughes' life. *Crow* itself is a gathering of what could be salvaged from the debris. These fragments from the first two-thirds of the story have been widely misinterpreted because readers lacked the necessary context of Crow's quest, the 'epic folk-tale' in which Crow was to have been transformed. Hughes came to regret not having provided this essential framework in some form, and always gave chunks of it whenever he read Crow poems. But he declined to publish this material until he gave me permission to do so in this book.

ACKNOWLEDGEMENTS

Hughes scholarship has been to date gratifyingly cooperative. During the 20 years this book has been in the making, I have received help of many kinds from more scholars than I can hope to name. It would be invidious to try to establish any priority, so I shall list some of them alphabetically: Nick Bishop, Roger Elkin, Colin Fraser, Nick Gammage, Mark Hinchliff, Fred Rue Jacobs, Claas Kazzer, Terry Gifford, Joanny Moulin, Colin Raw, Neil Roberts, Len Scigaj, Ann Skea, Steve Tabor. I should also like to thank Olwyn Hughes and Daniel Huws for the information they have generously supplied, and to acknowledge the great deal I have learned from the many students with whom I have studied Ted Hughes in adult classes.

'The Genesis of "The Dove Came"' is reprinted from *The Challenge of Ted Hughes*, by kind permission of Macmillan. The reprinting of the poem from the Rainbow Press edition of *Adam and the Sacred Nine* is by kind permission of Olwyn Hughes. All quotations from unpublished sources are by kind permission of Ted Hughes and the Ted Hughes Estate.

ABBREVIATIONS

ABS	Australian Broadcasting Corporation
ATH	Keith Sagar, *The Art of Ted Hughes*, Cambridge University Press, 1975
AS	Ann Skea
BBC TP	British Broadcasting Corporation Tape
BF	A. Stevenson, *Bitter Fame*, Viking, London, 1989
BS	Broadside
CUP	Cambridge University Press
DT	*The Daily Telegraph*
IOS	*Independent on Sunday*
KS	Keith Sagar
LE	Limited Edition
PBS	Poetry Book Society, London
PR	*Paris Review*, Interview, Spring 1995
SPJ	Hughes and McCullough (eds), *The Journals of Sylvia Plath*, Ballantine, NY, 1991
SPLH	A. Plath (ed.), *Sylvia Plath: Letters Home*, Harper and Row, NY, 1975
SW	J. Malcolm, *The Silent Woman*, Picador, London, 1994
TH	Ted Hughes
UU	E. Faas, *The Unaccommodated Universe*, Black Sparrow, Santa Barbara, 1980
WP	T. Hughes, *Winter Pollen*, Faber, London, 1994

A TIMELINE OF HUGHES' LIFE AND WORK
by Ann Skea

This list of Ted Hughes' publications, life events and interests is not comprehensive. It was compiled from books, newspaper articles, recordings, letters and notes to give an overview of important and formative influences that have helped to shape his work. It also suggests the date at which some of his works originated.

It is best used in conjunction with K. Sagar and S. Tabor, *Ted Hughes: A Bibliography, 1946–1995*, 2nd edn, Mansell, London, 1998.

1930
Born 17 August, Mytholmroyd, Yorkshire, to William Henry and Edith (née Farrar) Hughes. Sister (Olwyn) two years older; brother (Gerald) 'was ten years older than me and made my early life a kind of paradise ... which was ended abruptly by the war' (Letter to *AS*, November 1982, re. 'Two').
'...[B]rought up on his grandmother's farm' (Memoir, *DT*, 21 November 1998). 'My first six years shaped everything' (Interview, *DT*, 2 November 1998).

1937
Family moves to Mexborough, South Yorkshire. Owns a newspaper and tobacco shop.

1943
Begins at Mexborough Grammar School.

1945
First poems written. 'Zulus and the Wild West ... All in imitation of Kipling' (*UU* 20).

1946
First poems and prose pieces published in school magazine, *The Don*

and Dearne. An essay, 'Harvesting', contains seeds of later story, 'The Harvesting'.
Influenced by folk-tales, Shakespeare, Yeats, Hopkins, Virgil, Eliot, the 'very different rhythms of the King James Bible' (*WP* 5–6).

1948
Wins open exhibition to Pembroke College, Cambridge.

1949
Writes 'Song'. Begins two years of national (military) service. Stationed at a remote radar station at Fylingdales where he had nothing to do but read and reread Shakespeare and watch the grass grow. 'He literally knows Shakespeare by heart' (*SPLH*, 2 August 1956).

1951
Enters Pembroke to read English. 'I spent most of my time reading folklore and Yeats's poems' (*UU* 56). 'Beethoven's music was my therapy' (*PR* 85).

1952
Family returns to West Yorkshire to live at The Beacon, Heptonstall Slack.

1953
Fox dream. Drops English to study archaeology and anthropology (*WP* 8–9).

Publications (major publications in bold)	Work in progress, events, interests and influences

1954

'The Little Boys and the Seasons' (*Granta*) – pseudonym Daniel Hearing. 'Song of the Sorry Lovers' (*Chequer*) – pseudonym Peter Crew. 'The Jaguar' / 'The Casualty' (*Chequer*).

Graduates from Cambridge. Writes 'The Conversion of the Reverend Skinner', 'The Hag', 'Law in the Country of the Cats'.

1955

'The Woman with Such High Heels' (*Delta*). 'Comment on *Chequer*' (review – pseudonym Jonathan Dyce).

Living in London (Rugby St.) and Cambridge. Rose gardener, nightwatchman, zoo attendant, schoolteacher, reader for J. Arthur Rank. Planning to teach in Spain then emigrate to Australia (*SPLH*, 4 May). Reads a Penguin of American Poets 'that started me writing', 'infatuated with John Crowe Ransom' (*UU* 210). Writes 'The Thought-Fox', 'Secretary', 'Soliloquy of a Misanthrope', 'Billet-Doux', 'Fallgrief's Girlfriends', 'Two Phases', 'The Decay of Vanity', 'Childbirth' and 'Wind' (1955–6).

1956

Many *Hawk in the Rain* poems published, including 'Fallgrief's Girlfriends', and the poems that were to become 'Law in the Country of the Cats', 'Secretary' and 'Soliloquy of a Misanthrope', in the *St Botolph's Review.*

26 February – Launch of *St Botolph's Review*. Meets Sylvia Plath.
25 March – Second meeting with Sylvia.
16 June – Marries Sylvia Plath at St George the Martyr's Church, Bloomsbury.
June/July – In Spain. Writing animal fables. (*SPJ*, 'Benidorm').
August – To Heptonstall.
31 August – To Top Withens ('Wuthering Heights').
September – Audition for BBC poetry readings (*SPLH*, 28 September).
10 October – To London for BBC reading of Yeats's poems. Misses Sylvia at station (*SPLH*, 16 October;

1957
Many *Hawk in the Rain* poems
published.
April – 'O'Kelly's Angel' (story)
(*Granta*). May – 'Bartholemew Pygge
Esquire' (story) (*Granta*).
August – First *Lupercal* poem
published: 'Dream of Horses' (*Grecourt
Review*). September – **The Hawk in
the Rain**. December – 'Everyman's
Odyssey' (*Landmarks and Voyages*).

1958
Many *Lupercal* poems published
'invocations to writing', 'a deliberate
effort to find a simple concrete
language' (*UU* 209).

Birthday Letters, 'Fate Playing').
November – Living in Cambridge (55
Eltisley Ave.). Teaching English and
drama at local secondary modern
school. Sylvia Plath types out and
submits *The Hawk in the Rain* to
Harper's competition: 'I don't see how
they can help but accept this; it's the
most rich and powerful work since
Yeats and Dylan Thomas' (*SPLH*, 21
November). Astrology, horoscopes,
hypnotism, tarot and experimenting
with Ouija board. (*SPLH*, 28
October).

February – *The Hawk in the Rain* wins
Harper publication contest. Pan and
Ouija board (*SPLH*, 8 February).
Snatchcraftington, alphabetical fables
(*SPLH*, 24 February). Writes 'View of a
Pig', 'Quest' and 'Thrushes' at Eltisley
Ave. April – BBC reading (1 poem).
May – Hears Robert Frost reading at
Cambridge (*SPLH*, 24 May). June – To
Yorkshire. Then to USA (Wellesley
then Cape Cod). August – To
Northampton (337 Elm St.). Sylvia
teaching at Smith College. Meets Bill
and Dido Merwin.

Spring – Teaching at Amherst,
University of Massachusetts. 11 April –
Poetry reading at Harvard (*SPLH*, 22
April). 4 May – Meets Baskins
(Leonard and Esther). May – Reading
Creon in Paul Roche's *Oedipus* trans. at
Smith (*SPJ*, 19 May). June – Six
Lupercal poems recorded in USA. Rents
flat in Boston (Willow St., Beacon
Hill). July – Summons Pan with Ouija
board (*SPJ*, 4 July; *SPLH*, 5 July).
August – BBC (6 *Lupercal* poems).
December – Making wolf mask (*SPJ*,
28 December)

1959

Pike (*BS*) (*LE* 50). Many *Lupercal* poems published. Reviews: *Weekend in Dinlock*, Segal.

April – Awarded Guggenheim fellowship (*SPJ*, 23 April). Summer – Touring N. America by car. Had been pursuing Cabalistic and Hermetic interests for some time (*UU* 41). Doing 'exercises in meditation and invocation ... [from] magic literature' (*UU* 210). September – Yaddo Artists' Colony for 11 weeks. Writes 'Things Present', the last of the *Lupercal* poems. Meets Chou Wen-Chung, agrees to collaborate on *Bardo Thodol*. October – Writes *House of Taurus* (scrapped) 'symbolic drama based on the Euripides play *The Bacchae*' (*SPLH*, 7 October). Precursor to *Gaudete* (*ATH* 186–7). November – Revising *Meet My Folks* (*SPJ*, 1 November) December – Returns to England (Heptonstall).

1960

March – **Lupercal**. 'The Caning', 'Very fine, very difficult' (*SPJ*, 15 November), 'The Rainhorse', 'Sunday', 'Snow', 'The Harvesting' (stories).

Writing *Recklings* and *Wodwo* poems and radio plays. Writing and rewriting *Bardo Thodol* libretto (unperformed). Setting: Chou Wen-Chung. Dreams of *The Wound* action and text (*ABC* interview, 1976). February – Move to London (3 Chalcot Sq., Primrose Hill). Reading at Oxford Poetry Society (*BF* 184). March – Using Merwins' study *The Hawk in the Rain* wins Somerset Maugham award (*SPLH*, 24 March). *Lupercal* wins Hawthornden Prize (*SPLH*, 27 March). 1 April – Frieda Rebecca born. April – Dinner at T.S. Eliot's (*SPLH*, 26 April) 'one of the very great poets. One of the few' (*PR* 73). May – Meets Alan Sillitoe and his wife, Ruth Fainlight (*BF* 213).

June – Cocktail party at Fabers.
Photograph with Faber Poets (*SPLH*,
24 June), 'Duk-dam charm to call fools
in a circle' (*ABC* interview, 1976).
BBC accepts *House of Aries* (*SPLH*, 9
July). BBC – plays, stories and talks.

1961

March – *Dully Gumption's College
Courses*. 'Theology', 'a more
concentrated and natural kind of
poetry' (*UU* 211).
April – **Meet my Folks**. August –
Pamphlets for BBC broadcasts
Listening and Writing. Autumn – 'Miss
Mambrett and the Wet Cellar' (story).
Reviews: *Lochness Monster*, Dinsdale;
Living Free, Adamson; *The Cat in the
Hat Comes Back*, Seuss; *Barnaby and
the Horses*, Pender; *Timba*, *Gringolo*,
Koenig.

January – Thom Gunn to dinner
(*SPLH*, 1 January).
February – Sylvia Plath miscarries.
July – Reading (Poetry at the Mermaid,
London).
August – 'The Wound' written, 'a
Celtic-Gothic *Bardo Thodol*' (*ABC*
interview, 1976). Sells lease on London
flat to Wevills. Move to Devon (Court
Green).
November – BBC, *The Odyssey*, 'The
Storm' Book V (translation of Homer);
The House of Aries (play produced).
BBC – interview, talk, poems, school
broadcasts. Selector for Poetry Book
Society Choice.

1962

April – *Leonard Baskin* (Introduction).
May- *Selected Poems with Thom Gunn*.
June – 'The Poetry of Keith Douglas'
(essay). Introductions: *The Little Prince*,
St Exupéry; *Tarka the Otter*,
Williamson; *The Worst Journey in the
World*, Cherry-Garrard. Reviews: *The
Nerve of Some Animals*, Froman; *Man
and Dolphin*, Lilly; *Primitive Song*,
Bowra; *One Fish Two Fish*, Seuss; *The
Cat's Opera*, Dillon; *The Otter's Tale*,
Maxwell; *Animals of the Forest*, Vérité;
Close-up of a Honeybee, Foster; *Oddities
of Animal Life*, Roberts; *Imitations*,
Lowell; *Anthology of W. African Folk-
lore*, Jablow; *Everyman's Ark*, Johnson;
Here Come the Elephants, Goudey.

Gaudete – begun as a film script (*UU*
123). *The Chemical Wedding of
Christian Rosencreutz*, Andreas: 'for over
a year [this] became my prime source
of inspiration' (*BBC TP*, 21 January
1963).
17 January – Nicholas Farrar born.
February – BBC, *The Wound* (play
produced). Interest in shamanic
dismemberment, Bacchae and Orphic
myths (*BF* 320). Reading Nietzsche.
May – Wevills visit. Selling Daffodils
(*SPLH* 14 May).
June – Beekeeping (*SPLH* 15 June).
July – Reading for *Critical Quarterly*,
Bangor, Wales (*BF* 251). BBC – school
broadcasts, talk, poems, stories.

1963

January – *Here Today*, (introduction).
May – *Five American Poets* (ed.).
September – 'The Rock', (*The Listener*);
'The Poetry of Keith Douglas' (essay).
October – 'Ten Poems by Sylvia Plath'
(introduction). November – **How the
Whale Became** (fables); **The Earth-
Owl and other Moon People**; *'The Rat
Under the Bowler'* (essay). *Reviews:* I
Said the Sparrow, *West;* The World of
Men, *Baldwin;* Rule and Energy, *Press;*
Vagrancy, *O'Connor;* Emily Dickinson's
Poetry, *Anderson;* Folktales of Japan,
Seki; Folktales of Israel, *Noy.*

January – BBC, *Difficulties of a
Bridegroom* (play produced), based on
*The Chemical Wedding of Christian
Rosencreutz,* 'words, music and pictures
… the interest is in imagery and mood'
(*BBC TP*, 17 October 1965); 'a tribal
dream' (*UU* 212). February – Sylvia
Plath dies. Writes 'The Howling of
Wolves'. March – Writes 'Song of a
Rat'. September – BBC, 'The Rock'
(talk). BBC – interviews, poems, talks.

1964

January – 'The Howling of Wolves'.
February – *Selected Poems, Keith
Douglas* (ed.): (introduction).
March – 'The Suitor' (story).
April – **Nessie the Mannerless
Monster**; 'Dice' (poem in 8 parts).
Reviews: *Voss*, White; *Myth and
Religion of the North*, Turville-Petre;
The Collected Poems of Wilfred Owen,
Day Lewis; *Selections of African Prose*,
Whiteley; *The Heroic Recitations of the
Bahima of Ankole*, Morris; *Somali
Poetry*, Andrzejewski and Lewis; *The
Three Christs of Ypsilanti*, Rokeach;
Letters of Alexander Pushkin, Shaw;
Astrology, MacNeice; *Ghost and
Divining-rod*, Lethbridge; *Shamanism*,
Eliade; *The Sufis*, Shah (probably
written in 1962, see *BF* 320);
Mysterious Senses, Dröscher;
Heimskringla, The Prose Edda, Sturlson;
Gods, Demons and Others, Narayan.

Awarded lecturer's salary at University
of Vienna for 5 years, by Abraham
Woursell Foundation (*PR* 62).
February – BBC, *Dogs: A Scherzo* (play
produced). *Gaudete* film scenario
written. Writing *Eat Crow* (*UU* 212).
November/December – BBC, *The
Coming of the Kings* (play produced).

1965

January – 'Sylvia Plath' (note on *Ariel*).
March – *Ariel*, Sylvia Plath (ed.).

Helps to organize the first big Arts
Council International Poetry Festival.

April – 'The Genius of Isaac Bashevis Singer' (essay).
June – *Eat Crow* (play) (parts of *Difficulties of a Bridegroom*); *Modern Poetry in Translation* (editorial). Autumn – 'The Tiger's Bones' (play); 'Beauty and the Beast' (play). Reviews: *Faber Book of Ballads*, Hodgart; *Men who Marched Away*, Parsons; *Literature Among the Primitives, The Primitive Reader*, Greenaway.

Reading with Auden and Neruda (*PR* 73). September – BBC, 'The House of Donkeys' (re-telling of Japanese folk-tale). Reads 3 poems at Edinburgh Festival. October – BBC, reading 'Ghost Crabs', 'Waking', 'Gog III' from play *Difficulties of a Bridegroom*. November/December – BBC, *The Tiger's Bones; Beauty and the Beast* (plays produced). BBC – poetry readings, talks.

1966
Summer – 'Vasco Popa' (essay).
Autumn – 'On the Chronological Order of Plath's Poems' (notes).
October – *The Burning of the Brothel* (*LE* 300). Reviews: *Dylan Thomas Letters*, Fitzgibbon.

Crow poems begun at request of Baskin to accompany drawings, 'the way I wrote ... when I was about nineteen' (*UU* 121).
September – BBC, *The Price of a Bride* (play produced). BBC – poetry reading, talks.

1967
January – **Recklings** (*LE* 150).
April – *Scapegoats and Rabies* (*LE* 400).
May – **Wodwo** 'a descent into destruction of some sort' (*UU* 205).
August – *Animal Poems* (*LE* 100).
December – **Poetry in the Making** (broadcasts); 'Gravestones' (*BS*) (*LE* 40). First *Crow* poems published: 'Three Legends', 'A Battle', 'Lovesong'.

20 January – Alexandra Tatiana Eloise Wevill (Shura) born. July – BBC Poetry International '67 (speaking and reading; broadsheet and programme notes). September/October – BBC, *The Head of Gold* (play produced).

1968
February – **The Iron Man** (story): 'I just wrote it out as I told it over two or three nights' (*IOS*, 5 September 1993) March – *A Choice of Emily Dickinson's Verse* (introduction). July – *Yehuda Amichai: Selected Poems* (collaborated on trans.); *Beauty and the Beast* (play).
December – Many Crow poems published. *Five Autumn Songs* (*LE* 500). Reviews: *Folk-tales of Chile*, Dawson; *Hindoo Fairy Tales*, Frere; *The*

19 March – adaptation of Seneca's *Oedipus* performed (Old Vic): 'concentrated my writing ... useful in *Crow*' (*UU* 212). March – *The Demon of Adachigahara* (libretto), setting by Crosse, performed at Shrewsbury. May – BBC, *Sean, the Fool, the Devil and the Cats* (play produced); *Five Autumn Songs* written for and read at Harvest Festival, Little Missenden. Autumn – Reading poetry at Peacock Theatre,

Glass Man and the Golden Bird,
Manning-Sanders; *The Black Monkey,*
Hampden.

Dublin. BBC – poetry and play-
readings. The Arvon Foundation
established by John Fairfax and John
Moat: 'I thought the scheme was
unworkable'. Involved with first course
in Devon and was converted (Letter to
AS, August. 1993).

1969

February – *Vasco Popa: Selected Poems*
(introduction). December – **Seneca's
Oedipus** (adaptation). Many *Crow*
poems published.

February – *The New World* songs
commissioned (performed in 1972).
March – Househunting with Assia on
Tyneside. Last *Crow* poem, 'A Horrible
Religious Error', written on train from
Manchester after first televised reading.
Death of Assia and Shura. Co-director
of Poetry International. *The Battle of
Aughrim* recorded. Death of Hughes'
mother.

1970

January – 'The Chronological Order of
Sylvia Plath's Poems' (note in *The Art of
Sylvia Plath*). March – *The Martyrdom
of Bishop Farrar* (*LE* 100); 'Myth and
Education' I (US publication) (essay);
A Crow Hymn (*LE* 100).
August – 'Four Crow Poems' (*BS*) (*LE*
20).
September – **The Coming of the
Kings** (4 plays). October – **Crow:
from the Life and Songs of the
Crow**; *A Few Crows* (*LE* 75); *Amulet*
(*LE* 1); 'Fighting for Jerusalem' (*BS*)
(*LE* 1); *The Tiger's Bones* (play); *The
House of Donkeys* (part of the play);
Interview with Ekbert Faas (*UU*
197–208). Reviews: *Children's Games in
Street and Playground,* Opie; *The
Environmental Revolution,* Nicholson,
The God Beneath the Sea,
Garfield/Blishen; *The Book of
Imaginary Beings,* Borges.

May – Poetry D-Day (reading at the
Roundhouse).
August – Marries Carol Orchard.
September – Settings of two poems
performed at the Edinburgh festival:
'King of Carrion', 'Eros'. November –
Reads from *Crow* at ICA. BBC –
poetry readings, talks.

1971

March – *Shakespeare's Poem* (*LE* 150).
April – *Crow Wakes* (*LE* 200); *Poems with Ruth Fainlight and Alan Sillitoe*; Autumn Song (poster) ['Who Killed the Leaves?']; 'The Poetry of Ted Hughes' (sheets) (*LE*). May – *Fiesta Melons*, Plath (introduction) (*LE* 150); *Crossing the Water*, Plath (ed.); *Orpheus* (verse play).
September – *Winter Trees,* Plath (ed.) (note).
November – *Eat Crow* (*LE* 150); *With Fairest Flowers While Summer Lasts: Poems from Shakespeare* (ed.) (introduction) (*LE* 140); *A Choice of Shakespeare's Verse* (introduction). First formulation of the 'Tragic Equation'.

January – BBC, *Orpheus* (play performed). Olwyn Hughes founds Rainbow Press. Begins to look again at *Gaudete* material. The underworld, the 'most interesting part' of story narrative, 'trimmed itself down' (*UU* 214).
May/September – Accompanies Peter Brook to Shiraz Festival, Persia. *Orghast* performed: 'we orchestrated the sounds' (*ABC* interview, 1976). *The Conference of the Birds:* 'I wrote about 100 poems and scenarios for Peter Brook's company to improvise with' (Conversation with *AS*, 1995).
November – Reads at Manchester Poetry Centre.

1972

February – *Sunday* (story from *Wodwo*, separate publication by CUP).
September – *The Coming of the Kings* (script).
October – *Selected Poems 1957–67*; 'In the Little Girl's Angel Gaze' (*BS*) (*LE* 50).
November – *Orghast at Persepolis*, Smith (excerpts from play; ideas, language and myth); *Works in Progress 5* (Faas interview). Reviews: *A Separate Reality*, Castaneda.

August/September – 'The New World' (libretto), setting by Crosse, performed at the Three Choirs Festival (Worcester). Buys Moortown Farm (95 acres) and runs it with Carol and her father, Jack Orchard, who had owned a farm near Crediton (Conversation with *AS*, 1995).
October – 'Overwhelmed afresh' reading new Penguin selection of D.H. Lawrence's poems (Letter to KS).
December – BBC TV, *The Iron Man* read.

1973

July – **Orpheus** (play).
November – **Prometheus on his Crag** (*LE* 160); *Stones: Poems by Paul Merchant* (introduction) (*LE* 150).

March – *The Story of Vasco* performed (Sadler's Wells). April – Reads at Shakespeare Birthday Celebrations, Southwark.

1974

February – *The Story of Vasco* (libretto).
July - *Sean, the Fool, the Devil and the Cats* (script); *Beauty and the Beast*

Sees Baskin bird-drawings. Begins bird drama, *Cave Birds*: 'my starting point was the death of Socrates [and his] (script). September - **Spring, Summer, Autumn, Winter** (*LE* 140). *The House of Donkeys* (complete play). First *Cave Birds* poems published: 'The Summoner', 'The Executioner', 'The Risen'.

murder of the Mediterranean Goddess' (Letter to *AS*, November 1984).

1975

March – *The Interrogator* (*LE* 250) ('A Titled Vulturess'). May – Scolar Press edition of *Cave Birds* (10 poems written 1974–5). October – **Season Songs**. December – *Children as Writers 2* (foreword). A few *Gaudete* poems published.

April – Reading *Crow* poems at Cambridge Poetry Festival '[*Crow*] an expanded story for children' (Cambridge University recording). May – First Hughes exhibition staged in Ilkley. Reading at Hull University. 30 May – *Cave Birds* and *Lumb's Remains* performed (Ilkley Literature Festival): '[*Cave Birds*] a mystery play of sorts', '[*Lumb's Remains*] constitutes the Epilogue of a longish poem called *Gaudete*' (programme notes). June – BBC, *Cave Birds* read. Writes *Adam and the Sacred Nine*. Leases Lumb Bank to Arvon Foundation: 'I've poured a lot into it because I've seen what those courses can do for students' (Letter to *KS*).

1976

May - *Earth Moon* (*LE* 226). July – *Eclipse* (*LE* 250); 'Moon Hops' (*LE* 1). September – *Janos Pilinszky: Selected Poems* (co-ed.) (introduction); *Words Broadsheet Twenty-Five: Four Poets* ('The Virgin Knight') (*LE* 200). November – **Moon Whales**. 'Myth and Education' II (London publication) (essay); Arvon Foundation Conversation.

February – Death of Jack Orchard. March – Attends Adelaide Festival (readings and interviews). September – Reads with Pilinszky at Manchester Poetry Centre.

1977

May – **Gaudete**. June – *Chiasmadon* (*LE* 185); *Amen*, Yehuda Amichai

April – Finishing Elmet poems. July – Readings in USA.

(co-trans.) (introduction); *Johnny Panic and the Bible of Dreams*, Plath (introduction, postscript).
August – **Sunstruck** (*LE* 300).

August – Platform Performance of *Gaudete* (National Theatre).
September – BBC, introduces and reads *Season Songs*. October – Lectures on Herbert, Holub, Amichai and Popa at the Cheltenham Festival. Second interview with Ekbert Faas (*UU* 208–15). Awarded OBE.

1978

February – **Moon Bells**.
June – *Vasco Popa: Collected Poems* (introduction).
July – *A Solstice* (*LE* 100).
August – **Orts** (*LE* 200). October – **Cave Birds**; **Moortown Elegies** (*LE* 150); 'Moortown Elegies' (*BS*) (*LE* 100); 'The Head' (story).

Becomes president of Farms for City Children charity.
February – Reads at the Hobson Gallery, Cambridge. Recording for Norwich Tapes, Critical Forum Series: '[poetry/magic] is one way of making things happen the way you want them to happen'.
April – Reads at Lancaster Literature Festival. 'It's been a really scatty summer – too many people, too many dates & appointments' (Letter to *KS*).

1979

January – *The Threshold* (*LE* 100).
April – **Remains of Elmet** (*LE* 180), 'written in response to Fay Godwin's photographs … first poems reflected my mother's love of this area'. August – *Four Tales Told by an Idiot* (*LE* 450).
October – **Moortown**.
November – **Adam and the Sacred Nine** (*LE* 200), 'to conjure myself to be a bit more birdlike' (*PR* 72).
December – *Henry Williamson* (tribute) (*LE* 200); Morrigu Press (*BS*, 3 poems) (*LE* 30); 'Brooktrout' (*BS*) (*LE* 60); 'Pan' (*BS*) (*LE* 60); 'Woodpecker' (*BS*) (*LE* 60); 'In the Black Chapel' (*BS*) (*LE* 1500) for V & A exhibition; 'Wolverine' (*BS*) (*LE* 75); 'You hated Spain', 'Salmon Taking Times', 'The Earthenware Head'. Poems in *All Round the Year*, Morpurgo.

February – Reads at the Commonwealth Institute.
March – Reads at Leeds University.
May – ITV, reads poems from *Remains of Elmet*. July – 'We [*TH* and Nicholas] had a memorable three weeks in Iceland – very tough country. Caught some very big fish, & in plenty' (Letter to *KS*).
August/September – Working on several collaborations, with Richard Blackford (*The Pig Organ*), Peter Keen (*River*) and Leonard Baskin (*Under the North Star* and *A Primer of Birds*).
Voted best poet writing in English in small *New Poetry* poll (*BBC Internet News*, 1 January 1999).
September/October – Exhibition of 'Illustrations to Ted Hughes Poems'

at V&A.
December – Tribute to Henry
Williamson read at St Martin's in the
Fields.

1980

October – *The Reef and Other Poems*,
Sagar (introduction). 'Eagle' (*BS*) (*LE*
75); 'Mosquito' (*BS*) (*LE* 60); 'Tapir's
Song' (*BS*) (*LE* 15); 'Sky Furnace' (*BS*)
(*LE* 150); 'The Tigerboy' (story). *New
Poetry 6* (ed.) *Ted Hughes: The
Unaccommodated Universe*, Faas
(interviews, essays, reviews collected).

Fishing in Alaska with Nicholas.
April – *River* 'finished more or less'
(Letter to *KS*). Reads from *Remains of
Elmet* at Hebden Bridge. *The Pig Organ*
(libretto), setting, Blackford, performed
(Roundhouse, London) BBC – poetry
readings.
August – First International Hughes
Conference held in Manchester in
conjunction with major exhibition at
Manchester City Art Gallery.
November – Sets up and judges (with
Heaney, Larkin and Causley) the
Observer / Arvon Foundation Poetry
Competition: 'That's the last judging I
shall ever do. Ever. Ever. Ever. Ever.
Ever' (Letter to *KS*).

1981

March – **Under the North Star**.
July – **A Primer of Birds** (*LE* 250);
'Three River Poems' (*BS*) (*LE* 75);
'Cows' (*BS*) (*LE* 76); *The Way to Write*,
Fairfax and Moat (introduction);
Collected Poems, Plath (ed.)
(introduction); 'In Defence of Crow'
(essay).

Death of Hughes' father.
March/April – Spends a month in
Ireland where he catches his biggest
pike. December – 'Spent the best
(worst) part of this year involved in the
coils of the Plath journals … my own
compositions have been in hibernation
now for pretty well a year.… Just to
bring everything home together I made
a reselected poems' (Letter to *KS*).

1982

February – *New Selected Poems
1957–81*. July – *Wolf-watching* (*LE*
75); 'The Great Irish Pike' (sheets) (*LE*
26); *The Rattle Bag* (ed. with Seamus
Heaney); *The Journals of Sylvia Plath*
(co-ed.) (foreword); *Arvon Foundation*

October – Reads at Cheltenham
Literature Festival: 'I've told myself I
shall never read in public again' (Letter
to *KS*).

Poetry Comp. 1980 Anthology (co-judge) (part of intro.); *What Rhymes with Secret*, Brownjohn (foreword). Reviews: *Where I Used to Play on the Green*, Glyn Hughes.

1983
March – *The Achievement of Ted Hughes* (contains 30 uncollected poems). September – **River**. 'Mice are Funny Little Creatures' (*BS*) (*LE* 75); 'Weasels at Work' (*BS*) (*LE* 75); 'Fly Inspects' (*BS*) (*LE* 75); *Modern Poetry in Translation*, Weissbort (introduction).

January–March – Spends first three months writing 'The Hanged Man and the Dragonfly': 'I've sweated blood – as never' (Letter to *KS*). April/May – Works on *Flowers and Insects*. Visits Nicholas in Africa: 'a great, self-contained, blissful dream' (Letter to *KS*). Fishing in Scotland: '4 of us in 5 days caught 59 salmon' (Letter to *KS*). Attends Toronto Poetry Festival.

1984
June – **What is the Truth?**, 'written at the suggestion of C. and M. Morpurgo who run Farms for City Children' (*PBS Notes*, Autumn 1995). *The Complete Prints of Leonard Baskin* ('The Hanged Man and the Dragonfly' – introduction); *Where I Used to Play on the Green*, G. Hughes (introduction); *Britain: The World by Itself*, Perring and Press (poem and prose passage); 'Subsidy for Poetry' (essay).

June – Visits Ireland and festival in Orkney. August – 'I'm trying to add one or two things to *River* and to *Remains of Elmet*' (Letter to *KS*). October – Reads at Benefit Reading for Frances Horovitz. November – Reading tour to schools, including Hull, West Kirby and Oxford: 'Must have read to about 6000 or so, in all' (Letter to *KS*). Visits Egypt. December – Appointed Poet Laureate. Paul Muldoon said 'Who does he think he is? Calling himself "Ted" as if he went round in a cloth cap' (Conversation with *AS*, September 1997).

1985
Mokomaki (*LE* 50); *The Best Worker in Europe* (*LE* 150); *Sylvia Plath's Selected Poems* (ed.); *45 Contemporary Poems*, Turner (poem and essay); 'Putting a value on UK's salmon riches' (letter).

January – 'I've been chipping away at bits and pieces about Calder Valley' (Letter to *KS*). April – Reads at National Poetry Centre. May – Fishing in Scotland.

June – Visits Nicholas in Alaska:
'Called in on Victoria & Vancouver –
and realized that's where I ought to be
living' (Letter to *KS*). Wrote *The Cat
and the Cuckoo* there.
October – 'Just finished my mini-tour
of readings. Faber set it up – one in
each of their counties' (Letter to *KS*).
Also reads at Kent Literature Festival.

1986
August – *Ffangs the Vampire Bat and
the Kiss of Truth*. October – **Flowers
and Insects**. 'The Whistle'; 'Group';
'Circuit', poems by Sorescu (trans.);
William Golding, Carey ('Baboons and
Neanderthals' – essay); 'Children and
secretly listening adults' (letter); 'About
the Arvon Foundation' (notes).

January – ITV, *The Iron Man*, readings
by Tom Baker begin. 'This has been a
chaotic spring & summer. I've hardly
met myself, let alone anybody else. US
legal business [in connection with the
filming of *The Bell Jar*] boiling and
bubbling, among other slips of yew &
toads' eyes.… Then went to Spain – to
lay claim to my butt of sack' (Letter to
KS).

1987
August – *T.S. Eliot: A Tribute* (*LE* 150).
September – *The Cat and the Cuckoo*
(*LE* 2000, 250 signed): 'my wish was to
capitalise on a character study of the
creature. My model was runic knots …
mnemonic *quipus*' (*PBS Notes*, Autumn
1995). *The Complete Poems of Keith
Douglas*, Graham (introduction); *The
Singing Brink*, Dooley and Hunter,
(introduction); 'An Introduction to
"The Thought Fox"' (essay); 'To parse
or not to parse' (letter); 'On Sylvia
Plath's biographers' (letter); 'No chance
for fishery interests' (letter); 'The place
where Sylvia Plath should rest in peace'
(letter); 'Sylvia Plath: the facts about
her life and the desecration of her
grave' (letter); 'Where research becomes
intrusion' (letter).

March – 'I just spent 2 arduous weeks
writing a fresh Introduction to
Oxford's Keith Douglas' (Letter to *KS*).
Finished *Tales of the Early World*.
Summer – Fishes for steelhead on the
Deane in British Columbia.
November – Assembling *Wolfwatching*.

1988

June – **Tales of the Early World**
(fables). *An Anthology of Poetry for
Shakespeare*, Osborne (foreword); *First
and Always*, Sail (introduction); *Letters
to an Editor*, Fisher (includes letters
from *TH*).

Begins writing *The Iron Woman*: 'at one
point I was scared by it and had to
back off' (*IOS* 34).
June – To Alaska. September – Delivers
Eliot centenary address, 'A Dancer to
God'.
November – Reads at Armistice
Festival, Church of St Clement Danes,
London.

1989

September – **Moortown Diary**;
Wolfwatching: 'doubting my powers
and getting older. Of course both
wolves are caged and confined'
(Conversation with *AS*, December
1994). *In Praise of Trout*, Profumo
(foreword); Notes on *Wolfwatching*
(*PBS Bulletin*, Autumn 1989).

July – Begins writing *Shakespeare and
The Goddess of Complete Being* as *The
Silence of Cordelia*.
November – Visits Bangladesh for the
Asia Poetry Festival.

1990

Capriccio (*LE* 50); *Sean Hill's Gidleigh
Park Cookbook* (foreword); *Gabbiano*,
Pennati (facsimile of letter from *TH*);
Dear (Next) Prime Minister, Astley
(includes letter from *TH*); *Three
Contemporary Poets*, Dyson (includes 'A
Reply to Critics' and excerpts from
letter).

July – Second International Hughes
Conference in Manchester.
December – Suffers from shingles until
March 1991.

1991

Winning Words (judge) (foreword).

April – To Scotland.

1992

March – 'The Interpretation of
Parables' (article).
April – **Shakespeare and the Goddess
of Complete Being** (prose);
'Shakespeare and the Goddess',
'Battling Over the Bard' (reply to
review); 'Ted Hughes and the Plath
estate' (letter).

October – Cheltenham Literary
Festival reading, 'The Bear'. 'Just been
in Ireland, with Nicholas. Read at
Memorial Concert for George
Macbeth.... Then read for Field Day,
in Derry' (Letter to *KS*). 'Finished *The
Iron Woman*' (Letter to *KS*). Reviews:
Your World (winning photographs UN

June – **Rain Charm for the Duchy** (*LE* 280 and trade edn). September – **A Dancer to God** (tribute to Eliot). November – 'Your World' (essay) (*Observer Magazine*).

competition). BBC – poetry readings.

1993
May – *The Mermaid's Purse* (*LE* 100): 'not as warm as *The Cat and The Cuckoo*' (Conversation with *AS*, October 1993).
June – **Three Books**: 'Reading your book [*Ted Hughes: The Poetic Quest*] galvanised [Fabers] into publishing *Elmet*, *Cave Birds* and *River* as a single volume' (Letter to *AS*, August 1995).
September – **The Iron Woman** (story) 'a myth about writing a poem' (*IOS* 34); 'The Reckless Head' (*BS*) (*LE*); *Sacred Earth Dramas* (foreword); 'The Bear'; 'The Deadfall' (story).

February – 'I blundered into the pit of sorting out what exactly is going on in Coleridge's 3 poems – Kubla, Mariner, Christabel' (Letter to *KS*). March – Wilfred Owen Centenary at Oswestry. Talks about 'the catharsis of memorialising the dead in books' (*IOS* 34). Enthusiasm for Tony Buzan's experiments for developing brain and memory (*IOS* 32). August – 'Just going to Canada for a few days, do one or two readings' (Letter to *KS*). Reads with Tony Harrison in York.

1994
March – **Winter Pollen**. July – *Poetry* (in Macedonian) (*LE* 500).
October – **Elmet**: 'I deliberately made this version a collection about my family' (Conversation with *AS*).
November – *After Ovid*, Hoffman and Lasdun (includes 4 versions of *Metamorphoses* poems).
December – *Earth Dances* (*LE* 250); 'T.S. Eliot: the Death of St Narcissus' (introductory note).

Goes to the Macedonia Poetry Festival. 6 October – Reading for Poetry Day (National Theatre) with Simon Armitage ('The Earthenware Head', 'Anniversary', 'The Last of the 1st/5th Lancashire Fusiliers'). December – In London for Sacred Earth Drama Group meeting. Re. *The Mermaid's Purse* – Reg Lloyd 'disengaged from it and another illustrator found by Fabers' (Conversation with *AS*).

1995
March – **New Selected Poems**; *The Dream Fighter* (stories); PR interview with Drew Heinz; 'Sylvia Plath: the *Bell Jar* and *Ariel*' (essay).
August – *Spring Awakening* (*TH*'s version of Wedekind's play).

Sets aside his work on Alcestis to write a version of *The Oresteia* of Aeschylus 'the best thing I have ever done. I read it and wonder how I ever did it.' (Conversation with *AS*, September 1998).

September - *Shakespeare's Ovid* (*LE* 200).
October – **Difficulties of a Bridegroom** (stories); *Collected Animal Poems* (4 books); 'Football' (poem strip) (*LE* 499); 'Goku' (Creation story).

February – Reads at Bath Literature Festival; BBC TV, *The Dreamfighter*: reading by Bill Paterson. May – finishes his 'translation' of Wedekind's *Spring Awakening*, to be performed at the Barbican in August – 'powerful and relevant to modern youth' (Conversation with *AS*, October). BBC – poetry readings. Considers collating archive mss. in preparation for selling them. Asks *KS* and *AS* to help, but eventually decides he needs to do it himself. Writing more Ovid and writing 'about 100 poems about things I should have resolved thirty years ago. Should have written then, but couldn't' (Conversation with *AS*).

1996
Blood Wedding (*TH*'s version of Lorca's play); *A Choice of Coleridge's Verse* (ed.).

September – 'I also did 25 tales from Ovid's *Metamorphoses* – enjoyed that. A holiday in a rest home!!' (Letter to *AS*).
October – *Blood Wedding* performed (Young Vic), director Tim Supple: 'a difficult play to stage' (Letter to *AS*, September).
December – Translating *Sir Gawain and the Green Knight*: 'Did about 250 lines in 2 days, for *The School Bag*, so thought I'd do the rest in 10. Mistake!' (Letter to *KS*).

1997
Tales from Ovid. 'Shaggy and Spotty' (story): 'found in my archive … a story I told the children when they were about two and just jotted notes' (Conversation with *AS*, September). *By Heart* (ed) (introduction): 'it worked for Nicholas when he was at school' (Conversation with *AS*, September). *The School Bag*, (ed. with Seamus Heaney).

Discussion of the South Bank Mind Olympics and Ted's teaching in a similar course run in Liechtenstein. Warner Bros., making animated version of *The Iron Man*, abandon Pete Townsend and David Thacker's musical version: 'Pete says the script is nothing like my own writing' (Conversation with *AS*, September).

September – Moortown Farm sold.
Talks about *Birthday Letters*:
'autobiographical.… I chose two dates
[for possible publication] using
horoscopes, April 23 or an earlier one'
(Conversation with *AS*).
October – 'I've put together about 90
pieces about S.P. Still thinking whether
to pub. or not. Probably not, but it
would be a burden gone' (Letter to
KS).
November – Decides to publish
Birthday Letters: '<u>Don't speak about it</u> –
otherwise there'll be a whole Gallipoli
of entrenched weaponry mounted
ready. Totally vulnerable as it is' (Letter
to *KS*).

1998
January – **Birthday Letters**. *Phèdre*
(*TH*'s version of Racine's play); *Howls
& Whispers* (*LE*). Version of Euripides'
Alcestis sent to Barry Rutter of
Northern Broadsides (Conversation
with *AS*, September).
Winter – Interview published in *Wild
Steelhead and Salmon*.

January – *Birthday Letters* tops best
seller list; *Tales from Ovid* wins the
Whitbread Book of the Year prize.
March – *Tales from Ovid* wins the W.H.
Smith Literature Award. 'Just put
together about 250 of the best
translations of Yehuda Amichai. With
Daniel Weissbort' (Letter to *KS*). June –
'I'm just blocking out Gilgamesh for
Tim Supple to then convert to stage
action … I've translated Eurip's *Alcestis*
(did most of it before the *Oresteia*)'
(Letters to *KS*). *Phèdre* produced
(Malvern Literary Festival and
Almeida): 'I heard one woman say "I
wouldn't like to be Diana Rigg and have
to go through all that again tonight"'
(Conversation with *AS*, September).
October – *Birthday Letters* wins
Forward Prize for Poetry; appointed
member of the Queen's Order of Merit.
28 October – Ted Hughes dies.

1999
Tales from Ovid (acting version).
'The Prophet' (version of Pushkin's poem from Weissbort's trans.).
The Mermaid's Purse (trade edn).
Aeschylus: **The Oresteia**.
Euripedes **Alcestis**.

January – *Birthday Letters* wins T.S. Eliot Prize for Poetry, the South Bank Award for Literature, the Whitbread Prize for Poetry and the Book of the Year prize.
April – Tim Supple's adaptation of *Tales from Ovid* opens at Swan theatre, Stratford.
13 May – Memorial Service at Westminster Abbey.
September – *Oresteia* opens at National Theatre. International conference on Hughes planned for Lyon in February 2000.

CHAPTER ONE
The Mythic Imagination

In his address at the Memorial Service for Ted Hughes at Westminster Abbey, Seamus Heaney claimed that as DNA is the genetic code for the human body, so myth is the poetic code for the human spirit. By myth he meant not only the great body of named myths we have inherited from the ancient world, but any imaginative work that consciously or unconsciously takes on an identifiably mythic shape.

The choice of mythic subject matter or imagery is, of course, no guarantee of the release of 'mythic imagination'. Myth can be used as a short-cut to prefabricated 'profundity' (*Star Wars*); it can degenerate into fantasy (Tolkien); it can seduce a genuine poet to inflate his themes into cosmic incomprehensibility (Blake). Hughes writes:

> Obviously many poems take myths as their subject matter, or make an image of a *subjective* event, without earning the description 'visionary', let alone 'mythic'. It is only when the image opens inwardly towards what we recognize as a first-hand as-if-religious experience, or mystical revelation, that we call it 'visionary', and when 'personalities' or creatures are involved, we call it 'mythic'. (*Shakespeare*, rev. edn 35)

The ancient myths have stayed alive, and new or recycled myths will forever be created precisely because of myth's continuing power to 'open inwardly' in this way, giving access to subjective experience in a way that makes it not only easier to understand and handle, but also, by giving it a context of accumulated human experience and a grounding in the permanent features of the human psyche, easier to communicate. It does not allow the reader, as some 'confessional' poetry does, to stand aside from the recorded experience, regarding it as unique to the unbalanced, even in some cases psychotic,

1

subjectivity of the poet. For Hughes the greatest exemplars of such mythic imagination in English are Shakespeare, Coleridge and Eliot.

The disease

The history of Western civilization has been the history of man's increasingly devastating crimes against Nature, Nature defined not only as the earth and its life forms, powers and processes, but also as the female in all its manifestations, and as the 'natural man' within the individual psyche. It is the story of Man's mutilation of Nature in his attempt to make it conform to the procrustean bed of his own patriarchal, anthropocentric and rectilinear thinking. In his review of Max Nicholson's *The Environmental Revolution* Hughes firmly linked the ecological crisis to the role of the poet and to the myth that subsumes all other myths, the myth of the quest.

> The story of the mind exiled from Nature is the story of Western Man. It is the story of his progressively more desperate search for mechanical and rational and symbolic securities, which will substitute for the spirit-confidence of the Nature he has lost. The basic myth for the ideal Westerner's life is the Quest. The quest for a marriage in the soul or a physical reconquest. The lost life must be captured somehow. It is the story of spiritual romanticism and heroic technological progress. It is a story of decline. When something abandons Nature, or is abandoned by Nature, it has lost touch with its creator, and is called an evolutionary dead-end. (*WP* 129)

Man will always live by myths, true or false. But the twin myths of Reformed Christianity and technological progress (supporting each other in their fanatical rejection of Nature) have proved to be false because they involve hubristic lies about the supremacy of Man to Nature. In the first of his two 'Myth and Education' essays, Hughes analyses, for example, the false myth of St George and the Dragon, a recipe for disaster (first kill the dragon; ask questions later, if at all), since the dragon is Nature.

The most important role for the poet is to challenge the false myths we all live by and offer true myths which involve the inward journey and the painful acquisition of self-knowledge, which illuminate and purge the dark interior, and which help us to discover 'a proper knowledge of the sacred wholeness of Nature, and a proper alignment of our behaviour within her laws' (or, as Hughes put it elsewhere, 'to realign our extreme, exclusive attitude with our natural environment and our natural biological supply of life'):

> When the modern mediumistic artist looks into his crystal, he sees always the same thing. He sees the last nightmare of mental disintegration and spiritual emptiness. ... This is the soul-state of our civilization. But he may see something else. He may see a vision of the real Eden, 'excellent as at the first day', the draughty radiant Paradise of the animals, which is the actual earth, in the actual Universe: he may see Pan, the vital, somewhat terrible spirit of natural life, which is new in every second. Even when it is poisoned to the point of death, its efforts to be itself are new in every second. This is what will survive, if anything can. And this is the soul-state of the new world. But while the mice in the field are listening to the Universe, and moving in the body of nature, where every living cell is sacred to every other, and all are interdependent, the Developer is peering at the field through a visor, and behind him stands the whole army of madmen's ideas, and shareholders, impatient to cash in the world. (*WP* 130)

All the quest myths, however far the quest hero may travel, end where he started, under his own coat. They are internal voyages of self-discovery. The quest myth that most deeply influenced Hughes was *The Conference of the Birds,* in which the questing hero, the hoopoe, together with the ragged remnant of his band of birds, arrives finally at the mountain-top where the fabulous Simmurgh is to reveal the secret of it all. But the Simmurgh can tell them nothing they do not know already, and reveals himself to be but a mirror or conflation of themselves. Yet their journey and sufferings have not been in vain, since they return sadder and wiser birds, bearing healing truths for those who had stayed behind or fallen by the way-side.

It could be argued that a 'living myth' is not a new myth but a rediscovery and release of the power of the oldest myths. In *The Myth of the Goddess* Baring and Cashford write:

> Nature is no longer experienced as source but as adversary, and darkness is no longer a mode of divine being, as it was in the lunar cycles, but a mode of being devoid of divinity and actively hostile, devouring of light, clarity and order. The only place where the voice of the old order breaks through, though so dis-guised as to be barely recognizable, is where the inspiration of poetry re-animates the old mythic images. (298)

The old order breaks through, either by consciously reanimating the old mythic images or by allowing them to well up from the depths of the psyche, in a surprisingly high proportion of the greatest imagina-tive writers of our tradition. It is 'barely recognizable' today only because we have been conditioned not to recognize what is staring us in the face. So Auden looked at the great body of mythic imagery within and behind Yeats and called it mere silliness.

> Do you remember that article about Yeats in the *Kenyon Review*, where Auden dismissed the whole of Eastern mystical and reli-gious philosophy, the whole tradition of Hermetic Magic (which is a good part of Jewish Mystical philosophy, not to speak of the mystical philosophy of the Renaissance), the whole historical exploration into spirit life at every level of conscious-ness, the whole deposit of earlier and other religion, myth, vision, traditional wisdom and story in folk belief, on which Yeats based all his work, everything he did or attempted to bring about, as 'embarrassing nonsense'? (*TH* to *KS*, 30 August 1979)

And Philip Larkin gazed blankly at the 'common myth-kitty' and dis-missed it as irrelevant to his own or any other poet's concerns, thus castrating his own poetry and criticism. His best poems are about his desperate need for the spiritual healing he allowed his lesser self to spurn.

What has kept the old consciousness alive through the thousands of years of its gradual rejection and persecution, in spite of the obliteration of the beliefs and rituals of nature religions and the total desacralization of modern life in the West, has been art, myth and, especially, poetic literature. That ancient vision of atonement is preserved in myth, and both preserved and perennially recreated in art. The purpose of art is to preserve it, and imaginative art cannot do otherwise, since the very nature of the creative imagination is holistic; its primary function is to make connections, discover relationships, patterns, systems and wholes.

There is now widespread agreement that we must try to develop a new holistic, biocentric vision incorporating the latest insights of imaginative (and computerized) science. This can be attempted in two ways, through deep ecology and through imaginative art. In the work of Ted Hughes they are essentially the same.

Imagination

Imagination seeks to respiritualize Nature, to heal the split in the human psyche, replacing anthropocentric with biocentric consciousness, to provide the only viable religion for the new millennium.

A work of imagination shares with a living creature or the ecosystem itself the characteristic of not being reducible to its parts, or explicable in terms of the technique of its manufacture. It cannot be exhausted by analysis. It is a system of interrelationships which, since it extends far beyond the words on the page, engages with everything else in the reader's conscious and unconscious experience, and is therefore virtually infinite. It is a microcosm, a model of the universe. The living poem is the opposite of a well-wrought urn (or billiard-ball in Lawrence's comic terminology) complete in itself; it sends out countless roots and tendrils, ripples, shock-waves, shrapnel, grapnels, to touch, engage, disturb, grapple with the world, and with a different matrix of experiences, beliefs, values, psycho-biological make-up, in each reader. In relation to *Shakespeare and the Goddess of Complete Being* Hughes wrote: 'I want my readers to approach it with the

cooperative, imaginative attitude of a co-author.' This seems to me
the only valid approach to any imaginative work.

Imagination is not a separate faculty which some are born with. It
is what happens when the faculties we all have are freed from their
usual bonds and divisions, resist the process of training and indoctri-
nation, and speak out with the voice of nature – the voice of human
nature of course, but not a human nature that defines itself in con-
tradistinction to the rest of life; the voice of a man or woman, but not
one who represses the anima or animus that is their continuity in
consciousness. The language of the imagination is necessarily holistic and biocentric. It is grounded simultaneously in the depths of the
artist's being and in the external universe. It breaks down the walls of
egotism, sexism, nationalism, racism, anthropocentrism. It expresses
relationships and wholes. Its language is metaphor and symbol. The
literary imagination connects all the severed halves – inner and outer,
self and other, male and female, life and death, Man and Nature.
Every metaphor is a stitch in the suture.

Imaginative speech is essentially metaphorical. For the process of
making metaphors Wordsworth made this astonishing claim:

> This principle is the great spring of the activity of our minds
> and their chief feeder. From this principle the direction of the
> sexual appetite and all the passions connected with it, take their
> origin: it is the life of our ordinary conversation; and upon the
> accuracy with which similitude in dissimilitude and dissimili-
> tude in similitude are perceived, depend our taste and moral
> feelings. (*Preface to the Lyrical Ballads*)

Metaphor is the linguistic equivalent of touch. It is the link, the
bridge, the meeting, the marriage, the atonement, bit by bit recon-
structing the world as a unity, blissfully skipping over the supposed
chasms of dualism. Hughes speaks of it as 'a sudden flinging open of
the door into the world of the right side, the world where the animal
is not separated from either the spirit of the real world or itself'
(*Shakespeare* 159). Lawrence speaks of poetry as a 'magical linking
up':

The religious way of knowledge means that we accept our sense-impressions, our perceptions, in the full sense of the word, complete, and we tend instinctively to link them up with other impressions, working towards a whole. The process is a process of association, linking up, binding back (religio) or referring back towards a centre and a wholeness. This is the way of poetic and religious consciousness, the instinctive act of synthesis. (*Apocalypse* 190)

Imagery is the body of our imaginative life, and our imaginative life is a great joy and fulfilment to us, for the imagination is a more powerful and more comprehensive flow of consciousness than our ordinary flow. In the flow of true imagination we know in full, mentally and physically at once, in a greater, enkindled awareness. At the maximum of our imagination we are religious. And if we deny our imagination, and have no imaginative life, we are poor worms who have never lived. (*Phoenix* 559)

The images that most consistently achieve this magic are symbols. Jung valued the symbol highly as providing the necessary third ground on which the otherwise polarized halves of the psyche could meet:

What the separation of the two psychic halves means, the psychiatrist knows only too well. He knows it as the dissociation of personality, the root of all neuroses; the conscious goes to the right and the unconscious to the left. As opposites never unite at their own level, a supraordinate 'third' is always required, in which the two parts can come together. And since the symbol derives as much from the conscious as the unconscious, it is able to unite them both, reconciling their conceptual polarity through its form and their emotional polarity through its numinosity. (*Aion* 180)

The imagination is by no means the enemy of intelligence or civilization. Its function is to correct any imbalance which has come about in the psyche, to reconcile and harmonize the warring, artificially polarized elements. What we call intelligence is often merely the analytical and manipulative aspects of intelligence developed to the exclusion of, at the cost of, all other aspects – intelligence cut off from its sustaining and validating connections with the rest of the psyche, with emotion and spirit, with the body, and with everything outside itself. Yeats said: 'God save me from thoughts men think in the mind alone.' If thought were a matter of mind only, man would be a windowless monad, an ego-bound obscenity. Such thinking is what Blake called 'single vision and Newton's sleep'. It is the insanity of the clever imbeciles of science, business and government who have brought the world to its present condition.

At a reading Hughes explained how it had come about that a poem ('Tiger-psalm'), which had begun life (in the sixties) as a dialogue between Socrates and Buddha, had ended up as a dialogue between machine-guns and a tiger:

> The whole abstraction of Socrates' discourse must inevitably, given enough time and enough applied intelligence, result in machine-guns ... machine-guns descending directly from a mechanical, mechanistic development of logicality which grows from the abstraction of dialectical debate.

The ultimate in 'applied intelligence' and 'mechanistic development of logicality' was perhaps the computer-based systems analysis of the Rand Corporation which largely directed American foreign policy in the 1960s – perhaps the apogee of disembodied reason in our history, when the computerized dialectical debate focused on what figure of American losses in a nuclear war, between 15 and 100 million, would be 'acceptable' or 'sustainable'. Dean Acheson said of American policies and actions at that time: 'The criteria should be hard-headed in the extreme. Decisions are not helped by considering them in terms of sharing, brotherly love, the Golden Rule, or inducing our citizens into the Kingdom of Heaven' (quoted in Stein, *Peace on Earth* 281). Of the brinkmanship of the Cuban missile crisis Acheson said: 'Moral talk did not bear on the problem.' Nor did it bear on American action in Vietnam. In 1964 the analysts assured the US government that a war in Vietnam could be quickly won. When in 1967 the Rand Corporation's computer was asked when the war would end, it replied that America had in fact won it in 1964. Perhaps the most realistic literature of the sixties was the so-called 'absurd' fiction of Heller and Vonnegut.

And 'applied intelligence' has in store for the early years of the next millennium all the incalculable perils of global warming, of genetic engineering, of water wars. American and Russian scientists are spending billions of dollars a year on a project to abolish night by stringing across the sky vast artificial moons, each a hundred times brighter than the real moon. This will destroy all the ecosystems that depend on the age-old rhythm of night and day. And it is not just moonshine, since the first such moon, Znamya 2.5, will be launched before the end of the millennium. It is lunacy. We are also promised soon the first human clone, and the creation of life in the laboratory from purely synthetic components.

What is normally thought of as thinking, all those methods of 'thinking' that have been developed over the centuries in Western civilization, whose dualistic assumptions have been built into the very structure of our language, has specialized in separating things from each other, then separating the parts, analyzing, vivisecting, compartmentalizing, until it has drastically weakened our capacity for thinking in a way that puts things together, makes connections, perceives patterns and wholes. For most of the history of the human race the language of myth and folk-tale was to some extent generally understood, and understood to have a relevance not only to metaphysical truths, but to the health of the race and to the practical business of living. This has largely gone, except as it is perennially recreated by great imaginative art.

Imagination's goal is atonement, the healing of the split between the mind and the rest of our faculties. Starting from the narrow world we all inhabit, with its hubristic human perspectives and habitual complacencies, the imagination reaches inward towards the roots of our being and outward towards the powers of the non-human world. We know that all mirrors held up to nature, even by scientists, are distorting mirrors. All descriptions of nature are coloured by attitudes, are partly descriptions of the contents of the observer's own psyche projected onto the receptive face of nature. For the scientist this might be a problem, but for the artist it is the whole point of his art. Hughes develops the case:

> The character of great works is exactly this: that in them the full presence of the inner world combines with and is reconciled to the full presence of the outer world. And in them we see that the laws of these two worlds are not contradictory at all; they are one all-inclusive system; they are laws that somehow we find it all but impossible to keep, laws that only the greatest artists are able to restate. They are the laws, simply, of human nature. And men have recognized all through history that the restating of these laws, in one medium or another, in great works of art, are the greatest human acts. ... So it comes about that once we recognize their terms, these works seem to heal us. More important, it is in these works that humanity is truly formed. And it has to be done again and again, as circumstances change, and the balance of power between outer and inner world shifts, showing everybody the gulf. The inner world, separated from the outer world, is a place of demons. The outer world, separated from the inner world, is a place of meaningless objects and machines. The faculty that makes the human being out of these two worlds is called divine. That is only a way of saying that it is the faculty without which humanity cannot really exist. It can be called religious or visionary. More essentially, it is imagination which embraces both outer and inner worlds in a creative spirit. (*WP* 150–1)

But before imagination can operate in this way upon the outer world, it must make the necessary inner and outer connections to allow creative energy to flow through the body and all its faculties. The artist as physician must first heal himself.

Myth

Metaphors and symbols, the natural language of the imagination, have a natural tendency to form dynamic combinations. As though they wanted to communicate something urgent, they strive to acquire the capacity to change and develop in time which is characteristic of narrative or drama. When a set of powerful symbols have fully developed their potential for dramatic narrative, we can call them a myth. A myth, in other words, is a story in which not only the figurative language that might be used in the telling, but the very characters, actions, settings, properties, are, whatever else they may be, symbolic.

Moreover, these stories tend to gravitate towards a very few closely related shapes which seem to operate as paradigms of crucial, archetypal human psychological or spiritual processes. We can speak, for example, in relation to mythic literature, of the death and dismemberment which leads to resurrection, of the quest motif, of the shamanic flight, of the pranks and follies of fools and tricksters, of the healing of the disabling wound and regeneration of the wasteland, of the trial, punishment and redemption of the criminal, of the slaughter of the goddess by her son/consort, of Graves' white goddess and Lorca's *duende*, of the alchemical marriage, of the pursuit of what Blake called fourfold vision, of the Jungian process of individuation, and many more apparently wide-ranging paradigms. We will find that there is a great deal of overlap, that we are often using a different terminology for describing much the same thing.

It hardly matters where we begin, or in what order we look at these paradigms. Each throws up countless links to all the others. Together they weave a dense network of meanings which is the inherited wisdom of our culture, the accumulation of thousands of years of human effort to achieve some sense of the proper relationship between men and men, men and women, human beings and nature, created beings and the gods.

No great writer simply dips into the myth kitty for easy resonances. The imagination of the great writer is drawn, with or without his knowledge, towards these paradigms of human experience we all inherit. It will automatically, as an auto-therapeutic reflex, seize upon, adapt for its purposes, whatever myth or mythic paradigm seems at that moment to offer the greatest possibility of healing. As Hughes said in a discussion:

> I don't think it's possible to invent a story that your whole being
> doesn't need in this way of a myth that is trying to heal you. …
> You think of one myth rather than another because that myth
> is the one that belongs to you at that moment. You cannot cre-
> ate imaginatively anything that isn't made in healing yourself,
> otherwise it just isn't imaginative. ('Myth and Education I')

And in the first Faas interview he said that developing inwardly
means 'organizing the inner world or at least searching out the patterns there and that is a mythology' (*UU* 204).

The healing power of myths is partly a matter of connecting the
experience of the individual human being to the larger human and
non-human context. It was this quality, Lawrence wrote, that Hardy
shared with the great writers, Shakespeare or Sophocles or Tostoi:

> this setting behind the small action of his protagonists the ter-
> rific action of unfathomed nature; setting a smaller system of
> morality, the one grasped and formulated by human con-
> sciousness within the vast, uncomprehended and incompre-
> hensible morality of nature or of life itself, surpassing human
> consciousness. (*Study of Thomas Hardy*)

It is not that such writers write impersonally, striving for universality.
Far from it. It is an inward journey. The paradigms are located in the
depths of personal experience. But the paradigms can transform the
most apparently eccentric or unique experience into something uni-
versally recognizable, so that, for example, Kafka's fictional alter-ego,
K or Joseph K, simultaneously both expresses Kafka's unique personality and experience and enters the consciousness of the reader as the
prototypical alienated European of the modern era. So that Eliot's
'wholly personal grouse against life', as he called *The Waste Land*, is
received as distilling the cultural, psychological and spiritual experience of an age. Similarly, Hughes' personae – Crow, Prometheus,
Adam, Nicholas Lumb, the nameless protagonist of *Cave Birds* – are
all simultaneously unique expressions of Hughes' own nature and
experience and mythic prototypes easily recognized by any reader
willing to make connections with whatever body of myth, folklore

and imaginative literature he or she knows, and, more crucially, with his or her own inner depths to which the myths give access.

Different readers will give priority to different paradigms. I shall briefly describe, in relation to Hughes, some of the more common and central. But I shall deal only in passing with those that have been thoroughly described elsewhere.*

The Goddess

In the poems he wrote prior to the death of Sylvia Plath, Hughes is concerned primarily to try to cleanse the doors of his perceptions of Nature. In the last two thousand years Nature has become in Western consciousness a prowling mass of dangerous energies to insulate ourselves against, and a bottomless heap of resources to exploit. It could be increasingly marginalized, as our self-confidence increased; marginalized and at the same time polarized into an unacceptable face which civilized man had long risen above and could now safely ignore or control, and an acceptable face which could be domesticated and sentimentalized and incorporated into Christianity as the Wordsworthian pieties. All this Hughes tried to shed to reveal the true face of Nature. And that face, as it emerged from behind the veils, was monstrous.

The goddess first appears in Hughes' work as Isis, Mother of the Gods, speaking through the mouth of her hawk. This savage goddess ('The one path of my flight is direct / Through the bones of the living') is a far cry from the Isis who heals and resurrects the torn Osiris,

---

* See in particular Hirschberg, Scigaj, Bishop and Skea, and the following essays in critical anthologies: Sweeting, 'Hughes and Shamanism', Scigaj, 'Oriental Mythology in *Wodwo*', Ramsay, '*Crow*, or the Trickster Transformed', Bradshaw, 'Creative Mythology in *Cave Birds*', Sagar, 'Fourfold Vision in Hughes', in *The Achievement of Ted Hughes*; Porter, 'Beasts/Shamans/Baskin: The Contemporary Aesthetics of Ted Hughes', Scigaj, 'Genetic Memory and the Three Traditions of *Crow*', Gustavsson, 'Ted Hughes' Quest for a Hierophany: A Reading of *Crow*', in *Critical Essays on Ted Hughes*; Skea, 'Regeneration in *Remains of Elmet*', Scigaj, 'Ted Hughes and Ecology: A Biocentric Vision', in *The Challenge of Ted Hughes*.

then becomes his bride. Hughes' journey from one vision of the goddess to the other is the theme of chapter 4.

If Nature were indeed monstrous, then man, even if doomed never
to triumph over Nature, would be morally justified in attempting to
do so. But Hughes, unlike Tennyson, did not turn away from monstrous Nature in the belief that we have better alternatives in moral-
ity, civilization, art, and a religion of universal love. He persisted,
with the conviction of all true poets that Nature cannot be subdi-
vided, in the belief that if you reject the violence and ugliness, you
must also reject the creative energies and the beauty. The question he
asks in many of the *Wodwo* poems is whether it is possible to accept
Nature as a whole, to worship it, perhaps even to love it.

In this effort he was much helped by Robert Graves' *The White
Goddess*, which taught him to see the goddess as indivisibly triple: as
witch, crone, ogress, the sow that eats her own farrow; as erotic sex-
ually irresistible woman and procreant mother; and as beautiful vulnerable maiden. Her appearance at any given moment is largely
determined by the vision of the protagonist, who projects onto the
receptive face of Nature his own distorted preconceptions. If he is
afraid of the female, the goddess will appear fearsome to him. A black
American high-school girl once showed me a poem she had written:

> I am as nature is – ugly,
> When you see me ugly,
> Beautiful,
> When you see me beautiful.

We shall never see the goddess as beautiful if we bring expectations
that cannot encompass the beauty of blackness, of the snake, of the
predator at the moment of the kill. She is the mud-spattered 'black
Venus' of Peter Redgrove's poem 'The Idea of Entropy at Maenporth
Beach'. She is Lorca's *duende*:

> A few years ago, in a dancing contest at Jerez de la Frontera, an
> old woman of eighty carried off the prize against beautiful
> women and girls with waists like water, merely by raising her
> arms, throwing back her head, and stamping her foot on the

platform; in that gathering of muses and angels, beauties of shape and beauties of smile, the moribund *duende*, dragging her wings of rusty knives along the ground, was bound to win and did in fact win. ('The Theory and Function of the Duende')

The hero as criminal

It is unfortunate that the word 'hero', with its inevitable associations with bravery, nobility and greatness of soul, should have come to be used to describe the chief male character in any story, for many of the so-called heroes of myth, epic and drama are in fact criminals against Nature who should be viewed with horror as exemplars not of heroism but of hubris, or rather of hubris in their very heroism. Vaclav Havel writes:

> The natural world, in virtue of its very being, bears within it the presupposition of the absolute which grounds, delimits, animates and directs it, without which it would be unthinkable, absurd and superfluous, and which we can only quietly respect. Any attempt to spurn it, master it or replace it with something else, appears, within the framework of the natural world, as an expression of *hubris* for which humans must pay a heavy price, as did Don Juan and Faust. (*Living in Truth*)

Perhaps the most damaging perversity in our response to great literature has been our insistence on treating as heroes the anti-heroes, the criminals. Prometheus has been celebrated as winning Man his freedom from the tyranny of the gods. What Prometheus did was to teach Man to regard himself as autonomous, to regard nothing as sacred, to 'strike wounds in the divine environment' (Kerényi), to relegate nature to a heap of raw materials, to regard technology as the highest achievement, to probe Nature's deepest secrets and not hesitate to play with fire. In other words, Prometheus set the feet of the race on the road to where we now have to live.

We meet hubris in many of the protagonists of Greek tragedy –

Agamemnon, Creon, Oedipus and Pentheus for example; in Sir Gawain; in several of Shakespeare's most fascinating characters – Adonis, Theseus, Angelo, Hamlet, Macbeth, Prospero; in Gulliver, and the Man Who Loved Islands, and Pincher Martin; in the poets themselves as well as in their alter egos from the Ancient Mariner to Crow.

The crucial factor that makes the healing process potentially mythic is that the wound is self-inflicted, so that the healing process is simultaneously the trial and correction of a criminal. Hughes once said at a reading that he was always astonished by 'the extraordinary assumption by critics that they are the judges of literature, rather than criminals merely reporting on the judgments passed upon them by literature'. The great writers are far from being exempt from the criminality of their species and culture. The difference is that the writer recognizes his own guilt, puts himself in the dock, submits to correction by his own deepest self, the voice of nature within him, his imagination.

The creative writer is not a privileged being, a born judge or infallible seer. Writers who are concerned simply to castigate others for failing to live by their own superior values are lesser writers than those whose imaginative depth and honesty lead them to reveal, even when they are about quite other business, their own complicity in the crime against Nature and their own natures. Such writers earn an authenticity and universality lacking in propagandists for however good a cause.

The crime against Nature is there in Hughes from the beginning. But in the early poems it is a crime committed by others, the eggheads and egotists, who can harm only themselves, since they are to Nature but a few fleas on a lion, a few diseased leaves on a huge tree. Few people in the fifties believed that Man could seriously harm Nature, except in very small and localized ways. It needed ecology to demonstrate that you could not harm any part of Nature without harming the whole. Rachel Carson demonstrated the horrific effect of a single chemical, DDT, on the whole food chain. Man may not be able to draw up Leviathan with a hook, but he can draw up a great many Leviathans with exploding harpoons on factory ships. We know now that the sum of all the localized crimes can indeed poison the earth, the atmosphere, the multitudinous seas. And this knowledge is only the confirmation by science and our own direct experience of what has been evident to the poetic imagination for millennia, and is embodied in countless myths, folk-tales, poems. The commonest of all heroes is the one Joseph Campbell called 'The Hero with a Thousand Faces', the hero who hubristically sets himself above Nature and the gods, commits the archetypal crime against Nature and his own nature, is punished, virtually destroyed, but also corrected after a long quest in search of his bleeding victim which is also his true self. Prometheus was one of the earliest such heroes, who encouraged man by example to set himself above Nature.

The great imaginative writer may be one who has achieved a measure of fourfold vision – early Wordsworth, early Coleridge, Whitman, early Hopkins, later Yeats, later Lawrence, later Hughes. But that achievement is made at great cost. He is also likely to be the opposite, for much of his life, or in his more normal state – a cursed sufferer from single vision, from egotism, materialism, dualism, who differs from the rest of us in lacking our complacency, in knowing that he is sick and striving in his art to diagnose that sickness, to punish and to heal himself. The artist is a criminal like the rest, but differs from us in that his loyalty to his imagination forces him to acknowledge his guilt and seek correction. Rarely, he manages to get himself, to a degree, corrected.

We are all criminals in the sense that we have all persecuted, exploited or denied essential parts of ourselves, particularly that part which Jung called, in men, the anima. And that innermost self is representative of all that we persecute, exploit or deny in the outer world – women, 'undeveloped' peoples, animals, Nature herself. Hughes is careful not to accuse his protagonists of specific crimes. Their guilt lies rather in a state of being, a set of unconscious attitudes we all inherit, complacent and hubristic and inimical to Nature's laws. This state of being harms the goddess in three ways. It harms the actual women, her incarnations, with whom the protagonist comes in contact; it harms, directly or indirectly, the earth, its sacred creatures, its delicate web of interdependencies; and it harms the man's own anima, his daemon, the more creative, feminine part of his own nature.

By the time we reach *Crow*, Hughes' first major work after the death of Plath, the crime against Nature looms much larger than ever before, and is no longer a crime committed by 'them', certain identifiable types, but by all of us, to an extent that makes it seem to be a defect in the genetic code of the species, or at least the male of the species. But even if going on committing the crime is what it is to be human, humans also have the capacity to recognize their own criminality and do something about it. The writer hauls himself, as Everyman, into the dock of his own imagination, as Hughes quite literally does in *Cave Birds*, the continuation of the aborted *Crow*.

Imagination is the faculty that enables us to locate and release the violated prisoner, or at least to give her a voice. Those who are most successful in this we call poets. Initially, that voice may well be embittered, revengeful, destructive. It passes a harsh judgement on the poet, our representative. The punishment may be bloody, as in *The Bacchae* or *Gaudete*, terrifying, as in *King Lear* or 'The Ancient Mariner' or *Cave Birds*. But the pain and the fear, which may be real enough in some cases, are also symbolic of a process that is simultaneously destructive and creative, the breaking of the complacent, self-sufficient ego, which is the locus of guilt. Subsequently the voice becomes gentler, and the healing process can begin.

Beyond all this the artist must, of course, have the ability to communicate the whole experience through language in a way that produces an authentic miracle – that some sounds, or marks on a page, should transmit a healing and fertilizing power.

Hughes' fullest description of the myth of the goddess is to be found in *Shakespeare and the Goddess of Complete Being*. Here Hughes makes many attempts to summarize his approach. The best of these I can find is tucked away on pages 392–3:

> Confronting the Goddess of Divine Love, the Goddess of Complete Being, the ego's extreme alternatives are either to reject her and attempt to live an independent, rational, secular life or to abnegate the ego and embrace her love with 'total,

unconditional love', which means to become a saint, a holy idiot, possessed by the Divine Love. The inevitability of the tragic idea which Shakespeare projects with such 'divine' completeness is that there is no escape from one choice or the other. Man will always choose the former, simply because once he is free of a natural, creaturely awareness of the divine indulgence which permits him to exist at all, he wants to live his own life, and he has never invented a society of saints that was tolerable. In other words, always, one way or another, he rejects the Goddess. This is the first phase of the tragedy. Then follows his correction: his 'madness' against the Goddess, the Puritan crime ... which leads directly to his own tragic self-destruction, from which he can escape only after the destruction of his ego – being reborn through the Flower rebirth, becoming a holy idiot, renouncing his secular independence, and surrendering once again to the Goddess. From the human point of view, obviously the whole business is monstrous: tragic on a cosmic scale, where the only easements are in the possibilities of a temporary blessing from the Goddess (an erotic fracture in the carapace of the tragic hero) or of becoming a saint. There is a third possibility, in some degree of self-anaesthesia, some kind of living death. But man has no more choice in the basic arrangement than the blue-green algae.

Hughes calls this his 'tragic equation', though it is far from being some mechanical formula he has invented; it is no less than a complex, all-embracing myth, which Shakespeare forged out of his inheritance of classical mythology and gnostic and alchemical wisdom, all transformed in the crucible of his life and times, as his supreme attempt to convert apparently random and painful experience into a process of self-transformation:

> The secret of Shakespeare's unique development lies in this ability (in most departments of life it would be regarded as a debility) to embrace the inchoate, as-if-supernatural actuality, and be overwhelmed by it, be dismantled and even shattered by it, without closing his eyes, and then to glue himself back

together, with a new, greater understanding of the abyss, all within the confines of a drama, and to do this once every seven months, year after year for twenty-four years. (479)

And it is not only a matter of self-transformation. Shakespeare simultaneously expresses what Hughes calls 'the fundamental human challenge'. The equation is equally applicable, that is, not only to Shakespeare, but to the template of many of the classics of Western literature (including *The Oresteia*, the Theban plays of Sophocles, *The Bacchae*, *Sir Gawain and the Green Knight*, 'The Ancient Mariner', *Moby Dick*, *The Scarlet Letter*, Hopkins, Eliot, Golding and Hughes himself, especially *Crow*, *Cave Birds* and *Gaudete*), and to the present world predicament, the ecological crisis.

Going naked

The very act of transforming experience into art through the 'poetic' mastery of language itself exposes the artist to a new dimension of temptation, a new disguised form of criminality. The temptation is to process experience, in Lawrence's terms to cook it in the artistic consciousness, until it loses its savour, its very life and truth, and becomes another form of egotism. There is the temptation to succumb to the embrace of what Hughes called the 'maternal octopus' of the English poetic tradition, to produce your own version of what has been done so beautifully, so expressively, so powerfully, in the past; the temptation to write the sort of poetry that is currently valued, that critics and publishers seem to want; the temptation to put on display one's talents, as the young Yeats put all his circus animals on show in the full confidence that words obeyed his call; the temptation, having achieved some success, a readership, to repeat the same effects and write what Hopkins called Parnassian. Both Yeats and Lawrence at the time of the First World War were arguing that at such a time the poet could earn the right to be noticed only by going naked: 'Everything can go, but this stark, bare, rocky directness of statement, this alone makes poetry, today', Lawrence wrote in

1916. When Eliot read that 15 years later he responded with rare fervour:

> This speaks to me of that at which I have long aimed, in writing poetry; to write poetry which should be essentially poetry, with nothing poetic about it, poetry standing naked in its bare bones, or poetry so transparent that we should not see the poetry, but that which we are meant to see through the poetry, poetry so transparent that in reading it we are intent on what the poem *points at*, and not on the poetry, this seems to me the thing to try for. To get *beyond poetry*, as Beethoven, in his later works, strove to get *beyond music*. We never succeed, perhaps, but Lawrence's words mean this to me, that they express to me what I think that the forty or fifty original lines that I have written strive towards. (Matthiessen 90)

A few years later, at the beginning of another world war, Eliot wrote the line: 'The poetry does not matter' ('East Coker').

Ted Hughes had the same lesson to learn, the need for the self-abnegation by a famous poet of the pyrotechnics, the 'old heroic bang', on which his fame depended. He admired a generation of East European poets such as Popa and Pilinszky whose work was purged of rhetoric, deliberately impoverished, 'a strategy of making audible meanings without disturbing the silence' (*WP 223*). He sought a simplicity not of retreat or exclusion but on the far side of experience and complexity:

> This other rare type has the simplicity of an inclusion of everything in a clear solution. We recognize the difference, because we recognize in this latter kind that the observer has paid in full for what he records, and that has earned him a superior stake in reality, which is not common. Good folk rhymes have this kind of simplicity – experience itself seems to have produced them. … To succeed in any degree in producing it, a writer needs … a touch of that martial/ascetic brand of temperament – usually alien and even hostile to aesthetic sensibility – to provide the reckless drive towards essentials, and the readiness to

abandon the verbal charms of conventional poetry. (Introduction to *The Reef*)

The achievement of such nakedness is a shedding of what Lawrence called 'the full armour of their own idea of themselves', a form of ego-death. It is also a shedding of the husk that must split before the seed can germinate. From such humble beginnings whole new myths might grow.

Healing the Wound

Hughes' deepest discussion of the healing powers of the imagination is in his essay on Leonard Baskin, 'The Hanged Man and the Dragonfly'. Here he describes the process by which Baskin's greatest works miraculously transform the greatest imaginable horror, the hanged man, into something rich and strange, the dragonfly.

The process must begin with a kind of death, with full awareness, that is, of the nearness of actual death, 'the dead man behind the mirror', and the experience of the ego-death which would necessarily follow a full recognition and acceptance of that. Hughes was deeply influenced by Lorca, who wrote of the *duende*:

> The *duende* does not appear if it sees no possibility of death. ... In idea, in sound, or in gesture, the *duende* likes a straight fight with the creator on the edge of the well. The *duende* wounds, and in the healing of this wound which never closes is the prodigious, the original in the work of man. The magical quality of a poem consists in its being always possessed by the *duende*, so that whoever beholds it is baptized with dark water. Because with *duende* it is easier to love and to understand, and also one is *certain* to be loved and understood; and this struggle for expression and for the communication of expression reaches at times, in poetry, the character of a fight to the death. (136)

Baskin's hanged man is not a picture of death, but of an individual living a perpetual 'extreme moment', not of heightened powers of life, but of dead man nakedness, dead man last ditch helplessness, dead man exposure to the crowding infinities, getting to his feet only as a Lazarus, having had life stripped off him, and the ego and personal life plucked out of him, through the strange wound in the chest. (*WP* 92)

This figure appears frequently in Hughes, most notably as Prometheus on his crag and as the protagonist of *Cave Birds*, in, for example, 'The Knight'. Nor is it a picture of atrocity, designed merely to horrify. Because it is art it is also music, whose dark sounds are simultaneously horrible and beautiful. This music, Hughes claims, or what wells up out of this music, 'is also the sap of mathematical law, a secretion of the gulf itself – the organizing and creative energy itself':

> And so the very thing that makes it art, that gives it the ring of cosmic law and grips us to itself and lifts us out of our egoistic prison and connects, as it seems, everything to everything, and everything to the source of itself – is what makes it unpleasant. … It is, as it were, some ambiguous substance, simultaneously holy and anathema, some sort of psychological drug flourishing in the bloodstream.

Lorca called it *duende*; Hughes calls it *mana*: '*mana* as the goddess of the source of terrible life, the real substance of any art that has substance, in spite of what we might prefer'. *Mana* comes to the sufferer as the body's natural response to deep hurt, a healing medicine, a redemption. It must be paid for by that suffering. Hence all great art is tragic. Baskin's hanged man depicts the moment of unbearable pain, which is also the moment at which *mana* begins to flow. *The Hanged Man* is life-size – the largest woodcut ever made. As an engraver, Baskin literally wounds his subjects. 'It is the portrait of a total wound – head to foot one wound':

> And it is here in this woodcut, in the actual work of the blade, that we can find the meaning of Baskin's line. With deep labour, he is delivering his form from the matrix. He is liberating a body from the death that encloses it. Inevitably, one

imagines a surgeon's tranced sort of alertness, as he cuts…. And
as the scalpel cuts, *mana* flows. That is, seen from our point of
vantage, beauty flows. As if the blade, in prayer, were less a
honed edge, more a laying on of hands – a blessing – a caress –
and a glorification. The steel, under Baskin's care, is a balm
flowing into the wound

(…)

But in Baskin's imagination the Hanged Man is evolving further, and becoming something else too. That moment of
redemption, where healing suddenly wells out of a wound that
had seemed fatal, is not enough. The beauty of it has to
blossom. The dead man has to flower into life. And so this
skinned carcass, so wrapped and unwrapped in its pain, is
becoming a strange thing – a chrysalis, a giant larva. (92, 97)

And out of the chrysalis emerges the fragile beauty of the dragonfly:

The Hanged Man is a symbol of the first phase: *mana* nursed
from agony. And the Dragonfly is a symbol of the last phase:
the agony wholly redeemed, healed – and transformed into its
opposite, by *mana*.

This process is, of course, by no means unique to Baskin. Hughes
claims that it is the spontaneous response to private pain or tribal
calamity. He connects it to the mysteries of Eleusis – 'a stunning end-
of-all-things cry at the death of the god – which is also the cry of
incredulity, the ecstatic outcry at his simultaneous resurrection' – and
to the myths of Osiris, Prometheus, Job and the Holy Grail, to the
shaman's dream-journey 'from his difficult take-off and flight,
through obstacles and ordeals, to the source of renewal', to the mor-
phology of epic, 'its recurrent pattern of recognizable episodes …
wherever the saga tells, in one metaphor or another, of the search
for and the finding of *mana*'. A decade later he was to find the
classic literary expression of the paradigm in the ending of *Antony
and Cleopatra*:

What now remains, for this Osirian Antony, is for him to free
himself, wholly and finally, from that obsolete Herculean

Roman Antony, and emerge as his true self, the universal love god, consort of the Goddess of Complete Being, in so far as that can be incarnated in the body of the middle-aged Roman warrior, lover of a middle-aged, reckless, fearful queen. … While the drama portrays the self-destruction of the great Roman Antony on the tragic plane, it becomes, on the transcendental plane, a theophany, the liberation of Antony's Osirian Divine Love nature, under the 'magical' influence of the completeness of Cleopatra's. The play … begins with the love god fully formed but unacknowledged, trapped within the self-ignorant, military Herculean *bon viveur*, who is still confidently wrestling for political control of the Roman world. It ends with the crushed, empty armour of the former Herculean warrior, like an empty chrysalis, while the liberated love god, like an iridescent new winged being, lies in the lap of the Goddess, his love 'total and unconditional', reunited beyond life and death (in the high tomb) with the adoring Goddess. (*Shakespeare* 316–17)

Hughes' own *Prometheus on his Crag* undergoes a similar process, emerging finally from the shell (with the help of the vulture/midwife/goddess) of his crucified body as weightless as a dragonfly:

And Prometheus eases free.
He sways to his stature.
And balances. And treads

On the dusty peacock film where the world floats.

Many of the *Cave Birds* poems and the *Gaudete* epilogue poems (such as 'When the still-soft eyelid') are the verbal equivalent of Baskin woodcuts.

Lumb's agonies finally earn him the right to redeem a 'horrible world',

Where I let in again –
As if for the first time –
The untouched joy.

'The value and force of living myth'

The usual form of myth is the folk-tale, the narrative or epic poem, or the poetic drama (often, for the Greeks, a trilogy of such dramas). We can hardly conceive of all the painful transformations of a fully worked-out myth being contained in anything shorter than 'The Ancient Mariner'. Yet Hughes' imagination seemed most at home with the fairly short poem. Occasionally Hughes managed to get almost the whole myth into a single poem, but most of his poems, though they plug directly into one or more of the mythic paradigms I have been discussing, do not attempt to contain the whole process. Each poem is a station on the journey, a bulletin from the struggle. Consequently Hughes was attracted from the beginning to the poetic sequence. Some of the poems in *Lupercal*, most obviously 'Mayday on Holderness', were salvaged from an abandoned sequence about England, in which the unifying image was to have been a river – insofar as it was a specific river, the Humber. Hughes prefaced *Wodwo* with this note:

> The stories and the play in this book may be read as notes, appendix and unversified episodes of the events behind the poems, or as chapters of a single adventure to which the poems are commentary and amplification. Either way, the verse and the prose are intended to be read together, as parts of a single work.

He later described this adventure as 'a descent into destruction of some sort' (Faas 205), yet the last two poems at least clearly indicate an upward movement.

Hughes' most ambitious sequence, by far, was to have been *The Life and Songs of the Crow*, an epic folk-tale studded with hundreds of poems, in which Crow would recapitulate almost all the crimes and errors of humanity, undergo the descent into destruction, but finally, with the help of an Eskimo shaman, reconstitute himself and his female victim, and marry her. Having taken Crow through about the first two-thirds of his adventures and again just reached the point where Crow was beginning to make some progress, Hughes was stunned by the second tragedy in his life in March 1969. The wound was reopened. His own experience could no longer validate the healing process. Whereas in his works for children he was prepared to fabricate an up-beat ending – determined on principle to do so – he would never write a poem for adults that was not authenticated by his own experience. The published *Crow* was merely a selection of poems salvaged from the almost entirely negative phases of Crow's quest for humanity.

Crow, however, refused to die, and managed to complete his quest in slightly different terms as the nameless protagonist (cockerel/ crow/man) of *Cave Birds*. Though *Cave Birds* is Hughes' most complete sequence, and has been acclaimed by several critics as his most successful, it seems to me that its dependence on rather contrived and esoteric imagery drawn from alchemy puts it, as a sequence (there are several wonderful individual poems), to one side of the mainstream of Hughes' achievement, incompletely recycled through his own experience. Hughes himself came to feel this too: 'there's a funny atmosphere about them that I really dislike ... crabbed, dead, abstract'. When he proposed to drop from the sequence the several poems that stand outside the alchemical bird drama, I pleaded with him to retain them. He replied:

> I'd like to thank you for your remarks about *Cave Birds*, because they made me dig out those pieces I'd deleted, and so it comes about that I rediscover their rough virtues, so much better than what I tried to replace them with, as you so rightly complain, and I think probably better than the main sequence, certainly better than many of them. In fact now I look at them I realize they were the beginning of an attempt to open myself in a different direction, a very necessary direction for me, the only real direction, and I'm aghast at the time and density of folly that has passed since I lost sight of it.

Gaudete was another attempt to get the whole myth, but it is lopsided, the melodrama of the changeling Lumb overshadowing the story of the real Lumb so wonderfully, if obliquely, rendered in the Epilogue poems.

Moortown is a collection of short sequences, the farming poems, *Prometheus on his Crag*, *Earth-numb* and *Adam and the Sacred Nine*. In *Prometheus* the agony overwhelms the rather contrived ending. Adam is pleasing, but a little too formalized, formulaic. Hughes tried to overcome the limitations of the separate sequences by combining them with great care into a regenerative myth, which he described in a letter to me:

> The first part is a life embedded in mud, body of death etc., & seeds. *Prometheus* is what tries to wake up inside this. *Earth-numb* is his failing effort to come to terms with it. *Adam* is his succeeding means of coming to terms with it. That's the general plan. The whole drift is an alchemising of a phoenix out of a serpent. An awakened life out of an unawakened.
>
> Anything that was not satisfyingly inter-related, I kept out, or rather, it kept out. Prometheus is related to the main protagonist of *Earth-numb* – in his various phases. The Vulture not unrelated to the 9 birds. The death in the natural labouring external world of *Moortown*, which is mainly dung & death acting as a crucible for repeated efforts at birth, is a counterpoint to the 'birth', in a supernatural, spirit, inner world, of Prometheus. That's its symbolic role.
>
> It was a case of me finding the dominant pattern in all the stuff I had from 3 or 4 years, & making positive sense out of it, rather than negative. And as it turned out, I didn't have to wrench & remake anything, it was all there simply. What it lacks, as a single pattern, is a sense of purposive or dramatic motive. Maybe it's better that way. But it means its growing into other people will be a slow business – as it was with *Wodwo*.

Unfortunately, Ann Skea, one of the few readers with the imagination to divine such patterns, did not deal with *Moortown* in *The Poetic Quest* (a splendid book which, being published in Australia, has been largely ignored in England). Ann Skea has attempted, persuasively, to read *Remains of Elmet* as a complete regeneration myth, but to do so has had to rely on an ordering of the poems which is Fay

Godwin's, not Hughes'. It is, however, an ordering Hughes was willing to accept, and later recognized as better than his own two subsequent attempts to reorder the poems (in *Three Books* and *Elmet*).

As *Wodwo* and *Crow* got only the earlier stages of the myth, so *River* gets mainly the later, regenerative stages, completing the gradual transformation over Hughes' entire oeuvre from blood to mud to water to light.

We can say of Hughes what Hughes said of Eliot, that every poem must be read, chronologically, as part of 'the series which make up the poet's opus':

> The poet's each successive creation can be read as the poetic self's effort to make itself known, to further its takeover. This effort embodies itself in a complete visionary symbol of the poetic self and its separated predicament. The distinguished features of this kind of image are just these – that it is visionary, that it is irreducibly symbolic, and that it is dramatically complete. The successive visions evolve in time according to the way the poetic self evolves in its hidden life. (*WP*, 277)

When we look at the whole span of Hughes' work (as I try to do in chapter 4) we shall see how closely it fits most of the mythic paradigms I have been discussing. It also corresponds remarkably to the four-stage process leading to what Blake called fourfold vision.

Single vision is fallen vision, fallen, that is, from an assumed original, primal, unified vision, symbolized by Eden. At the Fall, which is both a curse we inherit and a process we re-enact in every life, Man is assumed to lose his ability to perceive anything in the spiritual dimension, anything as holy or miraculous. Hence it is a fall into sterile materialism and rationalism. He is assumed to lose his innocence, which is not simply his ignorance and inexperience but his flexibility, openness to experience, good faith, capacity for spontaneous authentic living; to lose his access to the Energies, either within himself or without. Fallen Man lives a second-hand life, a living death, in a self-made world of false rigidities and mechanisms of thinking and feeling and seeing. Single vision cannot see wholes, only fragments. It is analytic, compartmentalizing. It cannot see relationships and patterns and wholes, and is therefore solipsistic, reductive and dehumanizing, at the mercy of time and chance and death. Single vision is alienated, hubristic selfhood, and the achievement of twofold, threefold and fourfold vision are therefore stages in the annihilation of the self. The purpose is to regain Paradise – but it will not be the same Paradise. The new Paradise will be 'organized innocence' and atonement on the far side of experience and suffering and many inner deaths.

Single vision has been Western Man's common condition throughout historical time. Artists and prophets have always cried out against it. Only the symptoms change from age to age, and the artist must diagnose them afresh, for the new symptoms are usually hailed as signs of 'progress'. Blake saw the symptoms in the late eighteenth century as the deification of reason and the five senses (Locke), mechanistic science (Newton), the increasingly repressive Puritanism of the churches, and the first mills of the Industrial Revolution. It is not assumed that every artist is born with fourfold vision and never loses it. What he can never lose is the sense of something lost, and the obligation to struggle to recover it.

Blake's use of the suffix 'fold' implies that each stage depends upon and then subsumes the former. That is, the recovery of true vision, whereby we shall see things as they really are, can only be achieved by passing through all four stages, and in this order. Stage one is the recognition of the all-pervading symptoms of single vision as such, of the need to undertake the psychic or spiritual journey out of its dark prison, and to engage it in a lifelong battle. Stage two is the release of the energies that will be needed for this battle and this journey, energies that, denied and repressed, have become 'reptiles of the mind'. Stage three is the recovery of innocence. Stage four, the recovery of unified vision, will be a vision of the holiness of everything that lives.

What I am suggesting here is that Hughes' career has taken him this very route – not in a straight line, not without temporary diversions and retreats – there are endless recapitulations. The vision once achieved is not subsequently 'on tap': it has to be won again every time. If it is taken for granted, if short cuts are taken, it loses its valid-ity. Every insight must be paid for. Nevertheless, looking at the whole of Hughes' oeuvre, the paradigm fits.

And at the end of the quest there is always the return, when the hierophany must be turned into words as a healing gift for others. In 1987 Bo Gustavsson prophesied, on the basis of the clearly mythic shape of Hughes' career thus far, where his poetry would go next:

> Hughes' future development as a poet, if it is at all possible to speculate about such matters, will probably be in the direction of a poetry returning to everyday life. He will still be a mythic poet but a mythic poet who returns, like Campbell's questing hero, with the elixir of life or regenerative knowledge to share the life of ordinary people. Hughes will then write a poetry of mythic return to everyday life and by so doing he will complete his career as the foremost mythic poet of our age. The aim of this new phase of his career, following the two earlier phases of mythic descent and mythico-mystic initiation, will be to anchor his hierophanic awareness in everyday reality and so further broaden and clarify his awareness of the sacred. (*Critical Essays* 239)

And this is exactly what happened. After *River*, Hughes returned from Paradise, his spiritual home, to his ordinary home and familiar, indeed earliest themes. In *Wolfwatching* he writes again of the hawk and the wolf, but with a newly won poise, an unforced gentle strength. He returns to his own family history and particularly to the theme of the First World War in such poems as 'For the Duration', but with a new humility and deeper humanity. These qualities, this compassionate wisdom, informs many of his last poems: 'The Last of the 1st/5th Lancashire Fusiliers', 'Lines about Elias', 'Platform One'. These are no doubt the kind of poems Hughes would have continued to write had death not intervened.

Like Hughes, Joseph Campbell discusses the power of mythology and all creative art in biological terms:

> Mythological symbols touch and exhilarate centers of life beyond the reach of vocabularies of reason and coercion. The

light-world modes of experience and thought were late, very
late, developments on the biological prehistory of our species.
Even in the life-course of the individual, the opening of the eyes
to light occurs only after all the main miracles have been
accomplished of the building of a living body of already func-
tioning organs, each with its inherent aim, none of these aims
either educed from, or as yet even known to, reason; while in
the larger course and context of the evolution of life itself from
the silence of primordial seas, of which the taste still runs in our
blood, the opening of the eyes occurred only after the first principle of all organic being ('Now I'll eat you; now you eat me!')
had been operative for so many hundreds of millions of centuries that it could not then, and cannot now, be undone –
though our eyes and what they witness may persuade us to
regret the monstrous game.

  The first function of a mythology is to reconcile waking consciousness to the *mysterium tremendum et fascinans* of this universe *as it is*: the second being to render an interpretive total
image of the same, as known to contemporary consciousness.
(*Creative Mythology* 4)

The function of all art is 'the revelation to waking consciousness of
the powers of its own sustaining source'. Campbell claims that with
any writer whose realization of his own experience has been 'of a certain depth and import, his communication will have the value and
force of living myth' (*Creative Mythology* 4). Jung had said the same
in *The Spirit of Man*:

  The unsatisfied yearning of the artist reaches back to the primordial image in the unconscious which is best fitted to compensate the inadequacy and one-sidedness of the present.
  (…)
  Whenever the collective unconscious becomes a living experience and is brought to bear upon the conscious outlook of an
  age, this event is a creative act which is of importance for a
  whole epoch.
  (…)

He (the artist) has plunged into the healing and redeeming depths of the collective psyche. (82, 98, 105)

Jung believed, according to Baring and Cashford, that:

> if the conscious psyche of individuals or of groups (such as nations or even the human race as a species) has become distorted, then the unconscious psyche will, apparently intentionally, compensate for this distortion by insisting on an opposite point of view in order to restore the balance. (554)

Thus imagination is subversive, and the imaginative writer of sufficient courage says, in Melville's phrase, 'No, in thunder!' to the prevailing orthodoxies, unquestioned assumptions and shibboleths of his time. The dramatic festivals of ancient Greece virtually came into being in order to testify to the crime against Nature and warn of its inevitable consequences – consequences for the individual, for the state and for the race. Those protests and warnings have not hitherto been heeded. The truth is too uncomfortable, the implications too radically revolutionary.

We no longer need visionary artists to give us warnings; we are bombarded with warnings from every side. The role of the artist now is, more than ever before, to heal, to discover and embody possibilities of regeneration. In 1970 Hughes said that if our civilization was about to disappear, 'one had better have one's spirit invested in something that will not vanish. And this is a shifting of your foundation to completely new Holy Ground, a new divinity, one that won't be under the rubble when the churches collapse' (*UU* 207).

Aristophanes' *The Frogs* was performed at the Great Dionysia in 405 (possibly the same festival at which *The Bacchae* was performed), when it was obvious to the imaginative writers that Athenian civilization was about to vanish. *The Frogs*, for all its knock-about comedy, is almost as tragic in its implications for Athens as *The Bacchae*. The idea of the play is that since the three great poets, Aeschylus, Sophocles and Euripides, were all now dead, the only hope for Athens was to send Dionysos down to Hades to bring back the greatest of them. When Dionysos gets there, the ghost of Euripides asks him what he wants a poet for. 'To save the city of course', he replies. The comedy lies entirely in the idea that a dead poet might be brought back, not at all in the idea that a poet might save the city. The absolute seriousness of that proposition marks the difference in the status of the poet in Athenian society from our own. The idea that a poet could save us if listened to would now provoke almost universal laughter, not least among academics.

On 12 January 1999, the day on which it was announced that Hughes had won the T.S. Eliot prize, an article in *The Independent* asked Euripides' question 'What are poets for?', described Shelley's phrase 'unacknowledged legislators' as 'brash cockiness', and gave no hint that there could be any connection between poetry and the ecological crisis, the fate of our civilization or the life of the spirit.

Imaginative art would be in a privileged position to lead the way in our time if there were a large enough readership capable of responding appropriately to it. But the capacity for such a response had already in Lawrence's day become rare:

> The man who has lost his religious response *cannot* respond to literature or to any form of art, fully: because the call of every work of art, spiritual or physical, is religious, and demands a religious response. The people who, having lost their religious connection, turn to literature and art, find there a great deal of pleasure, aesthetic, intellectual, many kinds of pleasure, even curiously sensual. But it is the pleasure of entertainment, not of experience. ... They cannot give to literature the one thing it really requires – if it be important at all – and that is the religious response; and they cannot take from it the one thing it gives, the religious experience of linking up or making a new connection. (*Apocalypse* 155–6)

The greatest challenge to literature, education and literary criticism is to try to help readers to recover this faculty. As Lawrence writes:

> The great range of responses that have fallen dead in us have to come to life again. It has taken two thousand years to kill them. Who knows how long it will take to bring them to life. (78)

In the Faas interview in 1970 Hughes wrote of the call to the shaman to go to the spirit world:

> He goes to get something badly needed, a cure, an answer, some sort of divine intervention in the community's affairs. ... Poets usually refuse the call. How are they to accept it? How can a poet become a medicine man and fly to the source and come back and heal or pronounce oracles? Everything among us is against it. (*UU*, 206)

Hughes' assumption that the shamanic call and the poetic call are the same, that all great poems 'qualify their authors for the magic drum', seems less outlandish (as Paul Bentley has pointed out) in the light of Levi-Strauss's claim that an essential part of the undeniable effectiveness of shamanic procedures as cures lies in the shaman's ability to give the sufferer a language in which the sickness can be understood:

> The shaman provides the sick woman with a *language*, by means of which unexpressed, and otherwise inexpressible, psychic states can be immediately expressed. And it is the transition to this verbal expression – at the same time making it possible to undergo in an ordered and intelligible form a real experience that would otherwise be chaotic and inexpressible – which induces the release of the physiological process, that is, the reorganization, in a favourable direction, of the process to which the sick woman is subjected. (*Structural Anthropology* 198)

Perhaps since 1970 the claims made for myth by Hughes and Heaney have become a little less unthinkable, not because there is any wider appreciation of imaginative art, but because the poet is no longer alone. Art, science, philosophy, religion, are converging towards a common centre which we are now in a position to recognize as holistic, sacramental, a rapidly growing awareness that, in Coleridge's words, 'we are all one life'. No longer are poetic visionaries voices in the wilderness. Their vision, formerly seen as romantic or eccentric, is coming to be seen as the essential vision of the nascent world-age.

CHAPTER TWO
From Prospero to Orpheus

A relief map of a poet's childhood landscape is often an amazingly accurate map of that poet's psyche and imagination. That landscape is available to the poet not only as subject matter and 'local colour'; it can provide him with a fund of vital images, and with a paradigm for his understanding of life itself and his own inner being. If the business of the poet is, as Hughes has claimed, to find metaphors for his own nature, then the earliest images to present themselves as such metaphors are likely to be the contours, climate, flora and fauna of the first familiar place, especially if that place has been the family home for generations. Both Hughes and Plath became very aware of this, and wrote their own accounts of it. Plath's 'Ocean 1212-W' and Hughes' 'The Rock' appeared in *The Listener* within three weeks of each other in 1963.

The rock in Hughes' essay is Scout Rock, near his birthplace, Mytholmroyd, in the Calder Valley, from which the moors rise steeply on both sides, stretching to the north as far as Haworth.

> The most impressive early companion of my childhood was a dark cliff, to the South, a wall of rock and steep woods half-way up the sky, just cleared by the winter sun. This was the *memento mundi* over my birth: my spiritual midwife at the time and my godfather ever since – or one of my godfathers. From my first day, it watched. If it couldn't see me direct, a towering gloom over my pram, it watched me through a species of periscope: that is, by infiltrating the very light of my room with its particular shadow. (*Worlds* 122)

One feature similarly dominated Plath's childhood:

> My childhood landscape was not land but the end of the land – the cold, salt, running hills of the Atlantic. I sometimes think

36

my vision of the sea is the clearest thing I own. (*Johnny Panic* 177)

And again, the sea reached her when she was out of sight by infiltration:

> Even with my eyes shut I could feel the glimmers off its bright mirrors spider over my lids. I lay in a watery cradle, and sea gleams found the chinks in the dark green window blind, playing and dancing, or resting and trembling a little. (119)

This was not the sea of Melville. It was a sea not of depths (the 'whaled monstered sea-bottom' which fascinated Hughes) but of surface and mirrors, prismatic, not of relics but of jewels, not of sharks but of mermaids. Though this sea was capable of great violence, leaving spectacular wreckage and a dead shark in the geranium bed, 'my grandmother had her broom out, it would soon be right'. Nothing could disturb her sense that the sea's role in relation to herself was to bring her blessings, to lay its coloured magical tribute at her feet – 'the purple "lucky stones" I used to collect with a white ring all the way round, or the shell of a blue mussel with its rainbowy angel's fingernail interior'; nothing until the final sudden betrayal, the triumph of the real world:

> My father died, we moved inland. Whereon those nine first years of my life sealed themselves off like a ship in a bottle – beautiful, inaccessible, obsolete, a fine, white flying myth. (124)

Hughes, on the other hand, records that his first seven years were a struggle to escape from a curse, a shadow-trap:

> If a man's death is held in place by a stone, my birth was fastened into place by that rock, and for my first seven years it pressed its shape and various moods into my brain. There was no easy way to escape it. I lived under it as under the presence of a war, or an occupying army: it constricted life in some way, demanded and denied, and was not happy. Beneath it, the narrow valley, with its flooring of cricket pitch, meadows, bowling

greens, streets, railways and mills, seemed damp, darl   ⌐ ⌐ ⌐
satisfied. ... The final sensation was of having been ⌐app. ⌐
(*Worlds* 122)

He remembers the first time he made that escape, the climb with his
brother, at about six, to the top of the rock. He felt 'an alarming
exhilaration. I felt infinitely exposed, to be up there on the stage I had
been trying to imagine for so long'. Then, behind the immediate bar-
rier, were the high moors:

> Ultimately, the valley was surrounded by moor skylines, further
> off and higher than the rock, folded one behind another. The
> rock asserted itself, tried to pin you down, policed and
> gloomed. But you *could* escape it, climb past it and above it,
> with some effort. You could not escape the moors. They did
> not impose themselves. They simply surrounded and waited.
> (124)

Already the boy is being shaped to see life as a quest to discover and
reach whatever is over the edge of the known world.

> If any word could be found engraved around my skull, just
> above the ears and eyebrows, it would probably be the word
> 'horizon'. Every thought I tried to send beyond the confines of
> that valley had to step over that high definite hurdle. In most
> places the earth develops away naturally in every direction, over
> roads and crowded gradients and confused vistas, but there it
> rose up suddenly to a cut empty upturned edge, high in the sky,
> and stopped. I supposed it somehow started again somewhere
> beyond, with difficulty. So the visible horizon was the magic
> circle, excluding and enclosing, into which our existence had
> been conjured, and everything in me gravitated towards it.
> (125)

The spirit of the high moors was 'the peculiar sad desolate spirit that
cries in telegraph wires on moor roads, in the dry and so similar
voices of grouse and sheep, and the moist voices of curlews'. The light
up there was very different, 'at once both gloomily purplish and

incredibly clear, unnaturally clear, as if objects there had less protec-
tion than elsewhere, were more exposed to the radioactive dangers of
space, more startled by their own existence'. The spirit was eerie,
unpleasant, disastrous, too close to the stone, too close to death, yet,
like Lorca's *duende*, ultimately exultant.

> From there the return home was a descent into the pit, and
> after each visit I must have returned more and more of myself
> to the valley. This was where the division of body and soul, for
> me, began. (126)

The moors became, as for Emily Brontë, a spiritual home. His imagination needed the thrust of the Pennines:

> Those barrellings of strength are heaving slowly and heave
> To your feet and surf upwards
> In a still, fiery air, hauling the imagination,
> Carrying the larks upward.   ('Pennines in April')

The flora and fauna of the region carried a clear message to the
boy, that life was a continual struggle, against all the odds, merely to
survive. Yet the fact that it did, barely, survive was miraculous – that
the curlews could, apparently, live on air, that the polluted canal
beside his house could one day produce a trout ('an ingot', 'a trea-
sure', 'a free lord'),

> A seed
> Of the wild god now flowering for me
> Such a tigerish, dark, breathing lily
> Between the tyres, under the tortured axles
>   ('The Long Tunnel Ceiling')

that what humbled these hills had also raised

> The arrogance of blood and bone,
> And thrown the hawk upon the wind,
> And lit the fox in the dripping ground.   ('Crow Hill')

Hughes told Ekbert Faas that all the forms of natural life were 'emis-
saries from the underworld'. In the 1995 *Paris Review* interview,

Hughes was asked why he chose 'to speak through animals so often'.
He replied:

> I suppose, because they were there at the beginning. Like par-
> ents. Since I spent my first seventeen or eighteen years con-
> stantly thinking about them more or less, they became a
> language – a symbolic language which is also the language of
> my whole life. It was ... part of the machinery of my mind
> from the beginning. They are a way of connecting all my deep-
> est feelings together. So, when I look for, or get hold of a feel-
> ing of that kind, it tends to bring up the image of an animal or
> animals simply because that's the deepest, earliest language that
> my imagination learned. (81)

A year later, in the Negev interview, he added: 'It was a symbolic language that became attached to my own emotions and remained. My
first six years shaped everything'.

The fox quickly became Hughes' personal totem, the perennial
victim but also the unquenchable flame. His attempts to keep
orphaned fox cubs were disastrous. He was fascinated by those men
who chose (like his own grandfather Crag Jack) to renounce the complacencies of the civilized world and throw in their lot with the non-
human creation; and by those whom the turmoil of history had
thrown over the top into the no-man's-land of trench warfare. The
images with which his father and uncle, both wounded hair's-breadth
miraculous survivors of the First World War, filled the imagination
of the growing boy were not difficult to match with those flooding
his experience from the natural world around him.

That is one way of looking at those first seven years; but it is only
part of the truth, a part perhaps more coloured by self-conscious
adult recollection than another view, which seems closer to the consciousness of such a young child, and much closer, remarkably parallel, to the experience of Sylvia Plath over those same first seven years.

By far the most important relationship of Hughes' Mytholmroyd
years was with his brother Gerald, ten years his senior. Gerald was
adept at all the things Ted wanted to do – camping, lighting fires,
using a rifle. Ted was his eager retriever as he shot anything that

moved. They went camping together in the nearby beautiful valleys, such as Hardcastle Crags and Crimsworth Dene. These times were bliss for the young Ted, these places paradisal:

> Two stepped down from the morning star.
> The stolen grouse were glowing like embers.
> The dew split colour.
> And a cupped hand brimmed with cockcrows.
> …
>
> Then the stream spoke oracles of abundance
> And the sun poured out at their feet.

But when Hughes was seven and his family moved to Mexborough in South Yorkshire, Gerald did not go with them. He cut loose to become a gamekeeper in Devon – the happiest year of his life. He spent most of the war in Africa. After the war he emigrated to Australia and got married there. Gerald had been his guide, not only physically, to the secret, magical places, but the spirit guide into the unfallen animal world for the apprentice shaman:

> The guide flew up from the pathway.
>
> The other stood still.
>
> The feather fell from his head.
> The drum stopped in his hand.
> The song died in his mouth. ('Two')

This loss of the elder brother was, of course, nothing like as traumatic an experience as Sylvia Plath's loss of her father at the same age. But, combined, as it was, with the loss of the whole landscape of his childhood, it was a watershed, sealing off those years as a dream of innocence.

In the event, there were equally magical places near Mexborough, such as Old Denaby, where Hughes tried to sustain the dream, at first alone, later with a school friend who shared his obsession with fishing and shooting. Though the landscape of South Yorkshire was less dramatic than that of West Yorkshire, the fauna was even more so.

Hughes lived within walking distance of both the Don and the Dearne, and would frequently leave home early enough in the morning to give himself time to investigate the wildlife of these rivers. There was a stretch of the Don where the river in spate had scooped out large hollows between places where the root systems of trees held the soil in place. Hughes found that if he silently climbed up the side of one of these hollows and peeped over the edge, there would frequently be some creature there. On one occasion, as he climbed one side of the hollow, quite unknown to him a fox was climbing the other. They arrived at the ridge simultaneously, and looked into each other's eyes from a distance of a few inches. For a split second, which seemed timeless, Hughes felt that the fox had leapt into his head, supplanting his own provisional human nature with its own definitive foxhood. This was the kind of experience he most wanted from the natural world, encounters with another, deeper reality, with something so totally other as to be sacred, yet also able to speak as nothing else could to his own depths, depths below all conditioning and education. Indeed, school and nature came to seem opposites, one the place where he should be incarcerated and disciplined according to artificial rules, the other the place where, in Emily Brontë's words, his 'own nature would be leading'; and this became the subject of some of his boyhood poems:

> But when evenings came for working where was I? – In some place lurking
> In the woodlands, always shirking any thing that needed ink.

At 11, Hughes discovered in the school library Henry Williamson's *Tarka the Otter*, which became his bible for two years until he almost knew it by heart. That book showed him how the poetic imagination could not only express but deepen and enrich one's response to the natural world. Alongside Kiplingesque sagas about Zulus or the Wild West, he began to write his own poems about fishing and shooting. Miss McLeod, his first form mistress at Mexborough Grammar School, took an interest in his writing. Then a young English teacher, Pauline Mayne, picked out a line in a poem he had shown her about a wildfowling expedition, a line describing the hammer of the wildfowler's gun breaking in the cold 'with a frost chilled snap'. 'That's poetry', she said. 'If that's poetry', he thought, 'I can give you no end of it.' Since writing poems about nature needed ink, such poems became the link between his truant disposition and his developing literary interests.

After the departure of Gerald, Hughes' older sister Olwyn became an important influence. Hughes wrote to me:

> His absence left me to my sister – who took his place as my mentor. She was the prodigy at school. – And I see now she had marvellously precocious taste in poetry. When my teacher began to make remarks about my writing my mother went out and bought a whole library – 2nd hand – of classic poets. All the Warwick Shakespeares, & everything after. Eventually Olwyn got me into the Shakespeare. They coached me, somehow – perpetual expectations. ... So all that started up alongside my shooting & fishing obsession. The later teachers – Pauline Mayne and John Fisher – became close friends of my mother's & Olwyn's & of mine, of course. So, I was in that cooker from age of about eleven – and totally confident that I belonged in it, so by 16 I had no thought of becoming anything but writer of some kind, certainly writing verse.

In one sense, this was a wonderful education for a budding poet. But in another, it meant that, like Sylvia Plath (though in a much less extreme and damaging way), Hughes was now 'in the cooker' of the literary and academic expectations of the women who surrounded him, women he loved and admired. Yet there remained throughout his adult life a hankering for the lost dream world, a suspicion that in going down the road of grammar school and university he had sacrificed another life altogether, the possibility of emulating his brother by becoming a gamekeeper or emigrating to Australia. What he later found most attractive about Henry Williamson when he met him was that 'he was untamed, and he was free'.

Writing poems, even when they were not about animals, was capturing animals by other means:

In a way, I suppose, I think of poems as a sort of animal. They have a life of their own, like animals, by which I mean that they seem quite separate from any person, even from their author, and nothing can be added to them or taken away without maiming and perhaps even killing them. And they have a certain wisdom. They know something special ... something perhaps which we are very curious to learn. Maybe my concern has been to capture not animals particularly and not poems, but simply things which have a vivid life of their own, outside mine. (*Poetry in the Making* 15)

Another boyhood poem is called (with considerable poetic licence) 'On Catching a 40 lb Pike'. Not far from his home was the site of an ancient monastery, with a pond 'as deep as England' in which were huge and ancient pike, which the young Hughes would fish for at night:

> It held
> Pike too immense to stir, so immense and old
> That past midnight I dared not cast
>
> But silently cast and fished
> With the hair frozen on my head
> For what might move, for what eye might move.
> The still splashes on the dark pond,
>
> Owls hushing the floating woods
> Frail on the ear against the dream
> Darkness beneath night's darkness had freed,
> That rose slowly towards me, watching.   ('Pike')

Fishing became, very early, the perfect metaphor for the poetic act as Hughes came to understand it. Concentration on a float has the same effect of dissolving the ego as concentration on a poetic subject.

All the little nagging impulses, that are normally distracting your mind, dissolve. They have to dissolve if you are to go on fishing. If they do not, then you cannot settle down: you get bored and pack up in a bad temper. But once they have dissolved, you enter one of the orders of bliss. ... At every moment your imagination is alarming itself with the size of the thing slowly leaving the weeds and approaching your bait. Or with the world of beauties down there, suspended in total ignorance of you. And the whole purpose of this concentrated excitement, in this arena of apprehension and unforseeable events, is to bring up some lovely solid thing like living metal from a world where nothing exists but those inevitable facts which raise life out of nothing and return it to nothing. (*Poetry in the Making*, 60–1)

The imagination is an antenna projected from the known self into the darkness of the unknown, from which it can haul into consciousness and articulation whatever horrors or marvels live there. And the metaphor works equally well whether the darkness is the world beyond the human or the darkness of the poet's own unconscious. The results suggest that the Great Outer Darkness (which spells God), is the same as the small inner darkness, since 'what you find in the outside world is what's escaped from your own inner world' (as Hughes said in an interview). What might rise from the depth of a pond and what might rise to consciousness in a dream are the same thing. Every gaze into outer darkness is also a 'shut-eyed look / Backward into the head' ('The Bull Moses'). Every fox is a thought-fox.

The poet's job is hence to release as many as he can of the caged beasts of his being, at least as a prerequisite, before he can do anything else, such as understand, control or recognize those energies. The opposition between those caged energies and the world of analytical intellect came to a head in Cambridge. Cambridge English stopped me writing poetry for 16 years. It had the same effect on many others, including Hughes. In his second year, exhausted by the effort to start an essay on Dr Johnson, Hughes at last gave up and went to bed. Immediately he dreamed that his door opened and there entered 'a figure that was at the same time a skinny man and a fox walking erect. ... Every inch was roasted, smouldering, black-charred, split and bleeding. Its eyes ... dazzled with the intensity of the pain.' It left its bloody footprints on the unwritten page, then said to him: 'Stop this – you are destroying us' (*WP* 9). The following night an erect leopard entered his bedroom and silently pushed him backwards over a chair.

> I connected the fox's command to my own ideas about Eng. Lit., & the effect of the Cambridge blend of pseudo-critical ter-minology and social rancour on creative spirit, and from that moment abandoned my efforts to adapt myself. I might say, that I had as much talent for Leavis-style dismantling of texts as anybody else, I even had a special bent for it – nearly a sadis-tic streak there, – but it seemed to me not only a foolish game, but deeply destructive of myself. (Letter to *KS*, 16 July 1979)

Hughes took these dreams so seriously that at the end of the year he transferred from English to archaeology and anthropology, a study that introduced him, among many other things, to the international currency of theriomorphic images. The fox, the wolf and the jaguar escaped from the furnace into his poems.

Sylvia Plath continued to feel an alien in a world she had been sys-tematically unprepared for, like the protagonist of Lawrence's 'The Princess'. At 18 she wrote:

> After being conditioned as a child to the lovely never-never land of magic, of fairy queens and virginal maidens … the beautiful dark-haired child (who was you) winging through the midnight sky on a star-path in her mother's box of reels … all this I knew, and felt, and believed. All this was my life when I was young. To go from this to the world of 'grown-up' reality. … To feel the sex organs develop and call loudly to the flesh; to become aware of school, exams, bread and butter, marriage, sex, compatibility, war, economics, death and self. What a pathetic blighting of the beauty and reality of childhood. (*Jour-nals* 20–1)

Apart from the sea, nothing in Plath's childhood landscape seems to have impinged on her. It seems to have been a landscape from which disturbing wildness had been effectively removed, safe, tame, controlled. Nature provided no alternative values to nurture. And the values of nurture were that the purpose of life is personal success earned by hard work and measured in fame and money.

The purpose of Plath's childhood poems was the same as her grandmother's broom, to make everything all right. Her poetic creations provided the insulation of comforting myths, of universal approval. They were part of the process of weaving her 'web of happiness'. They fortified the sense of the centrality and security of selfhood, compensating with their display of the mastery of words and forms for any disturbance life might have caused. At the age of 14, Plath astonished her English teacher by handing in a group of poems, of which he most admired a poem called 'I Thought That I Could Not Be Hurt', which contains the lines:

> Then, suddenly my world turned gray,
> and darkness wiped aside my joy.
> A dull and aching void was left
> where careless hands had reached out to destroy
>
> my silver web of happiness.
> The hands then stopped in wonderment,
> for, loving me, they wept to see
> the tattered ruins of my firmament.   (*Letters Home* 34)

The devastating experience that had produced this agony was the accidental smudging of one of her pastel drawings by her grandmother. The poems were read in class and highly praised. Sylvia commented:

> I was overjoyed, and although I am doubtful about poetry's effect on the little strategy of 'popularity' that I have been slowly building up, I am confident of admiration from Mr. C!

Popularity became part of her larger strategy of 'success'. Her doubts about the contribution poetry could make to this pushed her towards the short story. Hughes writes:

> Her ambition to write stories was the most visible burden of her

life. Successful story-writing, for her, had all the advantages of
a top job. She wanted the cash, and the freedom that can go
with it. She wanted the professional standing, as a big earner, as
the master of a difficult trade, and as a serious investigator into
the real world. ... So her life became very early a struggle to
apprentice herself to writing conventional stories, and to hammer her talents into acceptable shape. 'For Me', she wrote,
'poetry is an evasion from the real job of writing prose.' (*Johnny
Panic* 2–3)

She tried to judge her poems by the same criteria of saleability ('I
depend too desperately on getting my poems, my little glib poems,
so neat, so small, accepted by *The New Yorker*', she wrote a week
before meeting Hughes).

Some of Plath's pre-Cambridge poems were astonishingly
accomplished. She had already mastered some of the most difficult
forms, such as the villanelle. It was Plath, not Hughes, who con-
signed everything she had written before their meeting to juvenilia.
She knew that her prodigious technical skill was not releasing, was
perhaps building an elaborate prison for, the deeper self, the creative
energies.

Plath and Hughes met each other's poetry before they met each
other. The first poems Plath published in Cambridge were 'Epitaph
in Three Parts' and '"Three Caryatids without a Portico" by Hugo
Robus. A Study in Sculptural Dimensions', which appeared in
Chequer in January 1956. Hughes and several of his friends, including David Ross, Daniel Weissbort and Daniel Huws, were circulat-
ing a fortnightly critical *Broadsheet* in reaction against the Cambridge
poetry magazines, which seemed to them to favour lifeless form at
the expense of the charge and charm they recognized as the real thing.
They seized on 'Caryatids' as representing the worst sort of preten-
tious arty empty formalism. They 'concocted / An attack, a dismemberment, laughing' ('Caryatids 2'). In his review of that issue of
Chequer in *Broadsheet* Huws wrote: 'Of the quaint and eclectic art-
fulness of Sylvia Plath's two poems my better half tells me "Fraud,
fraud", but I will not say so; who am I to know how beautiful she may

be.' (In fact both Hughes and Huws had been told how beautiful she was by Lucas Myers, who had already met her.) Unfortunately, 'Caryatids' was Plath at her worst:

> In this tercet of torsos, breast and thigh
> slope with the Greek serenity
> > of tranquil plaster;
>
> each body forms a virgin vase,
> while all raise high with regal grace
> > aristocratic heads;
>
> these maidens would support with valor
> a portico that weighed the pillar
> > of classic sister,
>
> but such a trial is not granted
> by the gods: behold three daunted
> > caryatids.

It was the only Plath poem Hughes ever read 'through the eyes of a stranger':

> It seemed thin and brittle, the lines cold.
> Like the theorem of a trap, a deadfall – set.
> I saw that. And the trap unsprung, empty.
> I felt no interest, no stirring
> Of omen. In those days I coerced
> Oracular assurance
> In my favour out of every sign.
> So missed everything
> In the white, blindfolded, rigid faces
> Of those women. I felt their frailty, yes:
> Friable, burnt aluminium.
> Fragile, like the mantle of a gas lamp.
> But made nothing
> Of that massive, starless, mid-fall, falling
> Heaven of granite
> > stopped, as if in a snapshot,
> By their hair.   ('Caryatids 1')

He missed, naturally enough, the irony of the fact that the first Plath poem he read should be one in which she is asking the gods to send down a vast stone weight upon her head. In the story 'The Deadfall', Hughes describes a deadfall:

> a big flat stone like a flagstone, big as a big gravestone, leaned outwards, on end. It was supported, I saw, by a man-made contraption of slender sticks. Tucked in behind the sticks, under the leaning slab, lay a dead wood pigeon, its breast torn, showing the dark meat. … It was the first deadfall I had seen set. … My brother explained how it worked. How one light touch on the tripstick would collapse the support and bring the great stone slam down flat – on top of whatever was under it.

What was destined to spring that deadfall was a fox. 'Epiphany', as we shall see, suggests that another fox was to spring the deadfall of his as-yet-undreamed-of marriage.

Plath herself, as she sat among the ruins of her poem demolished by Huws, and of her brittle life invaded by Hughes, was much more aware of the tragic potential of the situation. 'Conversation Among the Ruins' begins: 'Through portico of my elegant house you stalk / With your wild furies', and ends with the speaker rooted to his black look,

> the play turned tragic:
> With such blight wrought on our bankrupt estate,
> What ceremony of words can patch the havoc?

The subliminal image in this poem is of the Lady of Shallott, weaving her beautiful magic web from images of the real world selected for their beauty and serenity, and defused by their quadruple distance from that reality – the formal art of the tapestry transforming images in a mirror reflected from a window looking out over a pastoral landscape, until the whirlwind, the irresistible masculine force of Lancelot, smashes mirror and loom, breaks the curse, but at the same time exposes the Lady to a harsh reality she cannot live with. So Plath had developed her ceremony of words (a month before meeting Hughes she wrote of her thesaurus 'that I would rather live with (it) on a desert isle than a bible' (*Journals* 97), her penchant for writing about the world reflected in works of art, her architectural imagery and structures, to prevent the 'whirlwind' of real days from breaking into her magic castle – yet at the same time desperately, fearfully, wanting to be released from it, and recognizing Huws as 'an ally of the generous creative opposing forces' (97).

After a visit to her psychiatrist, Plath wrote: 'I fear oppressive and crushing forces. ... I re-create the flux and smash of the world through the small ordered word patterns I make' (131). Hughes used poetry for exactly the opposite purpose, to smash through the layers of protective insulation, of 'order and ordinary', to let in the 'wandering elementals'.

Hughes' earlier poem 'Wind' might have been about precisely this. The fragile window trembles to come in under intolerable pressure from a wind that would sweep away books, thoughts, normal human relationships, all sense of the security and centrality of selfhood; shatter the house itself, the carefully built structure of civilization (which Castaneda calls the *tonal*) with which we try to insulate ourselves against the energies without and within (which Castaneda calls the *nagual*, and Lorca the *duende*).

> As long as his *tonal* is unchallenged and his eyes are tuned only for the *tonal*'s world, the warrior is on the safe side of the fence. He's on familiar ground and knows all the rules. But when his *tonal* shrinks, he is on the windy side, and that opening must be shut tight immediately, or he would be swept away. And this is not just a way of talking. Beyond the gate of the *tonal*'s eyes the wind rages. I mean a real wind. No metaphor. A wind that can blow one's life away. In fact, that is the wind that blows all living things on this earth. (Castaneda, *Tales of Power* 176)

Plath's first impressions of Hughes were recorded in imagery of wind:

> We shouted as if in a high wind, about the review. ... He said my name, Sylvia, in a blasting wind which shot off in the desert behind my eyes, behind his eyes, and his poems are clever and terrible and lovely. ... I dream a banging and crashing in a high wind. (*Journals* 111–14)

In 'The Queen's Complaint' she wrote: 'All the windows broke when he stalked in.' And in the journals she recorded the impact of his poetry as both a release and a violation: 'Ted can break walls … and in my mind I am ripped to bits by the words he welds and wields' (142).

Castaneda's word 'warrior' is perhaps apposite for Hughes, who had already instinctively adopted a view of the poet as quest hero, as one who, on behalf of the race, undergoes an ego-death, purifies himself for the quest into the unknown, the 'opening', the pitch dark where the animal runs; who goes, at great cost and risk, to 'negotiate with whatever happens to be out there'. Such a view of the role of the poet has, of course, major implications for form and language. Far from seeking to perfect a 'ceremony of words' to distance and defuse experience, Hughes had from the start sought words that 'cannot be outflanked by experience' because they are inseparable from it, exist in the same dimension as rock or wind or blood or death (a kind of language he found in the Border Ballads). While Plath searched her thesaurus, Hughes plundered Anglo-Saxon and dialect for the words and rhythms he needed. He struggled to free himself from 'the maternal octopus of the English poetic tradition'.

> It is a return to an alliterative poetry that, pounding, brutal and earthbound, challenges the Latinate politeness of artificial society with ruthless energy and cunning, and so drags the Latinate words into its unruly, self-ruling world that even *they* come to sound northern and Germanic. The pummelling trochees and lead-weighted, bludgeoning spondees have a mesmeric effect, beating and rooting out of us those once apparently safe underlying rhythms of rhetorical and philosophical discourse, mental scene-painting and nostalgic or evocative reflection, with which the iambic pentameter is so closely associated. Quite literally, by asserting the naked, deeper rhythms of our Germanic (and also onomatopoeic) heritage, Ted Hughes is taking the English language back to its roots. (from '"Natural" Rhythms and Poetic Metre', an unpublished essay by A.S. Crehan)

It was precisely this diction and these rhythms Sylvia found in the

Hughes poems she read before meeting him, poems that made her determined that she *would* meet him, that he might be the one to help her 'make something tight and riding over the limits of sweet sestinas and sonnets' (as she wrote a few hours before meeting him, at the launch of the *St Botolph's Review*). One of the four Hughes poems in the first and only number of that review was 'Soliloquy of a Misanthrope' in which he expresses his preference for 'every attitude showing its bone, / And every mouth confessing its crude shire', and the prophetic 'Fallgrief's Girl-friends', where Fallgrief determines to seek no more than a 'muck of a woman' to match his 'muck of a man', only to be frustrated by outrageous fortune:

> he meant to break out of the dream
> Where admiration's giddy mannequins
> Lead every sense to motley; he meant to stand naked
> Awake in the pitch dark where the animal runs,
> Where the insects couple as they murder each other,
> Where the fish outwait the water.
> > The chance changed him:
> He has found a woman with such wit and looks
> He can brag of her in every company.

It was this persona that Plath decided to inflate still further and enrol in the overblown melodrama she records in her journal, not, at first, as the marauding black panther, but as understudy for Richard Sassoon, who was wisely extricating himself. The real Hughes matched this persona physically, but had assumed it in some of his poems partly to compensate for his actual shyness and reticence, his sense, in Cambridge, of his own provinciality and inexperience. Hughes never saw the journals until after Plath's death.

Hughes' poems (she no doubt soon read all he had written – about half the poems in *The Hawk in the Rain*), were initiations into a world totally foreign to Plath, characterized by what seemed to her a magical closeness to the natural world. She responded to the poems in much the same way as to the creatures he introduced her to or invoked for her. Plain hawthorns were mysteries, common mallards unearthly:

> You were a camera
> Recording reflections you could not fathom.
> I made my world perform its utmost for you.
> You took it all in with an incredulous joy
> Like a mother handed her new baby
> By the midwife.   ('The Owl')

Hughes accepted the role she had cast him in before even meeting him, not the as yet unsuspected role of substitute father, but the role of the hero who would release her real self from its prison, the mid-wife of that rebirth.

At the first opportunity after their return from their honeymoon in Spain, Hughes took Plath to Yorkshire, which he believed she would find 'therapeutic'. Her immediate response suggested that this was so. She wrote to her mother of the 'most magnificent landscape', claiming to be a 'veritable convert to the Brontë clan':

> I have never been so happy in my life; it is wild and lonely and a perfect place to work and read. I am basically, I think, a nature-loving recluse. Ted and I are at last 'home'. (*Journals* 268–9).

Hughes was not so sure. Uncle Walt took them to Top Withens (the setting of *Wuthering Heights*). Hughes saw this in retrospect as having been something of a test for Plath. How would she respond to what, for him, was holy ground? Would she share any of his sense of spiritual kinship with the ghost of Emily Brontë? ' – how would you take up now / The clench of that struggle?' It was, perhaps unfortunately, an idyllic day. Walter encouraged Sylvia's 'transatlantic elation'. She climbed a tree for a snapshot.

> What would stern
> Dour Emily have made of your frisky glances
> And your huge hope?   ('Wuthering Heights')

Plath recorded in her journal 'the furious ghosts nowhere but in the heads of the visitors and the yellow-eyed shag sheep' (148–9).

On a later visit to Yorkshire Plath found herself out alone at night in less benign weather. The long wind pared her down 'to a pinch of flame'.

> All the night gave her, in return
> For the paltry gift of her bulk and the beat
> Of her heart, was the humped indifferent iron
> Of its hills, and its pastures bordered by black stone set
> On black stone ... but before the weight
> Of stones and hills of stones could break
> Her down to mere quartz grit in that stony light
> She turned back.   ('Hardcastle Crags')

Far from being 'home', this was the most alien environment Plath had experienced, the exact concrete embodiment of her recurrent nightmare 'of being crushed in a huge dark machine, sucked dry by the grinding indifferent millstones of circumstance' (*Journals* 131). The idea of living in Yorkshire was dropped, and they returned to London.

The immediate effect on Plath's poetry was devastating. Her dissatisfaction with her previous work became a sweeping, self-castigating contempt, so that eventually even her finest poems such as 'Circus in Three Rings' and 'Two Lovers and a Beachcomber by the Real Sea' were rubbished as products of 'the old crystal-brittle and sugar-faceted voice'. Instead she tried to adopt Hughes' voice, with all its aggressive monosyllabic diction and wrenched syntax. There are several striking acts of ventriloquism, such as 'Spinster' and 'Strumpet Song':

> Walks there not some such one man
> As can spare breath
> To patch with brand of love this rank grimace
> Which out from black tarn, ditch and cup
> Into my most chaste own eyes
> Looks up.

Hughes knew that this would not do. His job was to help Plath to find her own true voice, and neither of them had any idea what that might sound like.

Of one thing Hughes was sure, that he did not want Plath to become a 'confessional' poet. In 1966 he wrote:

> Her poetry has been called 'confessional and personal', and connected with the school of Robert Lowell and Anne Sexton. She admired both these poets, and knew them personally, and they both had an effect on her, and she shares with them the East Massachusetts homeland. But the connection goes no further. Her poetic strategies, the poetic events she draws out of her experience of disintegration and renewal, the radiant, visionary light in which she encounters her family and the realities of her daily life, are quite different in kind from anything one finds in Robert Lowell's poetry, or Anne Sexton's. Their work is truly autobiographical and personal, and their final world is a torture cell walled with family portraits, with the daily newspaper coming under the door. The autobiographical details in Sylvia Plath's poetry work differently. She sets them out like masks, which are then lifted up by dramatis personae of nearly supernatural qualities. The world of her poetry is one of emblematic visionary events, mathematical symmetries, clairvoyance, metamorphoses, and something resembling total biological and racial recall. And the whole scene lies under the transfiguring eye of the great white timeless light. (*UU* 180)

In other words, Hughes believed that the best poetry was the most imaginative, and that the closer poetry stayed to the 'facts' of autobiography and the details of daily life, the less scope was left for the operations of imagination. It seemed to him that only by marshalling the full powers of imagination could 'deadly negatives' be transformed into 'triumphant positives'. If a writer were unable to get beyond the autobiographical, they were likely to 'simply stay as they were, a recurrent stuck dream that simply goes on delivering its inescapable blow' (Letter to *KS*). His models were Shakespeare and Coleridge. This was how, in *Crow*, Hughes began, after a three-year silence, to try to escape from the deadfall of Plath's death.

After 1966 Hughes became less hostile to confessional poetry. In the *Paris Review* interview of 1995 he admitted that the masks, the symbols, the analogies, of the kind of poetry he had always preferred, could be seen as a kind of cowardice, a fear of going naked, a 'strategy of concealment, of obliquity':

> The novelty of some of Robert Lowell's most affecting pieces in *Life Studies,* some of Anne Sexton's poems and some of Sylvia's, was the way they stripped off the veiling analogies. Sylvia went furthest in the sense that her secret was most dangerous to her. She desperately needed to reveal it. You can't overestimate her compulsion to write like that. She had to write those things – even against her most vital interests.

Yet, even while admiring the courage and recognizing the necessity for such poems, Hughes continued to believe that a less personal and naked expression might have produced even better art:

> Once you've contracted to write only the truth about yourself – as in some respected kinds of modern verse, or as in Shakespeare's sonnets – then you can too easily limit yourself to what you imagine are the truths of the ego that claims your conscious biography. Your own equivalent of what Shakespeare got into his plays is simply foregone. (69–70)

And not only better art. It might also have served Plath's 'vital interests' better – even have saved her life.

Of course, the influence of Hughes on Plath was by no means a one-way affair. 'I see now that when we met, my writing, like hers, left its old path and started to circle and search.' She introduced him to American literature.

> But our minds soon became two parts of one operation. We dreamed a lot of shared or complementary dreams. Our telepathy was intrusive. (77)

One effect of the relationship on Hughes was to make him much more self-conscious about his own work, more interested in articulating his position and reading works of anthropology and psychology which could provide him with a firm launch-pad. He began to devise exercises they could do together, which proved as useful to himself as to Plath. Hughes tried to take her back to what for him had always been the elements of poetry, as one might teach a complete beginner. We hear his voice in the *Journals*:

> Poems are bad to begin with: elaborate ones especially: they freeze me too soon on too little. Better, little exercise poems in description that don't demand philosophic bear traps of logical development. Like small poems about the skate, the cow by moonlight, a la the Sow. Very physical in the sense that the worlds are bodied forth in my words, not stated as abstractions, or denotative wit on three clear levels. Small descriptions where the words have an aura of mystic power: of Naming the name of a quality: spindly, prickling, sleek, splayed, wan, luminous, bellied. Say them aloud always. Make them irrefutable. (163)

Most of the exercises in *Poetry in the Making* probably had their origin as exercises devised primarily for Plath. In 1957 Plath wrote, obviously echoing Hughes:

> All I need to do is work, break open the deep mines of experience and imagination, let the words come and speak it all, sounding themselves and tasting themselves. (162)

In the first chapter of *Poetry in the Making* Hughes was to write:

> Imagine what you are writing about. See it and live it. Do not think it up laboriously, as if you were working out mental arithmetic. Just look at it, touch it, smell it, listen to it, turn yourself into it. (18)

It was a terrible struggle for Plath to wean herself off long-established habits of composition. Several months after the marriage she was planning a novel: 'Then I can write slowly, rewriting each chapter, carefully with a subtle structured style. If I can ever find a subtle structured style' (*Journals* 155). In the 'Writing a Novel' chapter of *Poetry in the Making* Hughes recommends 'letting your imagination

go and following it with your pen as fast as you can'. Together they
worked at 'headlong, concentrated improvisation on a set theme'.
Limits were set, perhaps one side of paper and ten minutes:

> These artificial limits create a crisis, which rouses the brain's
> resources: the compulsion towards haste overthrows the ordi-
> nary precautions, flings everything into top gear, and many
> things that are usually hidden find themselves rushed into the
> open. Barriers break down, prisoners come out of their cells.
> (*Poetry in the Making* 23)

That final image is clearly much more appropriate to Plath than to a
class of schoolchildren, and reveals the true origin of these exercises.

Other exercises were more esoteric, less appropriate for schoolchildren, such as efforts to exploit dream material, and to obtain
assistance from the stars or the Ouija board. They asked whatever it
was that spoke to them through the Ouija board (it called itself Pan,
not the Great God Pan, but a little spirit that lived in the bottom of
an iceberg) to suggest subjects for poems. To Hughes Pan suggested
an otter. Though he had always been fascinated by otters, he had not
yet attempted to write about them. He produced a good poem, and
read it to Pan. Pan was not satisfied, and offered to help if he would
write a second part. Part I is an evocation of a creature neither fish
nor beast, of neither land nor water, in Lawrencean free verse, half-
quoting Lawrence's 'Snake': 'Like a king in hiding'. The second part
as published is a tighter rhyming poem about the even more important frontier the otter straddles, between life and death:

The otter belongs

In double robbery and concealment -
From water that nourishes and drowns, and from land
That gave him his length and the mouth of the hound.

In London there was to be another incident which only with hind-
sight could be seen as an even more crucial, more ominous test than
the visit to Top Withens – this time a test for both of them. The title

of Hughes' poem 'Epiphany' suggests a sudden revelatory encounter with something recognized as sacred. It is another encounter with a fox, this time a helpless captive cub in the middle of London, in the possession of a man who is trying to sell it for a pound. In both the previous encounters with foxes we have noted, the fox has embodied values alternative to, and under desperate pressure from, the outer conditions of Hughes' life – school, university, now marriage.

Like all the best poetic symbols, like Lawrence's birds, beasts and flowers, Hughes' creatures are very real, even to the 'sudden sharp hot stink of fox'. So Hughes' anecdote of the fox-cub, like Lawrence's of the snake, works perfectly at the level of realism. How could a man take a fox-cub home to a wife, any wife, let alone one completely out of touch with wildlife, trying to cope with a new baby in a tiny London flat? But the poem, as the title tells us, is about something else:

> Then I walked on
> As if out of my own life.
> I let that fox-cub go. I tossed it back
> Into the future
> Of a fox-cub in London and I hurried
> Straight on and dived as if escaping
> Into the Underground. If I had paid,
> If I had paid that pound and turned back
> To you, with that armful of fox -
>
> If I had grasped that whatever comes with a fox
> Is what tests a marriage and proves it a marriage -
> I would not have failed the test. Would you have failed it?
> But I failed. Our marriage had failed.

Clearly, if Hughes were still talking only of adopting a fox-cub, such a test of a marriage would be grossly unreasonable. The crucial phrases are 'as if out of my own life' and 'whatever comes with a fox'.

In 1915 Lawrence described the cyclamens of Lake Garda as 'little living myths that I cannot understand'. He knew that to come to such understanding was the greatest possible achievement in life or art. It was only by recognizing the superior reality, the sacredness, of unfallen creatures, that their meaning could be released. An adequate response to the blueness of a gentian then requires the question: 'What, in me, can answer to this blueness?' Every creature is a message about God:

> In the very darkest continent of the body, there is God. And from him issues the first dark rays of our feeling, wordless, and utterly previous to words; the innermost rays, the first messengers, the primeval, honourable beasts of our being, whose voice echoes wordless and forever wordless down the darkest avenues of the soul, but full of potent speech. Our own inner meaning. (*Study of Thomas Hardy* 205)

And poetry is the nearest we can get to that potent speech. In '*Orghast*: Talking Without Words', Hughes says much the same thing:

> The luminous spirit (maybe he is a crowd of spirits), that takes account of everything and gives everything its meaning, is missing. Not missing, just incommunicado. But here and there, may be, we hear it.
>
> It is human, of course, but it is also everything else that lives. When we hear it, we understand what a strange creature is living in this Universe, and somewhere at the core of us – strange, beautiful, pathetic, terrible. Some animals and birds express this being pure and without effort, and then you hear the whole, desolate, final actuality of existence in a voice, a tone. There we really do recognize a spirit, a truth under all truths. (*WP* 124–5)

Hughes asks what in him can answer to this fox-cub. He identifies the fox with his own inner meaning, his authenticity, the ultimate truth of his being, the god or luminous spirit in him, the *nagual*, the *duende*. It is that part of each of us that the pressures of living in our society, the compromises demanded by relationships and domestic responsibilities, force us to walk away from, to ignore or repudiate, to condemn to suffering or death by neglect.

These meanings are reinforced if we make the connection between

'Epiphany' and 'The Golden Bird' as recorded by the brothers Grimm. In our culture we can hardly respond to the word 'epiphany' without registering the more specific meaning of the Feast of the Epiphany, or Twelfth Night, the story of the quest of the three kings (bearing three precious gifts) for a transforming encounter with the divine. In 'The Golden Bird' three men embark on a difficult quest for the golden bird, with no idea where to look or how it is to be caught. The men go one at a time on a quest that is doomed for the first two, and almost for the third and youngest, because far from bearing gifts or seeking the divine, they are impelled by mere worldly greed. Success is possible, but only by listening to the wisdom of the fox, which is the voice of their own innermost being. The fox insists on stripping away all the values symbolized (in a materialistic, spirit-less world) by gold. They must not, he tells them, be dazzled by appearances, wealth, comfort, but must choose the 'poor and mean', the dirty and shabby, over the rich, pleasant and beautiful. But the reconstructed self which is capable of choosing the shabby wooden cage over the golden cage, the old leather saddle over the golden saddle, would no longer be capable of devoting a life to obtaining possession of a golden bird, a golden horse and a golden girl. It is dressed as a poor man that the youngest son finally gains admission to the home from which he has been excluded by his grasping brothers.

The Magi, on the other hand, were questing for a new birth, their own as well as the Saviour's. In Eliot's poem, their quest involves a 'cold coming' through unknown territory, at 'just the worst time of the year'. They have sacrificed their former selves and values, 'the old dispensation', the 'summer palaces' and 'silken girls'. They had to overcome the voices in their ears that it was all folly. How otherwise could they hope to recognize as sacred, as King of Kings, a naked child surrounded by beasts in a lowly stable? Their success is not mea-sured in wealth or happiness. They return to their kingdoms to be henceforth alienated from their people, wishing for 'another death'.

On the realistic surface, the main sacrifice Hughes had made in his pursuit of the golden girl was to accept what he took to be Plath's ambitions for himself also. He had been amazed when, on asking the

Ouija the question he assumed Plath would want to ask, 'Shall we be famous?', she had reacted with fury:

> 'And give yourself to the glare? Is that what you want?
> Why should you want to be famous?
> Don't you see – fame will ruin everything.'
> I was stunned. I thought I had joined
> Your association of ambition
> To please you and your mother,
> To fulfil your mother's ambition
> That we be ambitious. Otherwise
> I'd be fishing off a rock
> In Western Australia.   ('Ouija')

The figure of the mother acquires an almost folk-tale status as she attempts to provide a new wardrobe for the bride and groom appropriate to her ambitions for them. For the wedding she brought Plath a 'pink wool knitted dress', but Hughes wore his old thrice-dyed black cord jacket ('No ceremony could conscript me / Out of my uniform'), so that he felt like 'the Swineherd / Stealing this daughter's pedigree dreams'. The blue flannel suit Plath wore for her first class when she began teaching at Smith College Hughes came to see as a 'mad, execution uniform':

> I watched
> The strange dummy stiffness, the misery,
> Of your blue flannel suit, its straightjacket, ugly
> Half-approximation to your idea
> Of the proprieties you hoped to ease into,
> And your horror in it.   ('The Blue Flannel Suit')

Seeing her stiffen into it, he saw 'the lonely / Girl who was going to die'.

Proprieties of dress merged into those of behaviour and, of course, poetry. Gently, humorously, for the best of motives, those who were confident that they had Plath's best interests at heart sought to curb the disturbing new wildness of her verse. In March 1957 Olive Higgins Prouty wrote to her:

> Someone remarked to me after reading your poem 'Pursuit' in
> the *Atlantic*, 'How intense'. Sometime write me a little poem
> that isn't intense. A lamp turned too high might shatter its
> chimney. Please just *glow* sometimes ... (*BF* 85)

At the time it seemed to both Hughes and Plath that such comments
were inimical to the very distinction of Plath's work, which lay in the
fact that 'she saw the world in the flame of the ultimate substance and
the ultimate depth' (*UU* 181–2).

Hughes' first attempt to explain to himself and others what had happened to Plath's poetry during their marriage came with the publication of *Ariel* only two years after her death. He spoke of the
compulsive pattern-making of her early work, her 'obsession with
intricate rhyming and metrical schemes ... almost perverse, with their
bristling hurdles', and contrasted this with the momentum of her late
work, 'charged with terrific heat, pressure and clairvoyant precision'.

> But the truly miraculous thing about her will remain the fact
> that in two years, while she was almost fully occupied with chil-
> dren and house-keeping, she underwent a poetic development
> that has hardly any equal on record, for suddenness and com-
> pleteness. The birth of her first child seemed to start the
> process. All at once she could compose at top speed, and with
> her full weight. Her second child brought things a giant step
> forward. All the various voices of her gift came together, and for
> about six months, up to a day or two before her death, she
> wrote with the full power and music of her extraordinary
> nature. (*WP* 162)

We know now that the development had been far from sudden or
miraculous, but had been worked at assiduously by Plath with
Hughes' help and encouragement for the several years of their marriage. Nor does Hughes here even hint that there might be any connection between her nature, her poetic power, and her death. These
are precisely the connections that were being made simultaneously by
Robert Lowell in his introduction to the American edition of *Ariel*.

In the harshest poems (such as 'Lady Lazarus' and 'Daddy') he recognizes 'the strident rasp of the vampire – a Dido, Phaedra, or Medea'. He admires the feverish energy, 'yet it is too much; her art's immortality is life's disintegration. ... These poems are playing Russian roulette with six cartridges in the cylinder.' He refers to her 'last irresistible blaze', her 'appalling and triumphant fulfillment'. In comparison, Hughes' comments seem evasive.

Five years later, in his 'Notes on the Chronological Order of Sylvia Plath's Poems', the birth to which he refers is not that of Plath's children, but of Plath herself: 'The new birth is requisitioning all nature to its delivery.' Hughes is now more open about his own input:

> At this time [1959] she was concentratedly trying to break down the tyranny, the fixed focus and public persona which descriptive or discursive poems take as a norm. We devised exercises of meditation and invocation. (*The Art of Sylvia Plath* 191)

He describes also deliberate exercises in experimental improvisation on set themes:

> She had never in her life improvised. The powers that compelled her to write so slowly had always been stronger than she was. But quite suddenly she found herself free to let herself drop, rather than inch over bridges of concepts. (192)

He describes one such exercise from 1962:

> Opposite the front of our house stands a church. Early one morning, in the dark, I saw the full moon setting on to a large yew tree that grows in the churchyard, and I suggested she make a poem of it. By midday, she had written it. It depressed me greatly. It's my suspicion that no poem can be a poem that is not a statement from the powers in control of our life, the ultimate suffering and decision in us. It seems to me that this is poetry's only real distinction from the literary forms that we call 'not poetry'. And I had no doubt that this was a poem, and perhaps a great poem. (193–4)

There is no attempt to explain that sentence: 'It depressed me greatly.' Clearly he was thrilled that she had, as it were, completed her apprenticeship, had produced one of her first great poems, over which he had no control, wanted no control. If she was to fulfil her potential as a great poet, her poems must speak her fate, even when that statement was far from what either of them wanted to hear. The same darker note was sounded the following year in a piece in the *Observer*:

> The poetry of the *Ariel* poems was no surprise to me. It was at last the flight of what we had been trying to get flying for a number of years. But it dawned on me only in the last months which way it wanted to fly. (*WP* 165)

Hughes' introduction to Plath's *Collected Poems* added nothing. Presumably he wanted the poems to speak for themselves. In his foreword to Plath's *Journals* in 1982, Hughes tried to put his finger on the very moment when he first heard the Ariel voice. He claims to have heard it for the first time in the summer of 1959:

> Her real self showed itself in her writing, just for a moment, three years earlier (than the *Ariel* poems), and when I heard it – the self I had married, after all, and lived with and knew well – in that brief moment, three lines recited as she went out through a doorway, I knew that what I had always felt must happen had now begun to happen, that her real self, being the real poet, would now speak for itself, and would throw off all those lesser and artificial selves that had monopolized the words up to that point, it was as if a dumb person suddenly spoke. (*Journals* xii)

They were lines from the ending of 'The Hermit at Outermost House' :

> Still he thumbed out something else.
> Thumbed no stony, horny pot,
>
> But a certain meaning green.
> He withstood them, that hermit.

Rock-face, crab-claw verged on green.

Gulls mulled in the greenest light.

It was no great poem, but he wrote of it: 'It has the comic goblin, the tricksterish spirit, the crackling verbal energy, that was the nymph-form – a lot of Caliban in it – of *Ariel.*' (*The Art of Sylvia Plath* 190). The first poem-length breakthrough came a few months later, with the final part of 'Poem for a Birthday' – 'The Stones' – 'where the voice of Ariel can be heard clearing its throat'. Then came a struggle of two and a half years, including *The Bell Jar*, before the emergence, finally, of 'the first true Ariel poem', 'Elm', where 'some bigger suggestions pushing through a constricted, suppressive group of lines about an elm tree ... transformed her whole technique, and located her true subject matter' (*WP* 210).

But it was in the long essay on Plath's *Journals*, published in *Grand Street* in 1982, that Hughes developed his position most fully. Here Hughes for the first time puts Otto Plath, Sylvia's father, at centre stage. Here Hughes accepts the imagery of fire, that Plath was 'forcing herself deeper into some internal furnace', that he was deliberately stoking that furnace, but tends to deny, in his prose, that it was other than an alchemical workshop where the crucible was part of a classic Jungian process of individuation:

> We have spoken of this process as a 'nursing' of the 'nucleus of the self', as a hermetically sealed, slow transformation of her inner crisis; and the evidence surely supports these descriptions of it as a deeply secluded mythic and symbolic inner theatre (sometimes a hospital theatre), accessible to her only in her poetry. One would like to emphasize even more strongly the weird autonomy of what was going on in there. It gave the impression of being a secret crucible, or rather womb, an almost biological process – and just as much beyond her manipulative interference. And like a pregnancy, selfish with her resources. ... The process was, in fact, a natural and positive process, if not the most positive and healing of all involuntary responses to the damage of life: a process of self-salvation

– a resurrection of her deepest spiritual vitality against the odds of her fate. (*WP* 180–2)

The subject matter of the *Ariel* poems, he says, 'didn't alarm her':

> Why should it, when Ariel was doing the very thing it had been created and liberated to do? In each poem, the terror is encountered head on, and the angel is mastered and brought to terms. … She had overcome, by a stunning display of power, the bogies of her life. (188)

We are perhaps now in a better position to understand the difference between Lowell's account of *Ariel* and Hughes'. For Hughes it is the story of 'how a poetic talent was forced into full expressive being, by internal need, for a purpose vital to the whole organism' (184). Lowell, reading *Ariel* for the first time as the work of a dead poet, making no distinction, not having the information to make any such distinction, between the pre- and post-1963 poems, assumes a necessary continuity which Hughes denies. This is clearest in his essay on 'Sheep in Fog', the crucial importance of which is inseparable from its being Plath's only poem to span that divide. Hughes there insists that what he means by 'the Ariel voice' is the voice of those pre-1963 poems Plath herself collected under that title. The later poems, which he decided to add to her collection, were not the voice of the escaped triumphant survivor, but a new voice, embittered and desperate, disabled by a new fatal combination of circumstances from coping with a last attack by the seemingly defeated forces.

That is the story as Hughes had consistently told it in cool prose, acknowledging the risk and cost, but ultimately not questioning that embarking on and carrying through this process was, in spite of the ending, of the fact that 'her new self could not ultimately save her', vindicated by *Ariel*. That is not to say, of course, that a book of great poems is worth a young life. It is to say that the alternative to that temporary triumph over her fate would have been to go down to it without even the satisfaction of making a fight of it. Hughes' many descriptions of this process are confidently positive, barely troubled by any doubts that the process was as clearly a moral duty as Prospero's duty to release Ariel from the cleft pine.

Hughes' insistence that 'it was a process of integration start to finish' involved making a complete separation between Plath's poetry and her death, and consigning the latter to the realm of pure accident. He claimed in a 1981 letter to me (which must have been written at about the same time as his *Grand Street* essay) that her death was 'not at all essential to the poems':

> I read those Ariel poems as a climb – not a fall. A climb to a precarious foothold, as it turned out. But she was knocked off again by pure unlucky combination of accidents.

He enumerated these accidents and developed his case at great length in order to counteract 'the notion of her as a young woman hurtling to disintegration shedding rags of poetry – leaping into Aetna & bursting into flames as she fell'. Hughes argued this case again and again very persuasively, almost convincingly. But his very insistence perhaps indicated that his main concern was to convince himself, to hold at bay the totally different account which was to erupt in the nineties in the poems he came to call *Birthday Letters*, where the very same images that constituted his positives in the prose (the pregnancy, the 'internal furnace') now constitute (particularly in 'Suttee' and 'The God') the most irredeemably destructive and horrific elements of his vision.

The 'Sheep in Fog' essay was written in 1988. But in his last prose account, 'Sylvia Plath's *Collected Poems* and *The Bell Jar*', written in 1995, the balance had shifted a great deal. The positive account is still there, fully and strongly stated: 'the author's psychic autobiography, the creation-myth of the new person that had emerged in the "Poem for a Birthday" and that would go on in full cry through *Ariel*' (*WP* US edn 468), reinterpreted here in terms of the Osiris myth. But now the positive and negative elements are no longer described as phases, the one replacing the other at a specific date, the end of 1962, but as two levels, the upper, purposive level, and a lower level of 'unalterable truth'.

The 'positive' aspect of the ritual holds good only on that upper level – where her shaping will is in control, where the ritual magic is choreographed according to plan, and the rebirth is hopeful.

On the lower level it was only a seeming and temporary triumph:

> When she tries to impose her protective, positive interpretation and nurse the germ of an authentic rebirth, in her nativity ritual, the material itself is doing something quite different. ... The symbolism discloses a pattern of tragedy that is like a magnetic field in the very ground of her being. ... The simultaneity of the two levels, and the bewildering fact that each level speaks in the equally-real-or-symbolic terms of the other, produces the paradox that makes the novel, the poems and the author truly tragic. (480–1)

When we turn to *Birthday Letters* we find that the lower level, the pattern of tragedy, takes over almost exclusively. Given that the poems were written over a long period, with no thought of publishing them as a collection, let alone a sequence, there is amazing richness and coherence of imagery. All the interwoven strands of imagery – dreaming, sleepwalking, the labyrinth, acting parts in an already written play (or merely dangling as puppets, or manipulated as glove puppets by immense hands), drowning, burning, blood – lead to the same inexorable finale, the same triumph of death (in the person of the dead father) over everything that can be set against it.

The most obvious difference is that the rational and objective accounts in prose take for granted a world in which the actors have a measure of freedom and control. This assumption is completely absent from the poems, which are darker, more confused and doubtful, more fatalistic. The characteristic tone of the poems is of ironic resignation. Everything Hughes and Plath thought they were doing as free intelligent individuals was in fact part of a tragic drama written in the stars before they even met:

> Nor did I know I was being auditioned
> For the male lead in your drama. ('Visit')

> That day the solar system married us
> Whether we knew it or not.   ('St Botolph's')

In the prose, as we have seen, Hughes argued that the process of releasing the Ariel voice at almost any cost was justified by the outcome, which was 'the birth of her new creative self'; that we can see in 'The Stones', for example, 'how the substance of her poetry and the very substance of her survival are the same'. In the poems the imperatives of poetry and those of survival, or at least of a successful marriage ('the life that might have bonded us / Into a single animal, a single soul'), are seen as mutually exclusive, the imperatives of poetry drowning out those of life. An experience of rare plenitude (fishing, in fact), happiness and togetherness is described in these terms:

> It was a visit from the goddess, the beauty
> Who was poetry's sister – she had come
> To tell poetry she was spoiling us.
> Poetry listened, maybe, but we heard nothing
> And poetry did not tell us. And we
> Only did what poetry told us to do.   ('Flounders')

In 'The Minotaur' Hughes actually traces a skein leading directly from his own advice to Plath that the destructive energies of her daily life ought to be going into her poems (where, in his prose accounts, they would have responded to that release and expression by becoming creative) to her death. When she is being violently aggressive towards him, he says to her: 'Get that shoulder under your stanzas / And we'll be away.' But in retrospect had he thereby given her goblin 'the bloody end of the skein' that that unravelled their marriage?

> Left your children echoing
> Like tunnels in a labyrinth,
>
> Left your mother a dead-end,
> Brought you to the horned, bellowing
> Grave of your risen father –
> And your own corpse in it. ('The Minotaur')

It is, finally, her pen that takes everything from her. Her poetry, he claims, 'with its blood-sticky feet', follows her from the bloody shrine of her dream life in her father's grave. Her book is merely 'the empty mask / Of the Genie' ('Totem'). Ariel is present and happy at Plath's 60th birthday reunion. 'Only you and I do not smile' ('Freedom of Speech').

In the poems the note of triumphant rebirth is gone entirely. Instead the tragic end of the story colours everything leading up to it, like a Hardy novel. The poems speak of 'your floundering / Drowning life and your effort to save yourself':

> Alone
> Either of us might have met with a life.
> Siamese-twinned, each of us festering
> A unique soul-sepsis for the other,
> Each of us was the stake
> Impaling the other. ('9 Willow Street')

Admittedly, these lines describe a particularly difficult period in the relationship; but even the whole controlling myth, presented in the prose as that of Jungian alchemical rebirth, is here the opposite, 'the myth we had sleepwalked into: death':

> 'Find the core of the labyrinth.' Why? What opens
> At the heart of the maze? Is it the doorway
> Into the perfected vision? Masterfully
> The voice pushed us, hypnotized, bowing our heads
> Into its dead ends, its reversals,
> Dreamy gropings, baffled ponderings,
> Its monomaniac half-search, half-struggle,
> Not for the future – not for any future -
>
> Till it stopped. Was that the maze's centre?
> Where everything stopped? What lay there?
> The voice held me there, by the scruff of the neck,
> And bowed my head
> Over the thing we had found. Your dead face. ('Fishing Bridge')

In poem after poem we find Hughes sleepwalking, groping, like an actor without a script, or with the wrong script, or finding himself playing the wrong role. The role Hughes had chosen for himself was that of Prospero in *The Tempest*, with Plath, naturally, as Ariel. He spoke of Plath's poetry as 'the story of Ariel's imprisonment in the pine, before Prospero opened it' (*WP* 178). Plath certainly regarded Hughes as a magician. His familiarity with the animal world was, to her, 'a mystery of peculiar lore and doings':

> Anything wild, on legs, in your eyes
> Emerged at a point of exclamation
> As if it had appeared to dinner guests
> In the middle of the table. ('The Owl')

He made his world perform its utmost for her entertainment. His masterpiece was the summoning of an owl. Yet early in *Birthday Letters* Hughes repudiates the role of Prospero, claiming to have been altogether the wrong 'witchdoctor' to manage either Plath or her Daddy:

> In my position, the right witchdoctor
> Might have caught you in flight with his bare hands,
> Tossed you, cooling, one hand to the other,
> Godless, happy, quieted.
>   I managed
> A wisp of your hair, your ring, your watch, your nightgown.
>   ('The Shot')

But who is, in fact, the 'male lead' in *The Tempest*? Is it Prospero, or Ferdinand, or even Caliban? The Hughes who introduces Plath to all the secrets of his world, which is the natural world, would perhaps have been recognized by someone to whom that world was less amazing as Caliban, before he has been brutalized, showing Prospero and Miranda 'all the qualities o' th' isle'. When Plath evoked Hughes in 'Faun' she brought him close to his beloved wodwo, and Shakespeare incorporated features of the wodwo into Caliban.

Aurelia Plath certainly tried to refashion Hughes as Ferdinand, a more suitable son-in-law. His unwillingness to disrupt his marriage with a fox-cub might be seen as submitting himself to the kind of emasculation Prospero demands of Ferdinand.

There are even glimpses of Hughes in the role of the naive Miranda:

> At twenty-five I was dumbfounded afresh
> By my ignorance of the simplest things.   ('Fulbright Scholars')

A sober star warns him to 'stay clear', but in his innocence he rushes to embrace and, of course, be betrayed by, a brave world new to him:

> You were a new world. My new world.
> So this is America, I marvelled.   ('18 Rugby Street')

These parallels with *The Tempest* were not imagined by Hughes after the event, but were consciously present to both Hughes and Plath from the beginning. Plath expressed her joy at the wedding in terms of Caliban's dream:

> You said you saw the heavens open
> And show riches, ready to drop upon us.
> Levitated beside you, I stood subjected
> To a strange tense: the spellbound future.
>   ('A Pink Wool Knitted Dress')

The spell that binds that future is not his. Nor can we exclude our knowledge of what came of Caliban's beautiful dream in his spell-bound future, hunted down by Prospero's hounds Fury and Tyrant.

As we have seen, in 1957/8 Hughes and Plath made frequent use of a Ouija board. Pan affirmed that there was a life after this life. When Plath asked how her father was, Pan replied: 'in plumage of raw worms'. Hughes' Prospero-like plan in using the Ouija had been, according to Plath's poem 'Dialogue Over a Ouija Board':

>   to dredge up
> Pools, prophesies and such from the unfathomed
> Bottom of your brain.

And of course to give Plath access to similar depths within herself. He recalls that during their sessions at the Ouija board, 'spirits' would regularly arrive with instructions for her from one Prince Otto, who was said to be a great power in the underworld. When she pressed for a more personal communication, she would be told that Prince Otto could not speak to her directly, because he was under orders from the Colossus. And when she pressed for an audience with the Colossus, they would say he was inaccessible. It is easy to see how her effort to come to terms with the meaning this Colossus held for her, in her poetry, became more and more central as the years passed. (*WP* 180)

It seems that to begin with Plath saw Hughes as a god of power who could control the world of spirits. In the copy of *The Colossus* which Plath gave to Hughes on its publication in 1960 she wrote: 'FOR TED of whom Colossus and Prince Otto learn their craft and art'. It is as though she trusted his most potent art to control these rough spirits and tame them for her poetic uses. But things began to go wrong with the Ouija sessions. For Plath the Ouija served merely as a mouthpiece for her father, now exalted to a potent god of the underworld, the ocean depths:

> It is a chilly god, a god of shades,
> Rises to the glass from his black fathoms.　　　　　　('Ouija')

Pan's messages to her were all invitations to join her father in those chilly depths. She intended at one stage to call her first collection *Full Fathom Five*:

> It relates more richly to my life and imagery than anything else I've dreamed up: has the background of *The Tempest*, the association of the sea, which is a central metaphor for my childhood, my poems and the artist's subconscious, of the father image – relating to my own father, the buried male muse and god-creator risen to be my mate in Ted, to the sea-father Neptune – and the pearls and coral highly-wrought to art: pearls sea-changed from the ubiquitous grit and sorrow and dull routine. (*Journals* 223)

What she does not say in the journal entry is that the poem 'Full Fathom Five' ends with her sense of exile from his sea-bed kingdom and desire for death by drowning:

> Father, this thick air is murderous.
> I would breathe water.

Pan stated that his favourite Hughes poem was 'Pike' ('I like fish') and his favourite Plath poem was 'Mussel Hunter' ('Kolossus likes it'), a poem about a heroic crab which suicidally turns its back on its appropriate element. Pan suggested that Plath should write about the Lorelei, because they were her 'own kin':

> The subject appealed to me doubly (or triply): the German legend of the Rhine sirens, the sea-childhood symbol, and the death-wish involved in the song's beauty. (*Journals* 246)

The poem ends:

> At the source
> Of your ice-hearted calling –
> Drunkenness of the great depths.
> O river, I see drifting
>
> Deep in your flux of silver
> Those great goddesses of peace.
> Stone, stone, ferry me down there.

All this material surfaces in Hughes' poem 'Setebos'. Here Hughes relinquishes the role of Prospero to Plath's mother 'flying her magic in / To stage the Masque and bless the marriage'. Hughes is Ferdinand: 'My wreckage / Was all of a sudden a new wardrobe, unworn'. Ariel 'our aura', Caliban 'our secret'. Sycorax is the presiding goddess 'in the wings / Of the heavens, like director / Studying the scenes to come'. When the script overtook them,

> I heard
> The bellow of your voice
> That made my nape-hair prickle when you sang
> How you were freed from the Elm. I lay

In the labyrinth of a cowslip
Without a clue. I heard the Minotaur
Coming down its tunnel-groove
Of old faults deep and bitter. King Minos,
Alias Otto – his bellow
Winding into murderous music. Which play
Were we in?

If this is a version of *The Tempest*, it is one in which not Prospero but
Setebos is restored to his kingdom, and claims Miranda as his bride.
Hughes reverts to a helpless Caliban:

I crawled
Under a gabardine, hugging tight
All I could of me, hearing the cry
Now of hounds.

The depression or chill or prickle of nape-hair which had been an
aside, a momentary digression in the prose, here becomes the whole
subject. In the prose Plath's singing how she was freed from the Elm
had been the triumphant birth-cry of Ariel. As recently as the 1995
essay the Elm had been celebrated as the locus of 'the essential mythic
drama', the Osirian resurrection, 'the actual achievement of transformation and rebirth, from the despairingly mourned death of love in
the father's coffin to the newborn voice and terrible vitality of the
bereft love returning to life, the awakening of *Ariel* itself' (*WP*, US
edn 475). And the dead father is still celebrated there as 'the presiding genius of her authentic self'. In the prose the elm is cast in the
role of the split pine from which Ariel is to be released. It is clearly
the doorway to the spirit world and the world of the dead of
ancient myth. In 'Childbirth', a poem written before he met Plath,
Hughes had recognized that the womb-door is a dangerous aperture.
Open it a 'furious inch' and 'all the dead could have got back'. Now
he records a 'worst dream ... your dream or mine?' in which 'you had
to lift / The coffin lid an inch' ('A Dream'). What comes up through
the elm-door in the form of a dark malign night-bird 'looking, with

its hooks, for something to love', is the spirit of the dead father, seeking not reconciliation and freedom, but total possession:

> And I sleepwalked
> Like an actor with his script
> Blindfold through the looking glass. I embraced
> Lady Death, your rival,
> As if the role were written on my eyelids
> In letters of phosphorus. With your arms locked
> Round him, in joy, he took you
> Down through the elm door.
> He had got what he wanted.
> I woke up on the empty stage with the props,
> The paltry painted masks. And the script
> Ripped up and scattered, its code scrambled,
> Like the blades and slivers
> Of a shattered mirror.   ('The Table')

In 'The God' he writes:

> The little god flew up into the Elm Tree.
> In your sleep, glassy-eyed,
> You heard its instructions. When you woke
> Your hands moved. You watched them in dismay
> As they made a new sacrifice.
> Two handfuls of blood, your own blood,
> And in that blood gobbets of me,
> Wrapped in a tissue of story that had somehow
> Slipped from you.

So the whole difficult labour, the attempt to free Ariel, the long alchemical process, has come to no more than 'finding your father for you and then / Leaving you to him' ('The Table').

Hughes himself accepted that this was a true account of the central theme of *Birthday Letters*:

> And yes, it's true – because I accepted her temperament & its
> apparent needs as a given set of facts, to be tended, humoured,

cared for, cured if possible in the long- term, and did not impose on her a whole new pattern of behaviour more actively extroverted & organized towards a disciplined engagement with the world, – I surrendered the chance to change her in other ways than by inward concentrated search for the essential voice of an essential self. If she had married a lawyer, a banker – as her mother wanted her to – well, God knows, maybe that would have been hopeless. God knows what way of life would have been better than the one we followed. Though in retrospect, it does read like the scenario written by her father, that she had to perform – and which I unwittingly directed so vigorously, with such fixed ideas, making such sacrifices, thinking we had all time ahead. (Letter to *KS*)

All the other strands of imagery lead to the same disaster. The imagery of fierce flames (in which they trusted the golden lotus could be planted) dominates the cover of *Birthday Letters* in one of their daughter's splendid paintings (balanced by the cool blue of Plath's 'kindly spirit', the jewel she lost). Prouty's image of the lamp turned too high had seemed at the time merely a failure of understanding, nerve and faith. But behind that homely image loomed the twin myths which came to obsess Plath, those of Phaeton and Icarus. In *Birthday Letters* Hughes develops that image to the nth degree. The process of burning away the old false self and verse gets out of hand, becomes a holocaust:

> I stepped back. That glare
> Flinging your old selves off like underthings
> Left your whole Eden radioactive.   ('Child's Park')

In the myth they thought they were enacting, Hughes' role was that of alchemist/midwife:

> In the myth of your first death our deity
> Was yourself resurrected.
> Yourself reborn. The holy one.   ('Suttee')

They were afraid of what they were doing:

> Yet it was the only thing you wanted.
> Night after night, weeks, months, years
> I bowed there, as if over a page,
> Coaxing it to happen.

They find themselves in the wrong myth, engulfed by flames, as the new 'babe all burning bright' appears 'scorched with excessive heat', like the sacrificial Christ-child in Southwell's 'The Burning Babe':

> And you had been delivered of yourself
> In flames. Our newborn
> Was your own self in flames.
> And the tongues of those flames were your tongues.
> I had delivered an explosion
> Of screams that were flames.

Plath did not want to be Christlike. She wanted fulfilment, not to be sacrificed as a 'child-bride / On a pyre', with the husband performing the part of the father:

> Both of us consumed
> By the old child in the new birth –
> Not the new babe of light but the old
> Babe of dark flames and screams
> That sucked the oxygen out of both of us.   ('Suttee')

What had gone wrong? Hughes believed unquestioningly in the Jungian process of individuation, derived, as it was, from Jung's study of those same quest narratives from world myth and folklore and literature with which Hughes himself was so familiar. He assumed that in this process Plath's all-too-evident obsessions, with her dead father and with death itself, would fall away as aberrations, products of the suppression of the true self, mere kindling in the pyre of her resurrection. But that did not happen. When Plath's dreams 'had burst their coffin' Hughes

> woke upside down in your spirit house
> Moving limbs that were not my limbs,
> And telling, in a voice not my voice,

A story of which I knew nothing,
Giddy
With the smoke of the fire you tended
Flames I had lit unwittingly
That whitened in the oxygen jet
Of your incantatory whisper. …
Then you wrote in a fury, weeping
Your joy a trance-dancer
In the smoke in the flames.
'God is speaking through me,' you told me.
'Don't say that,' I cried. 'Don't say that.
That is horribly unlucky!'
As I sat there with blistering eyes
Watching everything go up
In the flames of your sacrifice
That finally caught you too till you
Vanished, exploding
Into the flames
Of the story of your God
Who embraced you
And your Mummy and your Daddy -
Your Aztec, Black Forest
God of the euphemism Grief.   ('The God')

The true poetic voice, and therefore the true self that both Hughes
and Plath had striven so single-mindedly to release, Hughes had consistently referred to as Ariel. This was, of course, the name Plath
chose for her horse, and for her unpublished collection of poems. It
means, in Hebrew, God's lioness. Hughes knew well that the lioness,
any great cat, is an extremely dangerous symbol. In the Faas interview
he described his own jaguar poems as 'invocations of a jaguar-like
body of elemental force, demonic force':

> The tradition is, that energy of this sort once invoked will
> destroy an impure nature and serve a pure one. In a perfectly

cultured society one imagines that the jaguar- like elementals would be invoked only by self-disciplinarians of a very advanced grade. I am not one and I'm sure very few readers are, so maybe in our corrupt condition we have to regard poems about jaguars as ethically dangerous. (*UU* 199)

Despite his protestations, Hughes was a self-disciplinarian, poetically, of a relatively advanced grade. He had his methods, in his work, of keeping the energies he invoked under control:

> I wrote another jaguarish poem called 'Gog'. That actually started as a description of the German assault through the Ardennes and it turned into the dragon in Revelations. It alarmed me so much I wrote a poem about the Red Cross Knight just to set against it with the idea of keeping it under control ... keeping its effects under control. (200)

Hughes assumed that Plath, with his help, would find adequate controls for the energies they sought to release. Maybe if the crucial point had been reached earlier or later that might have been the case, but the moment was the worst possible, the moment of maximum rage, embodied in God's rampaging lioness. 'The symbol itself', Hughes wrote of the big cat, 'is unqualified, it is an irruption, from the deepest resources, of enraged energy – energy that for some reason or other has become enraged.'

Hughes records that Jung 'claimed to have detected in the dreams of Germans, between the wars, a rapidly increasing population of lions, panthers, big dangerous cats. Retrospectively, one interprets what that meant' (*WP* 263). Plath's love/hate relationship with her German father tapped that same vein of Nazism in her last poems.

Retrospectively it became possible for Hughes to interpret what all Plath's imagery meant. His study of the drafts of 'Sheep in Fog', for example, reveals a subliminal myth, the story of Phaeton, interpreted as the key to *Ariel*:

> Phaeton, son of a mortal woman and Apollo (the god of the Sun and of Poetry), took his father's Sun-chariot for a run, and the solar horses, under his half-mortal hands, ran out of control

through the heavens. The chariot, it might be supposed, was wrecked and he was killed. As an image of her Ariel flight in the chariot of the God of Poetry, which was also her attempt to soar (plunge) into the inspirational form of her inaccessible father, to convert her former physical suicide into a psychic rebirth, that myth is the parable of the book *Ariel* and of her life and death. (*WP* 200–1)

Four years later Hughes made the connection with the disastrous meltdown of Icarus:

> In her final correction of the last three lines (of 'Sheep in Fog'), the speaker, who in 'Ariel' had been the Phaeton figure urging the flying horse into the sun (triumphant, albeit 'suicidal' and doomed to fall), suddenly becomes an Icarus, whose melting world threatens to let her through 'into a heaven', not of the sun and freedom, but 'starless, fatherless, a dark water'. (*Shakespeare,* rev. edn 41)

These twin myths seem to have narrowed Plath's fate into a choice between a 'triumphant' death by fire or a defeated death by water.

The purpose of all serious poetry is to find a shape and meaning in the chaos of experience. For the whole of his career Hughes sought appropriate myths, or adaptations or amalgamations of myths, to help him in his effort to place his own little life in the context of permanent or recurrent experience in a world larger than the merely human. Both Hughes and, with his active encouragement and help, Plath made many such attempts. Their successes were temporary and subsumed by the final tragedy. *Birthday Letters* painfully records Hughes' continuing failure to make sense of those years. The alchemical myth of *The Tempest* cannot be made to serve as a template; nor do the models of some of his favourite poems such as 'The Burning Babe' and Owen's 'Strange Meeting' take him far. But the line in 'Otto' where Hughes refers to 'the dark adit / Where I have come looking for your daughter' hints that the true myth behind *Birthday Letters* (perhaps in a sense behind all his poems since 1963) had been the story of Orpheus and Euridice. In a message read for him at the award ceremony of the Forward Poetry Prize, Hughes said that in writing *Birthday Letters* over about 25 years he had 'tried to open a direct, private, inner contact with my first wife, not thinking to make a poem, thinking mainly to evoke her presence to myself and feel her there listening'.

The Orpheus story was the first that occured to Hughes after Sylvia Plath's death. He rejected it as 'too obvious an attempt to exploit my situation' (Letter to KS). He did, however, write a version for children in 1970. Here Orpheus' music is the music of happiness only, happiness deriving from Euridice. It makes even the trees and stones dance. But a voice in his ear, like the voice of a spider, tells him that 'everything must be paid for'. When Euridice dies – 'Her voice has been carried away to the land of the dead' – 'Orpheus' hand suddenly becomes numb'. (Hughes wrote no adult poems for three years.) At last Orpheus decides to go to the underworld to attempt to recover his wife. He uses his guitar like a shaman to make a road of sound to the bottom of the underworld, one note insanely repeated, gathering volume and impetus, and lands at the feet of Pluto, king of the kingdom of the dead. His wife, Pluto tells him, was the payment for his music. Orpheus plays a new music, a music not of beauty and happiness and life only, but of pain and all the cycles of death and renewal. This music causes Persephone herself to flower, the first time Pluto has seen her open since he snatched her from the upper world. Orpheus demands his own wife in exchange. Pluto cannot give him his wife: 'Your wife's body is crumbling to dust', but gives him her soul: 'Return to the world. Your wife's soul will be with you'. He returns, like so many of his heroes, 'a step, a step, and a step'. He cannot see or touch his wife, but he can hear her. She asks him to play for her:

> The music was not the music of dancing
> But of growing and withering,
> Of the root in the earth and the leaf in the light,
> The music of birth and of death.
> And the stones did not dance. But the stones listened.
> The music was not the music of happiness

But of everlasting, and the wearing away of the hills,
The music of the stillness of stones,
Of stones under frost, and stones under rain, and stones in the
sun,
The music of the seabed drinking at the stones of the hills.
The music of the floating weight of the earth.
And the bears in their forest holes
Heard the music of bears in their forest holes.
The music of bones in the starlight,
The music of many a valley trodden by bears,
The music of bears listening on the earth for bears.
And the deer on the high hills heard the crying of wolves.
And the salmon in the deep pools heard the whisper of the
snows,
And the traveller on the road
Heard the music of love coming and love going
And love lost forever,
The music of birth and of death.
The music of the earth, swaddled in heaven, kissed by its cloud
and watched by its ray.
And the ears that heard it were also of leaf and of stone.
The faces that listened were flesh of cliff and of river.
The hands that played it were fingers of snakes and a tangle of
flowers.

Hughes avoided the story for decades in his work for adults, even
conspicuously omitting it from his *Tales from Ovid*. But in his very
last work, his version of Euripides' *Alcestic*, (a work not commissioned like all his other 'translations', but a work on which he chose
to spend his increasingly precious time), feeling perhaps that in the
long agony recorded in *Birthday Letters* he had finally paid for the
right to lay claim to the story, he expanded a passing reference to
Orpheus, a single sentence in Euripides, to a twenty-seven line reca-
pitulation of the whole story (as he had earlier inserted the story of
Prometheus' release from the torment of the vulture).

Admetus has lost his wife Alcestis, and is consumed with guilt. He had mismanaged the situation. He had somehow let his wife's life slip through his fingers. Like Orpheus he had taken his happiness for granted:

> So much confidence. So many blessings.
> So much time!
> So many decades ahead of us.   (68)

He finds himself

> Thinking about Orpheus – in the thick of all this.
> Thinking of the impossible.
> How he went down there,
> Into the underworld, the dead land,
> With his guitar and his voice –
> He rode the dark road
> On the thumping of a guitar,
> A horse of music.
> He wrapped himself in his voice,
> Death-proof, a voice of asbestos,
> He went
> Down and down and down.
> You remember –
> He went for his dead wife
> And he nearly got her.   (22–3)

But for Admetus, in a play whose spirit of restoration is very like that of Shakespeare's last romances, the impossible happens. 'What was beyond belief' is accomplished: Alcestis is returned to him. Heracles says: 'She is yours. / All you thought you had lost – she is here'. Admetus' happiness is greater than ever, because now fully paid for:

> We have taken the full measure of grief
> And now we have found happiness even greater.
> We have found it and recognized it.   (83)

Out of the sufferings of Prometheus and Orpheus, out of the decades of pain, Hughes finally distills this positive vision. The last words of his last work are:

> Let this give man hope.

CHAPTER THREE
The Evolution of 'The Dove Came'

The way poetry is usually taught, artificially detaching the poem from the poet and from the whole creative process, encourages a belief that, as milk comes from bottles, so poems come from books. The complex and fascinating process by which they came into being and got into the books is totally ignored.

Though, as Hughes says, 'the poem can emerge of a sudden, complete and perfect, unalterable, taking the poet completely by surprise, as if he had no idea where it came from', there is widespread belief, particularly among the young, that this is how all poems are written, or should be written. Hughes would be the first to attest to the rarity of this experience. And even when it does happen, the poet more often than not *does* alter it. However, some poets have encouraged the growth of a mystique about how poetic inspiration works. There is Coleridge's suggestion in 'Kubla Khan' and its preface that once the poet has fed on honey-dew and drunk the milk of Paradise (marketed as laudanum in his day), even such complex poems as this will write themselves 'instantly', though a knock on the door is enough to break the spell. Elsewhere, Coleridge stated more temperately that the poem had been composed 'in a sort of reverie', which could be said of any poem. In fact, if a new Coleridge notebook turned up, it should not surprise us to find in it 20 drafts of 'Kubla Khan'. Though Dylan Thomas himself to some extent also fostered the myth of unpremeditated art, the fine frenzy, what Hopkins (speaking of Swinbume) called 'a delirium-tremendous imagination', critics should not have been as surprised as they were when the notebooks came to light after his death, revealing draft after draft transforming a poem beyond recognition. He laboured night after night at his craft or sullen art to produce the impression of 'spindrift pages'. He wrote to Henry Treece:

A poem by myself *needs* a host of images, because its centre is a host of images. I make one image, – though 'make' is not the word; I let, perhaps, an image be 'made' emotionally in me and then apply to it what intellectual & critical forces I possess – let it breed another, let that image contradict the first, make, of the third image bred out of the other two together, a fourth contradictory image, and let them all, within any imposed formal limits, conflict. Each image holds within it the seed of its own destruction, and my dialectical method, as I understand it, is a constant building up and breaking down of the images that come out of the central seed, which is itself destructive and constructive at the same time. But what I want to try to explain – and it's necessarily vague to me – is that the *life* in any poem of mine cannot move concentrically round a central image; the life must come out of the centre; an image must be born and die in another; and any sequence of my images must be a sequence of creations, recreations, destructions, contradictions.... Out of the inevitable conflict of images – inevitable, because of the creative, recreative, destructive and contradictory nature of the motivating centre, the womb of war – I try to make that momentary peace which is a poem. I do not want a poem of mine to be, nor can it be, a circular piece of experience placed nearly outside the living stream of time from which it came; a poem of mine is, or should be, a watertight section of the stream that is flowing all ways; all warring images within it should be reconciled for that small stop of time.

Reading back over that, I agree it looks preciously like nonsense. To say that I 'let' images breed and conflict is to deny my critical part in the business. (*Collected Letters* 281–2)

Hughes related this method to Thomas's larger purposes:

Every poem is an attempt to sign up the whole heavenly vision, from one point of vantage or other, in a static constellation of verbal prisms. It is this fixed intent, and not a rhetorical inflation of ordinary ideas, that gives his language its exaltation and reach. (*UU* 182)

Hughes had, at the very outset of his career, described his own method in very similar terms, when he spoke of 'the living and individual element in every poet's work':

> What I mean is the way he brings to peace all the feelings and energies which, from all over the body, heart, and brain, send up their champions onto the battleground of that first subject. The way I do this, as I believe, is by using something like the method of a musical composer. I might say that I turn every combatant into a bit of music, then resolve the whole uproar into as formal and balanced a figure of melody and rhythm as I can. When all the words are hearing each other clearly, and every stress is feeling every other stress, and all are contented – the poem is finished. (*UU* 163)

Though the language here ('formal and balanced a figure of melody') is influenced by the New Critics, and not the way Hughes would have expressed himself later, it describes adequately enough the method of an early poem such as 'The Thought-Fox'. It is clearly a time-consuming, paper-consuming process. Yet many young (and not-so-young) readers of 'The Thought-Fox' take literally the implication that such a poem could be written, without blotting a word, in the time it takes for the fox to cross the clearing, and with the poet having as little part in the business as the narrator who simply lets the fox enter his head and his fingers move automatically over the blank page. Many of Hughes' detractors write as though they believed all his poems to be instantaneous, automatic, lacking the application of his intellectual and critical forces – a hotchpotch of archetypes plundered from the myth-kitty. Seeds of poems (it is a *thought*-fox, not a poem-fox) and bits of poems do frequently come this spontaneous way, but an examination of Hughes' manuscripts reveals the protracted labour usually required to bring a poem from its first draft to its very different published text.

In the *Paris Review* interview Hughes was asked about the process by which his poems came to be written. He replied:

> Well, I have a sort of notion, just the tail end of an idea,

usually just the thread of an idea. If I can feel behind that a sort
of waiting momentum, a sense of some charge there to tap,
then I just plunge in. What usually happens then – inevitably I
would say – is that I go off in some wholly different direction.
The thread end of an idea burns away, and I'm pulled in on the
momentum of whatever was there waiting. Then that feeling
opens up other energies, all the possibilities in my head, I suppose. That's the pleasure, never quite knowing what's there,
being surprised. Once I get onto something I usually finish it.
In a way it goes on finishing itself while I attend to its needs. It
might be days, months. Later, often enough, I see exactly what
it needs to be, and I finish it in moments, usually by getting rid
of things.

There is no such thing as a typical Hughes poem. Each poem has
its unique kind of evolution. The number of drafts can vary from one
to 20 or 30. A poem can remain essentially the same through all its
drafts, or can be transformed beyond recognition. Most of a poem
can be there from the start, or only the merest hint. It is almost as
common for a poem to become shorter through its drafts as longer;
or it can grow long and then short again. It can come full circle and
end where it began. (The poet has here the advantage over the painter
or sculptor: if he decides that his first thoughts were best, they are not
lost.)

My choice of poem is almost random, since I am restricted to
those few poems I happen to have access to in all their drafts. I have
chosen from *Adam and the Sacred Nine* (written late 1975) 'The
Dove Came', which is fairly typical of Hughes' moderately complex
medium-length poems using theriomorphic imagery for psycho-spir-
itual purposes. Here is the final text:

The Dove Came

Her breast big with rainbows
She was knocked down

The dove came, her wings clapped lightning
That scattered like twigs
She was knocked down

The dove came, her voice of thunder
A piling heaven of silver and violet
She was knocked down

She gave the flesh of her breast, and they ate her
She gave the milk of her blood, they drank her

The dove came again, a sun-blinding
And ear could no longer hear
Mouth was a disembowelled bird
Where the tongue tried to stir like a heart

And the dove alit
In the body of thorns.

Now deep in the dense body of thorns
A soft thunder
Nests her rainbows.

When Hughes chose the order of the sections in *Moortown* – first the farming poems, then the *Prometheus* sequence, then *Earth-Numb*, and finally the *Adam* sequence, he intended that the whole book, like *Wodwo*, should constitute a 'single adventure', a progress from earth-bound suffering, through numbness to rebirth. So the *Prometheus* and *Adam* poems, as it were, bracket a very important phase of Hughes' career as he emerged from the horrors of *Crow* and the numbness of *Prometheus* into the painful and raw affirmations of *Adam*. *Adam and the Sacred Nine* is part of a larger process (which also includes *Cave Birds* and *Gaudete*) of reconstituting and resacralizing both the self and the world.

The manuscripts of 'The Dove Came' consist of 13 A4 pages, eight holograph and five typescript, two of these with holograph revision. With one exception (where there are two drafts of the opening), each page carries the whole poem. I have numbered 13 drafts, but these do not correspond to the 13 pages, since some of the holograph pages have two drafts, the original (not always wholly recoverable) and the interlinear, marginal and super-imposed revision (not always decipherable either), and some of the typescripts are merely fair copies. The published version constitutes a 14th, since it does not exactly correspond with the final manuscript. The drafts are undated, and there is no certainty that I have arranged them in the correct order.

Introducing a reading of several of the Adam poems on radio, Hughes said:

> All the creatures of the world come to him, telling him to pull himself together and get moving, but he just lies there, getting limper and limper. At last his creator can't stand it any longer, and so he sends down nine divine birds, to become his guardian, exemplary spirits. They are actually just ordinary birds, except for one, which is a Phoenix.

The dove he described simply as 'a gentle dove, forcing herself through all the opposition'. Strangely (given its crucial importance in the sequence), it was not one of the nine birds as Hughes first conceived the story, but replaced the kingfisher ('who sews the worlds together').

Each bird brings Adam a particularly clear example of a quality he will require if he is ever to achieve his full manhood. Each quality derives partly from the ornithological character of the species ('just ordinary birds'), partly from the character each bird has acquired in myth and folklore, which is not unrelated, since each bird that has acquired mythological status has done so at least in part by virtue of the observable characteristics of ordinary birds. There is no necessary distinction between 'ordinary' and 'divine'. And in *What is the Truth?*, after the farmer has described pigeons as pests fit for nothing but pigeon pie, the vicar comments: 'The holiest bird of all! What an end!' (58).

Doves are unique in being the only birds to feed their young on milk, a high-protein fluid called crop-milk. Since this can be produced at almost any time of year, they have no breeding season and raise several broods throughout the year. They copulate frequently and openly and were therefore thought to be lecherous and fertile. (The association with sexual love is built into our language with 'lovey-dovey', 'bill and coo' etc.) Presumably for this reason, the dove became sacred to the great goddesses Ishtar, Venus and Isis. The softness, warmth and milkiness of the dove's breast and its caressing call suggest all that is feminine, loving, maternal, protective. This aspect allowed its sacredness to be carried over into Judaic and Christian symbolism, where the dove symbolizes the Holy Spirit. In the Old Testament, the dove was the first creature to find land after the Flood, and is thereby closely associated with God's renewed covenant with mankind, symbolized by the rainbow (reflected in its prismatic plumage) (Genesis 9:13). In the Gospels the Spirit of God descends on Christ 'like a dove, and lighting upon him' when he is baptized by John the Baptist (Matthew 3:16). The Holy Ghost is traditionally pictured as a dove. For Hopkins the dove symbolized the perpetual daily renewal of the world: 'Because the Holy Ghost over the bent / World broods with warm breast and with ah! bright wings'. In both Christian and alchemical iconography the soul itself is frequently pictured as a dove. Proverbially, the dove symbolizes meekness and faithfulness. Nineteenth-century sentimental Christianity gave its qualities to Christ himself. Hughes would, of course, have been aware of the darker associations with Christ, the symbolism of the Holy Ghost as pentecostal fire and of Love as redemptive agony:

> The dove descending breaks the air
> With flame of incandescent terror
> Of which the tongues declare
> The one discharge from sin and error.
>
> (T.S. Eliot, 'Little Gidding')

The association with martyrdom and sacrifice is strengthened by our modern experience of the dove as living target, the extermination of the passenger-pigeon, the slaughter of wood-pigeons, of which *The Birdlife of Britain* says 'everyman's hand seems to be against them'.

By far the most important non-ornithological source for Hughes is Blake. Both *Prometheus on his Crag* and *Adam and the Sacred Nine* were first published by Olwyn Hughes' Rainbow Press, the emblem of which was Blake's illustration to Bryant depicting moon-arc, dove and rainbow. Both books, like most of Hughes' sequences of the 1970s, are reworkings of material which largely defeated Blake – attempts to find a simpler, more dramatic, more coherent, more poetic myth to embody the process by which Albion/Adam, fallen into the sleep of single vision, is gradually and painfully dismantled, reconstituted and awakened into the fourfold vision of Adam Kadmon, and reunited with his lost bride. Blake's defeated Albion is Hughes' Prometheus on his crag: 'Albion cold lays on his Rock … / Over them the famish'd Eagle screams on boney Wings' (*Jerusalem Plate* 94). In the third *Prometheus* poem Prometheus's shout shatters 'a world of holy, happy notions', symbolized by birds: 'The dove's bubble of fluorescence burst'. For Blake the dove symbolizes Albion's lost emanation, his threefold vision of innocence. Only Los, the poet, retains a vision of Jerusalem descending from heaven as a dove, and as a bride adorned for her husband Albion:

> I see thy Form, O lovely mild Jerusalem, Wing'd with Six
>   Wings
> In the opacous Bosom of the Sleeper, lovely Three-fold
> In Head & Heart & Reins, three Universes of love & beauty.
> Thy forehead bright, Holiness to the Lord, with Gates of pearl
> Reflects Eternity; beneath, thy azure wings of feathery down
> Ribb'd delicate & cloth'd with feather'd gold & azure & purple,
> From thy white shoulders shadowing purity in holiness!
> Thence, feather'd with soft crimson of the ruby, bright as fire,
> Spreading into the azure, Wings which like a canopy
> Bends over thy immortal Head in which Eternity dwells.
> I see the New Jerusalem descending out of Heaven,
> Between thy Wings of gold & silver, feather'd, immortal,
> Clear as the rainbow, as the cloud of the Sun's tabernacle.
>
> (*Jerusalem Plate* 86)

All these sources, and no doubt more esoteric ones, are available for Hughes to draw on, consciously or unconsciously, as he begins his poem. Through the drafts we can see the original images attracting others, falling away, undergoing manifold transformations, as Hughes struggles to let the dove force herself through all the opposition, most of which comes from Adam (Hughes, everyman, reader) himself.

Here is my attempt to recover the first draft:

The Dove

> Is the bubble the violet
> A breast of quiet lightning
> A thunder of softness, care
> And endearment, plundered by gods
> Arched wings
>
> A gateway of watchfulness
> Where the world plays
> With a child
>
> When they plucked her
> The stars floated off, and became unending They roasted her
> Then they disembowelled her
> Their mouths smoked.
> Her liver became an oracle.
>
> Her flesh still (?)
> (?) cave of slaughter. Her heart spoke, An oracle
> Of loving words
>
> Her heart became his tongue.
>
> He stood, drenched in her blood And hardening in the light.
>
> Still her words were his strength.

The first thing that strikes us is that not a line, not even a phrase, of this first draft survives into the published poem. Yet it is clearly the same poem. All the drafts, though they play many variations with the phrasing, begin with the dove's breast, its bulbous shape and its distinctive colouring. All the drafts retain the imagery of thunder and lightning, suggested, presumably, by the similar colour of thunder-clouds, the soft rumble of the voice, and the flash and clap of wings. Thunder and lightning also traditionally announce some interven-tion of the gods (usually angry, but in this case gentle) in human affairs. There is perhaps even a faint echo of the cosmic energies Frankenstein draws down to galvanize his inert monster, which then, all unknowing, kills an innocent child. The core of the poem, from the beginning, is the opposition between the imperative to love in the descending spirit, and the imperative to kill in the material world in which it is obliged to try to incarnate itself. How can Man, who is flesh little differentiated from mud, receive the bubble-delicate fluo-rescence of what the dove brings? The middle part of the poem throughout deals with the killing, disembowelling and eating of the dove, followed by the transformation of the dove's heart into the man's tongue. This alchemical transformation has something in com-mon with such pictures as the Boehme etching, known to Blake, of fallen Man awakening when a dove descends, pierces his breast and enters or becomes his heart, and also with those depictions of the soul leaving the body of a saint or martyr at death in the form of a dove emerging from the mouth.

The word 'bubble' is retained, in various combinations, through the first eight drafts. It is the right shape for a plump breast, has rain-bow colours, is extremely fragile and, moreover, exactly mimes the sound of a dove. But it has to be let go at last, probably because a bubble can only be knocked down once, if at all, does not bleed, and cannot be eaten, cannot force its way through anything, cannot live in the same world as thorns. The whole point about the dove's breast is that it is simultaneously substantial flesh and blood and insubstan-tial rainbow, both vulnerable and indestructible. The bubble falls between.

'Violet' comes and goes, but is finally retained in the splendid description of the dove's 'voice of thunder' as 'A piling heaven of sil-ver and violet'. 'Violet' is soft, but potentially violent, is closer than 'blue' (the alternative in draft 4) to the actual colour of thunder-clouds, and, being at the upper limit of human colour-vision, suggests, perhaps, that boundary between the seen and the unseen, the worlds of body and of spirit, where most of the events of these poems take place. Hughes continues for nine drafts to spell out the meaning of the dove's thunder as softness, care (later caresses) and endearments, but finds at last that these abstractions are redundant.

The next section also remains, little changed, until the tenth draft, when it disappears altogether. At the first revision it had become:

> Arched wings
> A gateway of watchfulness And lilac shadow
> Where a child plays with the world in the dust.

The dove is here presented as the guardian of a Blakean world of childish innocence. Though the word 'rainbow' does not appear until the fourth draft, the idea of the rainbow, symbolizing harmony and unfallen vision, must have been in Hughes' mind from the beginning. Blake's vision of childhood seems to blend with Lawrence's. When, in *The Rainbow*, Tom and Lydia Brangwen came together in perfect marriage, Tom knew 'that she was the gateway and the way out'. They created a rainbow arch of security for their child: 'Her father and her mother now met to the span of the heavens, and she, the child, was free to play in the space beneath, between.'

In Hughes' first draft, the dove is killed by anonymous adults. It comes as a shock to find that after the first revision, she is killed by the child. In the next draft we are told that he does so 'in childish unknowing', and in the fourth 'In childish dreaminess / He disembowels her / Looking for life'. This is the authentic Hughes world, where innocence is inseparable from slaughter. The childish, larval wodwo asks: 'Why do I find / this frog so interesting as I inspect its most secret / interior and make it my own?'

Draft 4 is already beginning to look like a finished poem, but evidently not the poem Hughes wanted to write:

> The bubble-blue dove
> Brings from heaven
> A breast of sleepy rainbows – the dove's lightning.

An air-stirring softness, caresses
And endearments. This is the dove's thunder.

Arched wings
A gateway of watchfulness
and lilac shadow
Where a child plays with the world in the dust
Soon he grows
He knocks her down, and he plucks her alive
The stars float off
Hardening and sharpening to enmity.
In childish dreaminess
He disembowels her
Looking for life.
His mouth smokes open
A cavern of hot slaughter
With her heart speaking inside it
A deathless oracle
Loving words to the child

Her heart is his tongue. His listening begins.

Though he stands drenched in her blood from head to foot
And hardening among stars
Her words are his strength.

This is the dove's milk.

The hardening of the stars and the child suggests not only a loss of innocence, but also a process of individuation, like something lifted from the flux, the forge, and cooling into its definitive form.

It seems that only when the child is drenched in the dove's blood from head to foot can he stand, come into his strength, and speak the word 'love'. Again there are echoes of the *Four Quartets*:

> The dripping blood our only drink,
> The bloody flesh our only food.   ('East Coker')

There are many accounts of pagan rituals where the worshippers are drenched in the blood of a sacrificial animal. Here is Frazer's account of an Attis rite:

> A bull, adorned with garlands of flowers, its forehead glittering with gold leaf, was driven onto the grating and there stabbed to death with a consecrated spear. Its hot reeking blood poured in torrents through the apertures, and was received with devout eagerness by the worshipper on every part of his person and garments, till he emerged from the pit, drenched, dripping, and scarlet from head to foot, to receive the homage, nay the adoration, of his fellows as one who had been born again into eternal life and had washed away his sins in the blood of the bull. (*The Golden Bough* 463)

There are, of course, important differences between what happens in the poem and such pagan rituals. The child is not a worshipper participating in a ritual. He knocks down the dove for no better reason than the Ancient Mariner shoots the albatross – on a whim, having nothing better to do; or rather, in accordance with the 'natural logic' (draft 8) which dictates that all creatures were created as food for other creatures, that any creature outside the ordered world of man is by nature his food, target or plaything. When Hughes was a child, his elder brother would wander the hills shooting anything that moved, and Hughes would act as retriever: 'He could not shoot enough for me' (*Poetry in the Making* 16). But even after compassion enters in, the killing goes on. Draft 8 adds 'tears ran from the saliva ducts', an echo of 'Crow Tyrannosaurus' – 'Weeping he walked and stabbed'.

The bull was the chosen sacrifice in the belief that the strength of the bull would pass into the worshipper, or the power of the god through his totemic beast. The dove can be destroyed all too easily, but the love it manifests in its willing sacrifice is sanctified, made absolute, by that sacrifice. The innocent child kills, and that fortunate fall into experience at its most destructive opens the way for his emergence into threefold vision, a vision of love. The Christian parallel seems inescapable. Not until Man has crucified God can he be redeemed by that same deathless God. This parallel is to become overt in draft 11.

Draft 10 again looks like a finished poem, neatly arranged in qua-
trains, and the first draft in typescript. It is noteworthy that the holograph of which the typescript is a fair copy has the deleted title 'The
Dove's Covenant'.

> The rainbows in the dove's breast are kindly.
> She has lightning too,
> When she claps her wings, it scatters like twigs.
> And the piling summer clouds of her voice, these are her
>   thunders.
>
> She said to the wolf-child: worship love only.
> The wolf-child knocked her down
> He disembowelled her, seeking the voice.
> His mouth smoked open, tears ran from the saliva ducts.
>
> A cave of hot slaughter.
> Inside, the heart, a glory
> Went on speaking.
> Loving words, a deathless oracle.
> The heart named him. The heart
> Had become his tongue moving
> Thickly and powerfully. His mouth closed.
> Dipped in fear, as in her blood, he emerged
>
> And stood in air,
> Hardening among stars.
> He spoke. And her words were his strength. This was the dove'
>   milk.

The opening has moved forward a little, with its scattering twigs and
piling clouds. The gateway of arched wings, hitherto the most con-
sistent part of the poem, has gone. But the surprising change here is
the sudden introduction of the wolf-child, mentioned in no other
draft. By a wolf-child are we to understand a child suckled by wolves?
If so, the imperative to worship love only would clash even more
strongly with 'natural logic' than in a normal child. Yet the normal-
ity of the child had seemed essential to the earlier versions. We could,

of course, question why there needs to be a child in the poem at all, since the dove is supposed to be visiting Adam, who never was a child. Blake seems to have smuggled the child in, and Hughes has been stuck with him, the poles of his poem having become murderous natural male innocence and sacrificial supernatural (or spiritualized) female innocence.

It is also surprising that the poem has made so little progress in ten drafts. In fact it seems to have lost a good deal of its original energy. 'Kindly' is inert. The dove's lightning and thunders have been reduced to purely descriptive metaphors. The dove loses in reality by having words put into its mouth. 'As in her blood' again reduces to an inert simile what had been a potent and literal drenching. The regular form of the poem seems to have tamed and diluted it. Nearly all the lines are now end-stopped, so there is no tension in the lineation, no momentum, no drama. The poem does not bear comparison with any of the other bird poems in the sequence.

But draft 11 throws out the child altogether, with much other dross, and the poem leaps forward almost to its final state.

The Dove Came

Her breast full of rainbows
She was struck down

The dove came, her wings clapped lightnings
That scattered like twigs
She was struck down

The dove came, her thunder
Piled like summer clouds and soft violet
She was struck down

She came with the flesh of her breast
She was eaten

She came with her blood richer than rubies
She was drunk

The dove came again, a blinding
Ear could no longer hear

Mouth was a disembowelled bird
Where the tongue tried to move, like a heart

The dove alit
In the body of thorns
Deep in the body of thorns
The dove of soft thunder
Nested her thunder.

This sudden coming clear may indicate some missing intermediate drafts, but in the absence of any evidence of that, we must assume that the advance is the result of two drastic decisions to make the whole poem about the dove (in line with the other eight bird poems), and to allow the Christian analogue to become a much more central determinant.

By putting the striking down of the dove in the passive and by having her struck down three times, Hughes suggests much more strongly that it is the fate of the dove to be struck down (as it was Christ's to be crucified) rather than any unusual cruelty in those who struck her down. The eating of the dove's flesh and drinking of her blood echoes the last supper:

> And as they were eating, Jesus took bread, and blessed it, and brake it, and gave it to the disciples, and said, Take, eat; this is my body. And he took the cup, and gave thanks, and gave it to them, saying, Drink ye all of it; For this is my blood of the new testament, which is shed for many for the remission of sins. (Matthew 26:26–8)

Yet the lines are not exclusively Christian, for they also echo the myths and folk-songs of the eating of fertility gods, such as Hughes draws on in 'The Golden Boy':

> With terrible steel
> They beat his bones from him
> With terrible steel

> They ground him to powder
> They baked him in ovens
> They sliced him on tables
> They ate him they ate him
> They ate him they ate him

And that apparent atrocity is actually the gift of life.

In the typescript the dove is 'big with rainbows', gravid with bless-ings, tokens of the covenant between Man and God. The dove alights, and nests, as doves do, in a dense thorn-bush, there to hatch no longer thunders but rainbows. The 'body of thorns' again suggests the crown of thorns which was the humble and painful token of the glory of Christ in his agony. Christ the king fisher of men sews the worlds together on the cross. The rainbow, reconciling the opposites of sun and rain, symbolizes that, or any other, atonement.

The dove is no legless bird of transcendence. She is spirit incar-nate. Her voice is also the soft thunder of a beating heart. Noah's dove was sent to find the landfall which would signify God's atonement with Man. On her first flight 'the dove found no rest for the sole of her foot'. It is no coincidence that the final poem of the *Adam* sequence is called 'The Sole of a Foot'. Here Adam is at last erect and reconciled to his earth-bound status. His foot says to the world-rock:

> I am no wing
> To tread emptiness.
> I was made
>
> For you.

The purpose of all these drafts and revisions was not to subject the material to 'craftsmanship', nor even, primarily, to produce 'a formal and balanced figure of melody and rhythm', which in many of the poems of this period would be totally inappropriate. It was a matter of throwing out all that could be thrown out, leaving only that which imperiously proves itself, the simplicity on the far side of complexity, the essential.

CHAPTER FOUR
From World of Blood to World of Light

Early in his career Hughes spoke of 'the terrible, suffocating, maternal octopus' of the English poetic tradition. But Hughes himself, despite his deep early involvement with the natural world, was never in much danger of being remade in the image of Wordsworth. The boy who was taken to a nearby pub to watch Billy Red catch and kill rats with his teeth, whose pet fox-cubs were torn apart by dogs before his eyes, who dreamed of being a wolf, was not likely to see Nature as Lucy Gray, rather as the sow that eats her own farrow. Nor did poetry first make its impact as mediated by Palgrave and his successors among schoolbook anthologizers, but with the unmediated violence of an Indian war-song chanted to him by his brother:

> I am the woodpecker,
> My head is red,
> To those that I kill,
> With my little red bill,
> Come wolf, come bear and eat your fill,
> Mine's not the only head that's red.   (*Poet Speaks* 87)

The nine-year-old Hughes felt he could do something like that.

Wordsworth sealed his spirit to the inevitability of decay and death. The years would only lead his dear sister from joy to joy; her mind would be, in after years, 'a mansion for all lovely forms', her memory 'a dwelling place / For all sweet sounds and harmonies' ('Tintern Abbey'). In the event she became an imbecile. Hughes is determined from the beginning to take a full look at the worst and accept it as Nature's norm:

> Minute after minute, aeon after aeon,
> Nothing lets up or develops.
> And this is neither a bad variant nor a tryout.

> This is where the staring angels go through.
> This is where all the stars bow down.   ('Pibroch')

The sound that haunted Hughes like a passion was:

> That cry for milk
> From the breast
> Of the mother
> Of the God
> Of the world
> Made of Blood.   ('Karma')

The first lines of the first poem in Hughes' first book, *The Hawk in the Rain*, plunge us into a world that is soon to become familiar:

> I drown in the drumming ploughland, I drag up
> Heel after heel from the swallowing of the earth's mouth,
> From clay that clutches my each step to the ankle
> With the habit of the dogged grave ...
>   ('The Hawk in the Rain')

The last lines of the last poem in his 1982 *Selected Poems* are a world away:

> So we found the end of our journey.
>
> So we stood, alive in the river of light
> Among creatures of light, creatures of light.
>   ('That Morning')

In this chapter I want to follow that journey, and look at some of the crucial stations in it.

The Hawk in the Rain is about Man, imprisoned in single vision as in his own body, looking out through the windows of his eyes at the surrounding energies, the 'wandering elementals'. He makes no effort to come to terms with them, as though that were unthinkable, but cowers, hides, peeps through his fingers, grips his own heart, runs for dear life. His only defence is poetry, where he can sit inside his own head and defend his ego with word-patterns.

'The Hawk in the Rain' pitches us into the thick of the battle
between vitality and death which Hughes claimed was his only subject. It is, in this poem as in many, a one-sided battle. Three of the
four elements seem to be in alliance with death. Earth, even the earth
of ploughland, is not fertile but a mass grave. Water drowns. Rain
falls not to engender new life but to convert earth to down-dragging
mud and to hack to the bone any head that presumes to raise itself.
Air manifests itself only as wind which kills any stubborn attempts at
life. The very language is a series of blows pounding life down. What
hope amidst all this for the fire of vitality or spirit? It is located only
in the eye of the hawk, which seems effortlessly, by an act of will, to
master it all, to be the exact centre, the eye of the storm, the 'master-
Fulcrum of violence'.

The hawk is as close to the inviolability of an angel as a living creature can be, yet the 'angelic eye' is doomed to be smashed, the hawk
to 'mix his heart's blood with the mire of the land'. The extinguishing of the hawk's fire, this mingling of mud and blood, as in the
trenches and bomb-craters of the First World War which his uncles,
by their stories, and his father, by his aching silence, had made the
landscape of the young Hughes' mind, is what death wants and
invariably gets in Hughes' poetry of the fifties and sixties. It is
what shoulders out 'One's own body from its instant and heat' ('Six
Young Men'). It is 'the dead man behind the mirror' (*UU* 171). Yet
the powerful ending of this poem comes to seem somewhat histrionic
when we compare it with the death of the buzzard in *What is the
Truth?*:

> Finally, he just lets the sky
> Bend and hold him aloft by his wing-tips.
>
> There he hangs, dozing off in his hammock.
> Mother earth reaches up for him gently.   (44)

Also the effect of 'The Hawk in the Rain' on the reader is far from
depressing. If the man trying to cross a ploughed field in a cloudburst
cannot be the 'master-Fulcrum of violence', the same man later sitting at his desk making a poem of the experience can.

I turn every combatant into a bit of music, then resolve the whole uproar into as formal and balanced a figure of melody and rhythm as I can. When all the words are hearing each other clearly, and every stress is feeling every other stress, and all are contented – the poem is finished. (*UU* 163)

This conception of art was very much in tune with the New Criticism fashionable in the fifties, and Hughes' early poems lent themselves to that kind of analysis. But it is an attitude to art he would soon have to modify radically. It is of a piece with the dualistic idea of creation by a sole male god. The goddess was heaven and earth, and cannot stand apart from nature. But the god who succeeded her makes nature out of inert materials, like an artist:

> In this way the essential identity between creator and creation was broken, and a fundamental dualism was born from their separation, the dualism that we know as spirit and nature. In the myth of the goddess these two terms have no meaning in separation from each other: nature is spiritual and spirit is natural, because the divine is immanent as creation. In the myth of the god, nature is no longer 'spiritual' and spirit is no longer 'natural', because the divine is transcendent to creation. Spirit is not inherent in nature, but outside it or beyond it; it even becomes the source of nature. So a new meaning enters the language: spirit becomes creative and nature becomes created. In this new kind of myth, creation is the result of a divine act that brings order out of chaos. (Baring and Cashford 274)

And within that metaphysic, art is Man's effort to bring further order out of chaos, to transform into music what would otherwise be uproar. Art becomes a contest against Nature.

This is true of even the best poems in *The Hawk in the Rain* such as 'Wind'. Here Hughes brilliantly mimes the distorting and levelling power of a gale, seeking to find words, like those of the Border ballads, 'that live in the same dimension as life at its most severe, words that cannot be outflanked by experience' (*WP* 68). His wind is real enough, and also carries much the same larger meaning as the wind

Castaneda's Don Juan calls the '*nagual*', a wind that threatens to obliterate the '*tonal*' – 'everything we know and do as men' (or in Hughes' words, 'book, thought, / Or each other'):

> Everyone's obsession is to arrange the world according to the *tonal*'s rules; so every time we are confronted with the *nagual*, we go out of our way to make our eyes stiff and intransigent. ... The point is to convince the *tonal* that there are other worlds that can pass in front of the same windows. ... *The eyes* can be the windows to peer into boredom or peek into that infinity. (*Tales of Power*, 172)

Insofar as he has the courage to 'peek into that infinity', Hughes displays the courage of what Castaneda calls a sorcerer:

> A leaf's otherness,
> The whaled monstered sea-bottom, eagled peaks
> And stars that hang over hurtling endlessness,
>   With manslaughtering shocks
>
>   Are let in on his sense:
> So many one has dared to be struck dead
> Peeping though his fingers at the world's ends,
>   Or at an ant's head.   ('Egg-head')

But the very skill Hughes exhibits in the control of language reinforces the tonal and keeps the wind out. The man who 'cannot entertain book, thought, / Or each other' can still write a splendid poem, with such finely crafted lines as: 'The wind flung a magpie away and a black- / Back gull bent like an iron bar slowly'.

The later Hughes will no longer erect such verbal barricades:

> And we go
>
> Into the wind. The flame-wind – a red wind
> And a black wind. The red wind comes
> To empty you. And the black wind, the longest wind
>
> The headwind
>
> To scour you.   ('The guide')

Given the landscape of mud and blood, the vast no-man's land, which is the world of Hughes' early poems, it is not easy for him to say how men should try to live in such a world. It is easier to say how they should not. What Hughes pours his most vehement scorn on is the egg-head's pride and 'braggart-browed complacency in most calm / Collusion with his own / Dewdrop frailty'; his spurning of the earth as 'muck under / His foot-clutch'; his willingness to oppose his own eye to 'the whelm of the sun' ('Egg-head'). Pride and complacency are man's commonest defences against receiving the full impact of the otherness and endlessness of the natural world. What Hughes is trying to say in this poem is, I take it, that the egg-head, in defending his tonal, his single vision, at all costs, is resisting birth, which requires the breaking of the ego-shell, because the wisdom that would then flood in would be accounted madness in our world of single vision. In *Moby Dick*, when the Negro boy Pip fell overboard, thought he had been abandoned, and was then rescued, he went about an idiot:

> The sea had jeeringly kept his finite body up, but drowned the infinite of his soul. Not drowned entirely, though. Rather carried down alive to wondrous depths, where strange shapes of the unwarped primal world glided to and fro before his passive eyes; and the miser-merman, Wisdom, revealed his hoarded heaps; Pip saw the multitudinous, God-omnipresent, coral insects, that out of the firmament of waters heaved the colossal orbs. He saw God's foot upon the treadle of the loom, and spoke it; and therefore his shipmates called him mad. So man's insanity is heaven's sense; and wandering from all mortal reason, man comes at last to that celestial thought, which, to reason, is absurd and frantic; and weal or woe, feels then uncompromised, indifferent as his God. (Ch. 93)

The tone of the poet's voice in 'Egg-head', however, is at the opposite pole from any divine indifference. The superiority of the poet manifests itself with just as much fervency and trumpeting as the egg-head is accused of. The style is confident and masculine and aggressive to the point of 'braggart-browed complacency'.

Such stylistic overkill is of a piece with the moral and sexual insen-
sibility of some of the worst poems of the 1950s such as 'Secretary',
'Bawdry Embraced', 'Macaw and Little Miss' and 'The Ancient
Heroes and the Bomber Pilot' (a poem glorifying the patriarchal sav-
agery of the Bronze Age).

In *Lupercal* we are again in a world of 'oozing craters' and 'sodden
moors', but this time with an awed acknowledgement that life is possible 'between the weather and the rock', that death and vitality are
manifestations of the same forces, generating as well as extinguishing
life:

> What humbles these hills has raised
> The arrogance of blood and bone,
> And thrown the hawk upon the wind,
> And lit the fox in the dripping ground.   ('Crow Hill')

Nor are these forces now felt as exclusively a downward pull and pressure:

> Those barrellings of strength are heaving slowly and heave
> To your feet and surf upwards
> In a still, fiery air, hauling the imagination,
> Carrying the larks upward.   ('Pennines in April')

(Though, as we are to see in 'Skylarks', to be flung upward is not necessarily an easier life than to be dragged down.)

Given such conditions, how to live? There is the example of the
horses patiently outwaiting the darkness of a 'world cast in frost' and
rewarded by a glorious sunrise. But that is a portion of eternity too
great for the eye of the narrator, who stumbles away from it 'in the
fever of a dream'.

Again, in 'November', he admires the 'strong trust' of a tramp
asleep in a ditch in the drilling rain and the welding cold, but this
patience is as hopeless as that of the corpses on the gibbet:

> Patient to outwait these worst days that beat
> Their crowns bare and dripped from their feet.

At the opposite extreme are the ancient heroes, the big-hearted, 'huge-chested braggarts' who spent their lives in war, rape and pillage, as if the answer were to try to beat ravenous Nature at her own bloody game. They are like the 'Warriors of the North', spilling blood

> To no end
> But this timely expenditure of themselves,
> A cash-down, beforehand revenge, with extra,
> For the gruelling relapse and prolongeur of their blood
>
> Into the iron arteries of Calvin.

Some heroes and geniuses are able to live as single-mindedly as thrushes or sharks, but the normal human condition is to be forever distracted from day-to-day living by the opposite pulls of heaven and hell, hope and despair, the dream of an 'unearthly access of grace, / Of ease: freer firmer world found' and the rude awakening from that dream,

> bearing
> Plunge of that high risk without
> That flight; with only a dread
> Crouching to get away from these
> On its hands and knees.   ('Acrobats')

Here, in a few lines, Hughes takes in the fall of Hopkins from the spiritual acrobatics of 'Hurrahing in Harvest' to the terrible sonnets; the fall of modernist vision from Wordsworth's egotistical sublime to Beckett's spiritual void.

There is, however, again some discrepancy between style and content. The style has all the necessary weight and strength to mime the pressure of the huge forces of the natural world upon the living organism. But the energies are invoked (often in the form of predatory beasts) with a sometimes overweening masculine confidence that they can be controlled by the imposed form of the poem itself. Were the poems really, as he thought at the time, containing the energies, or were they shutting out by their tightly closed forms energies which, had they come in, would have overwhelmed all pretence at art?

The style of *Lupercal* is confident of its ability both to evoke and control the energies, to plug in to the 'elemental power-circuit of the universe'. Hughes' imagination, purged of the poetic cult of beauty and the Wordsworthian sentimentalities, becomes a great intestine rejecting nothing:

> This mute eater, biting through the mind's
> Nursery floor, with eel and hyena and vulture,
> With creepy-crawly and the root,
> With the sea-worm, entering its birthright.

('Mayday on Holderness')

Thus the poet can clamp himself well onto the world like a wolf-mask, and speak with the voice of the glutted crow, the stoat, the expressionless leopard, the sleeping anaconda, the frenzied shrew, the roosting hawk – which is 'Nature herself speaking'. Yet again there is some discrepancy. We are told that the stoat 'bit through grammar and corset', that its 'red unmanageable life ... licked the stylist out of (the) skulls' of Walpole and his set ('Strawberry Hill'). But the poem that tells us so is a triumph of intelligence and style, in a volume of great stylistic achievement, orthodox grammar, corseted stanzas and even rhyming verse.

This discrepancy is also apparent in 'To Paint a Water Lily' with its elegant rhyming couplets. The poem is a verse exemplum of Carlyle's observations on Nature in 'Characteristics':

> Boundless as is the domain of man, it is but a small fractional proportion of it that he rules with Consciousness and Forethought: what he can contrive, nay, what he can altogether know and comprehend, is essentially the mechanical, small; the great is ever, in one sense or other, the vital; it is essentially the mysterious, and only the surface of it can be understood. But Nature, it might seem, strives, like a kind mother, to hide from us even this, that she is a mystery. ... Under all Nature's works, chiefly under her noblest work, Life, lies a basis of Darkness, which she benignantly conceals; in Life, too, the roots and inward circulations which stretch down fearfully to the regions

of Death and Night, shall not hint of their existence, and only the fair stem with its leaves and flowers, shone on by the sun, shall disclose itself and joyfully grow.

Hughes' example is the water lily, whose leaves are simultaneously the floor of the sunny, conscious world, accessible (visually) to any Sunday painter, and the roof of another, less colourful and 'aesthetic' world, the unconscious, inaccessible to all the senses, accessible only to the imagination. Hughes refuses merely to praise the rainbow colours of Nature (for which the painterly style of the poem is well suited), but strives to escape the tyranny of the eye and listen rather to the inaudible 'battle-shouts / And death-cries everywhere hereabouts'. He refuses to paint only the dragonfly alighting on the water lily if his imagination can see into the life of the pond and the horror nudging her root. However, in this poem at least, it can only gesture in that direction – 'Prehistoric bedragonned times / Crawl that darkness with Latin names'. The underwater world, the unconscious mind, is a closed book to the poet. There is no hint of the wisdom of Pip, of the shamanic journey into the 'regions of Death and Night' which Hughes' poems are later to become. In 'Photostomias' for example, this primitive deep-sea fish, also known as the dragon-fish, could well be described as having 'jaws for heads', but Hughes is there about deeper business than mere description of Nature's horrors, about the business of revealing that those horrors are also miracles, are also God:

> Jehova – mucous and phosphorescence
> In the camera's glare -
>
> A decalogue
> A rainbow.

In his 1977 interview with Ekbert Faas Hughes described writing 'To Paint a Water Lily': 'I … felt very constricted fiddling around with it. It was somehow like writing through a long winding tube, like squeezing language out at the end of this long, remote process.' He found in 'View of a Pig' 'a whole way of writing that was obviously much more natural for me than that water-lily-style'. Faas objected that 'To Paint a Water Lily' was 'one of the most beautiful poems in *Lupercal*'. Hughes replied:

> Maybe, but it isn't as interesting to me. And my follow-up to 'View of a Pig' was 'Pike'. But that poem immediately became much more charged with particular memories and a specific obsession. And my sense of 'Hawk Roosting' was that somehow or other it had picked up the prototype style behind 'View of a Pig' and 'Pike' without that overlay of a heavier, thicker, figurative language. ... All three were written in a mood of impatience, deliberately trying to destroy the ways in which I had written before, trying to write in a way that had nothing to do with the way in which I thought I ought to be writing. But then, that too became deliberate and a dead end. (*UU* 208–9)

'Pike' is a much better poem than 'To Paint a Water Lily', moving from the descriptive and narrative modes of total authorial command in the first nine stanzas into a more open dramatic mode, where what is being dramatized is precisely the fear arising from the speaker's ignorance of what is rising towards him out of the 'Darkness beneath night's darkness'. As Gaston Bachelard writes (not in relation to this poem):

> Night alone would give a less physical fear. Water alone would give clearer obsessions. Water at night gives a penetrating fear. ... If the fear that comes at night beside a pond is a special fear, it is because it is a fear that enjoys a certain range. It is very different from the fear experienced in a grotto or a forest. It is not so near, so concentrated, or so localized; it is more flowing. Shadows that fall on water are more mobile than shadows on earth. (*Water and Dreams* 101–2)

It is also the fear that what is rising towards him might be too monstrous, too alien, too ego-destroying for the poetry he is yet able to write to deal with. Fishing in deep water at night is the perfect image for the kind of poetry Hughes really wants to write, poetry which projects the most naked and unconditional part of the self into the nightmare darkness, not with the intention of bringing back trophies into the daylight world, but of confronting, being, if necessary, supplanted by, whatever happens to be out there. The poems about fishing and water tend to be those in which this is to be most fully achieved, culminating in 'Go Fishing'.

Hughes knew that the horror with which we view Nature 'red in tooth and claw' is in part a product of our own preconceptions ('What you find in the outside world is what has escaped from your own inner world') and our tendency to take 'portions of existence' (Blake) for the whole. He knew that not until we begin to understand Nature in its own terms will it show us any other face. Many of the poems in *Lupercal* are strategies for evoking, confronting and negotiating with the Powers. He forces himself and us to confront Nature at its most ugly, savage and apparently pointless, to look into 'the shark's mouth / That hungers down the blood-smell even to a leak of its own / Side and devouring of itself' ('Thrushes'). Perhaps Hughes was again remembering *Moby Dick*:

> They viciously snapped, not only at each other's disbowelments, but like flexible bows, bent round, and bit their own; till those entrails seemed swallowed over and over again by the same mouth, to be oppositely voided by the gaping wound. Nor was this all. It was unsafe to meddle with the corpses and ghosts of these creatures. A sort of generic or Pantheistic vitality seemed to lurk in their very joints and bones, after what might be called the individual life had departed. Killed and hoisted on deck for the sake of his skin, one of these sharks almost took poor Queequeg's hand off, when he tried to shut down the dead lid of his murderous jaw. 'Queequeg no care what god made him shark,' said the savage, agonizingly lifting his hand up and down; 'wedder Fejee god or Nantucket god; but de god wat made shark must be one dam Ingin'. (Ch. 66)

Blake felt much the same about the god who made the tiger.

One of the strategies Hughes adopted was his attempt to let Nature speak for herself through the mouth of a hawk in the most famous of his early poems, 'Hawk Roosting':

Actually what I had in mind was that in this hawk Nature is
thinking. Simply Nature. It's not so simple maybe because
Nature is no longer so simple. I intended some Creator like the
Jehovah in Job but more feminine. When Christianity kicked
the devil out of Job what they actually kicked out was Nature
... and Nature became the devil. He doesn't sound like Isis,
mother of the gods, which he is. He sounds like Hitler's familiar spirit. (*UU* 199)

The strategy does not work because Hughes cannot yet get behind
the fallen nature of our tradition, and therefore cannot render the
hawk's vision other than in terms of deranged human vision – the
vision of Canute or Richard of Gloucester or Hitler.

There are, of course, a great many animals in all Hughes' collections. It goes without saying that Hughes is a great animal poet. But
we must distinguish between the use he makes of animals in the early
poems and in the later. Most of the earlier animals are conscripted as
cannon-fodder in the doomed battle of vitality against death. They
are in the same trap as Man, but Hughes prefers to write about them
because they bellow the evidence which Man, except in moments of
extremity, tries to hide. Norman O. Brown takes Freud to task for
what he calls his 'metaphysical vision of all life sick with the struggle
between Life and Death':

> We need, in fine, a metaphysic which recognizes both the con-
> tinuity between man and animals and also the discontinuity.
> We need, instead of an instinctual dualism, an instinctual
> dialectic. We shall have to say that whatever the basic polarity
> in human life may be ... this polarity exists in animals but does
> not exist in a condition of ambivalence. Man is distinguished
> from animals by having separated, ultimately into a state of
> mutual conflict, aspects of life (instincts) which in animals exist
> in some condition of undifferentiated unity or harmony. (83)

Thus, as he gradually struggled free from his fatalistic dualism,
Hughes began to see the animal world as offering not primarily
images of sickness and struggle, but rather images of harmony even

between predators and their victims. Hughes' latest hawk is no murderous egomaniac; and the relaxed style takes off him the pressure to serve as a symbol of a savage god:

> And maybe you find him
>
> Materialized by twilight and dew
> Still as a listener -
>
> The warrior   ('A Sparrow Hawk')

As late as 1963, in a British Council interview, Hughes was still able to speak of his interest in poetry as 'really a musical interest' and of his desire to produce in his poems 'something final ... something that won't break down, like an animal'. Later he sought only to listen to and transcribe the music of that harp.

The early sixties was a period of intense experimentation in search of a poetry able to grope its way through that darkness without the map-grid of imposed form or the flash-light of rationality which would have scared away all its creatures. The most significant breakthrough at this time was 'Wodwo', first published in 1961. The success of the poem depends partly on the choice of persona – a 'little larval being' which might have just emerged from an egg or chrysalis, with human intelligence and curiosity, the human temptation to simply appropriate whatever it encounters, yet still naked and open, exposed and tentative – but mainly on finding the right voice for such a creature.

Rhymes, stanzas, 'poetic' effects of all kinds, rhetoric, have gone. And with them has gone the imposition of personality which those techniques had largely served. What we are left with is a very free verse, close to colloquial prose, flexible, responsive at every moment to the demands of the sense and to nothing else. It is a totally unforced utterance, a world away from the bludgeoning verse of 'The Hawk in the Rain'. The wodwo is no 'diamond point of will', no 'eye' or 'I' determined to keep things as they are: his 'I suppose I am the exact centre / but there's all this what is it ... very queer but I'll go on looking' denies the desirability of being a 'master-Fulcrum of violence' and at the same time the desirability of using the formal elements of poetry, its melody and rhythm, as a means of resolving the uproar, thereby sealing off the poem from the real world. No possible pattern is final or definitive or at the 'exact centre'. How can it be when 'there's all this'?

The language is reduced to a functional minimum from which, like the wodwo itself, it is now free to move out into new, less manipulative forms of expression: 'The nearest we can come to rational thinking is to stand respectfully, hat in hand, before this Creation, exceedingly alert for a new word' (*UU* 172).

This freedom seems to be related to a more inclusive, more holistic vision. 'Still Life', for example, begins as uncompromisingly as 'Pibroch', but we gradually realize that the bleak vision is not this time that of the poet himself, but that of 'outcrop rock' taking itself to be the exact centre, the one permanent exclusive reality. The poet stands to one side, saying 'but there's all this'. The less insistent style allows for a play of humour undercutting the claims of outcrop stone to be all there is, 'being ignorant of this other, this harebell',

> in which – filling veins
> Any known name of blue would bruise
> Out of existence – sleeps, recovering,
> The maker of the sea.

And in 'Full Moon and Little Frieda' we have balance instead of intolerable pressure, fullness instead of lack, unspilled milk instead of spilled blood, and a human being, albeit a child, in a reciprocal and rewarding relationship with a human world and a natural world at one with each other. The poetry here does not impose the momentary resolution, but mirrors it while remaining itself transparent, like water in a brimming pail.

The tragic events of February 1963 put an abrupt end to this atonement. Hughes was thrown back at a stroke into a much more deeply felt despair than ever before. It was as though he had seen the face of the goddess, who had blighted him and struck him dumb. It is the bloodiest of all the goddesses, Cybele, whom a Homeric hymn speaks of as she who 'loves the howling of wolves'. Before his three-year silence descended he wrote, however, 'The Howling of Wolves' and 'Song of a Rat'. The style here has gone very cold, metallic, each line the sharp tooth of a steel trap. The diction is a succession of blank monosyllables forced between teeth:

> The eyes that never learn how it has come about
> That they must live like this,
>
> That they must live

or

> The rat is in the trap, it is in the trap.

To dress such testimony up as 'poetry' (with the association of that word with 'pleasure' relentlessly insisted on by the BBC) would clearly be absurd, almost obscene. Great poetry is truth-telling, and the truth must be in the telling as much as in the authenticity of the vision. Pain, which otherwise is condemned to express itself in silence or inarticulate cries, has, in poetry, its only speech.

That speech will not be the speech of ordinary rational discourse. It searches for the buried world under the world, and for a speech beneath words. The poet opens himself to be 'pierced afresh by the tree's cry':

> And the incomprehensible cry
> From the boughs, in the wind
> Sets us listening for below words,
> Meanings that will not part from the rock.
>
> ('A Wind Flashes the Grass')

Meanings emerge from silence, from the blank unprinted page, sparely, one syllable for a line, in a voice that is not the commanding voice of the poet, but the faceless voice which issues the imperatives of living and dying to tree, gnat, skylark and man alike:

> A towered bird, shot through the crested head
> With the command, Not die
>
> But climb

Climb

Sing

Obedient as to death a dead thing.   ('Skylarks')

   Hughes described *Wodwo* as 'a descent into destruction'. He placed
the most up-beat poems at the end; but both 'Wodwo' and 'Full
Moon and Little Frieda' predate the death of Sylvia Plath. If we look
at the later poems in *Wodwo* and *Recklings* we are in a wasteland, a
dark intestine, pointless cycles of recurrence, a dark night of the soul,
a world very like that of Samuel Beckett. The 80-year-old woman
described in 'On the Slope' is at last defeated by the surrounding
hills. Like foxglove and harebell she accepts her fate with neither
protest nor hope:–

> But with the stone agony growing in her joints
> And eyes, dimming with losses, widening for losses.

   Now the window has come in, the wind of the nagual sweeps away
order and ordinary, and terrible energies are released. In *New Lines*
(ed. Conquest) John Holloway had warned his guest not to go down
to the sea at night: 'It makes no place for those ... who, to sustain our
pose, / Need wine and conversation, colour and light':

> (I) know, from knowing myself, that you will be
> Quick to people the shore, the fog, the sea,
>   With all the fabulous
> Things of the moon's dark side.   ('Warning to a Guest')

Hughes did go down to the sea, and what he found there were ghost
crabs:

> All night, around us or through us,
> They stalk each other, they fasten on to each other,
> They mount each other, they tear each other to pieces,
> They utterly exhaust each other.
> They are the powers of this world.
> We are their bacteria,
> Dying their lives and living their deaths.   ('Ghost Crabs')

The energies no longer need to be invoked. But when they come they are far too inhuman and overwhelming to handle. They supplant his normal consciousness, leaving him stripped of all defences and taken over by them. The 'elemental power-circuit of the universe' jams through him, blowing every fuse. Blake's symbol for the energies is the serpent or dragon. This is the face Hughes now sees on his god or not-god: the serpent as swallower of everything ('this is the dark intestine'), the dragon waiting with open mouth for the woman to deliver her child. Nature is 'all one smouldering annihilation', unmaking and remaking, remaking in order to unmake again. How could such a god be worshipped?

It is hard to say just when Hughes arrived at his spiritual nadir. Perhaps it came, poetically, in about 1967, in poems such as 'Existential Song' and 'Song of Woe'. The title of 'Existential Song' is ironic. The speaker asserts his existential freedom to transform his life by an act of will, to stop running for dear life as if he were 'nothing / But some dummy hare on a racetrack'. It is agony to wrench himself from his running, but he stops:

> He raised his fists
> Laughing in awful joy
> And shook them at the Universe
>
> And his fists fell off
> And his arms fell off
> He staggered and his legs fell off
>
> It was too late for him to realize
> That this was the dogs tearing him to pieces
> That he was, in fact, nothing
> But a dummy hare on a racetrack
>
> And life was being lived only by the dogs.

In 'Song of Woe' the speaker at last refuses to make yet another doomed bid to live within or even rebel against a nightmarish creation, to cling 'with madman's grip / To the great wheel of woe':

> Once upon a time
> There was a person
> Wretched in every vein –
> His heart pumped woe.
>
> …
>
> So he abandoned himself, his body, his blood -
> He left it all lying on the earth
> And held himself resolute
> As the earth rolled slowly away
> Smaller and smaller away
> Into non-being.   ('Song of Woe')

But the attempt to say goodbye to earth, to become light and shadowless is also doomed, like Crow's attempt to destroy his mother, the tree of which he is the topmost twig ('Revenge Fable'). In 'I Said Goodbye to Earth', Being itself is cruciform, yet the atoms in deep space are praying for incarnation, for life at any cost, as though it were better to be a man on a cross than not to be a man at all. The speaker hears the atoms praying:

> To enter his kingdom,
> To be broken like bread
> On a warm sill, and to bleed.

Hughes may have remembered the passage from Blake's *Vala* where the Human Odors arising from the blood of the terrible wine-presses of Luvah are driven by 'desire of Being':

> They plunge into the Elements; the Elements cast them forth
> Or else consume their shadowy semblance. Yet they, obstinate
> Tho' pained to distraction, cry, 'O let us Exist! for
> This dreadful Non Existence is worse than pains of Eternal
>   Birth'.   ('Night the Ninth' lines 736–9)

This acceptance of suffering, powerfully expressed in the essay on Popa in 1968, suggests the way out of total blackness which the post-war East European poets had found, and which Crow was intended to find:

The infinite terrible circumstances that seem to destroy man's importance, appear as the very terms of his importance. Man is the face, arms, legs, etc. grown over the infinite, terrible All. (*WP* 227)

The Energies manifested themselves to Hughes at that time as more dragonish and wantonly destructive than ever. He found it necessary, as Blake had done, to find a way to stand outside his own intolerable experience, to hold it at arm's length so as to see it whole, to objectify and systematize it as myth. Also he had to recapitulate, to go back to the very beginning and start his quest again, with harsher discipline, not to be seduced by beauty and by words, with fewer preconceptions, not even those that seem to define our humanity. He took Leonard Baskin's Crow-Man, gave him features from Eskimo, Red Indian and Celtic crow-lore, then hatched him, clueless, into our world, with the task of trying to understand it, and his place in it.

The intention was to use the figure of Crow as a means of recapitulating and correcting both his own errors and those of Western Man. Crow tries out or witnesses all the techniques of single vision – words and numbers, scripture and physics – the result is war, murder, suicide, madness. It seems that all the forms of language available to him in English, all the received, taken-for-granted, styles and discourses (including the rhetoric of Hughes' own early poems) are so inseperable from the lies, evasions, complacencies, sentimentalities, defunct ideologies, which they have been developed to express and enshrine, the moral rigidities and perversions of reformed Christianity, the spiritlessness of scientific rationalism and materialism, the blinkered hubris of anthropocentrism, male chauvinism, allegiance to all the wrong gods, heroes and codes, that they have ceased to have any purchase on anything Crow can recognize as real. Crow's language sheds everything we can recognize as poetry, as style. He tries to get back to what seems to him to be the irreducible starting-point: 'I eat, therefore I am.'

This incongruity of language and reality is laughable. Melville claimed that it was the duty of the imaginative writer to say 'No! In thunder' to the most cherished and unquestioned beliefs and values of his culture. Hughes, through Crow, says 'No!' in laughter – but it is a hollow, harsh, bitter laughter, close to despair, like Beckett's laugh 'at that which is unhappy'. It is in the spirit (most obviously in 'Criminal Ballad') of Blake's 'Excess of sorrow laughs'.

Crow's world has been compared with Beckett's. On the strength of *Crow* alone, this is understandable, though mistaken. In 1962 Peter Brook gave us a Beckettian *King Lear*. The interpretation worked well enough for the first three acts, but the last two, where the play begins to make its affirmations, had to be mangled. *Crow* is the equivalent of the first three acts of a five-act play, the last two acts of which were sketched out, partially written, but never published entire. In the light of what we know of the overall plan, it is clear that *Crow* was to have been as far removed from Beckett as the work of the post-war East European poets Hughes so much admired:

> At bottom, their vision, like Beckett's, is of the struggle of animal cells and of the torments of spirit in a world reduced to that vision, but theirs contains far more elements than his. It contains all the substance and feeling of ordinary life. And one can argue that it is a step or two beyond his in imaginative truth, in that whatever terrible things happen in their work happen within a containing passion – Job-like – for the elemental final beauty of the created world. Their poetic themes revolve around the living suffering spirit, capable of happiness, much deluded, too frail, with doubtful and provisional senses, so undefinable as to be almost silly, but palpably existing, and wanting to go on existing – and this is not, as in Beckett's world, absurd. It is the only precious thing, and designed in accordance with the whole universe. Designed, indeed, by the whole universe. ... They have managed to grow up to a view of the unaccommodated universe, but it has not made them cynical, they still like it and keep all their sympathies intact. They have got back to the simple animal courage of accepting the odds. (*WP* 221–2)

The first two-thirds of all quest narratives are composed of terrible happenings and 'torments of spirit'. The whole purpose is to demonstrate that that suffering can be the ground of that growth. Crow confronts the Energies always as something to be fought and killed – dragon, serpent, ogress – obstacles on his blundering quest. The bedraggled, scorched, exploded bird has to learn to survive the worst, to undergo and learn from dire punishments for his errors, failures and crimes (in his innocence which is also his guilt), and at last to get into a right relation with the female, who is also Nature and his own true demon. Crow's errant quest, his blind fear of the female, his failure to locate the Black Beast within himself, was to have become, after many adventures in which he is completely dismembered and reconstituted, a painful reintegration and a shamanic initiation ordeal. Crow's quest, though he does not himself know it, is ultimately the same as Hughes' quest, to achieve fourfold vision and thereby become fully a man, reborn into a redeemed world of joy.

The poems that were gathered in *Crow* (according to the dustwrapper 'from about the first two-thirds of what was to have been an epic folk-tale') are mainly about Crow's mistakes, his mutually destructive encounters with the Energies, his ego-death, his first glimmerings of conscience, his first tentative steps towards reconstituting himself and reinterpreting the world, with the help of his Eskimo guide. Hughes' intention, had the *Life and Songs of the Crow* been completed, was to bring Crow at last to a river he must cross. But his way is barred by a huge foul ogress who demands to be carried over on his shoulders. On the way her weight increases to the point where Crow cannot move. Then she asks him a riddle which he must answer before her weight will decrease to allow him to stagger a few more steps. This happens seven times. The first two questions are 'Who paid most, him or her?' and 'Was it an animal, a bird, or a fish?' Crow's answers, 'Lovesong' and 'The Lovepet', are about as wrong as they could be. But he comes to realize that these riddles are all about love, and are, in fact, recapitulations of his previous mistaken encounters with the female, onto whom he had projected the ugly and threatening contents of his own psyche, whom he had tried to kill or otherwise victimize. His answers gradually improve until, in his answer to the final question, 'Who gave most, him or her?', he gets it right. His answer is 'Bride and Groom', where the broken hero and his former victim begin 'with fearfulness and astonishment' tenderly to reassemble each other:

> So, gasping with joy, with cries of wonderment
> Like two gods of mud
> Sprawling in the dirt, but with infinite care
>
> They bring each other to perfection.

Crow reaches the far bank, and the ogress leaps lightly from his back transformed into a beautiful maiden, his intended bride.

But at the very moment when this upward process should have begun, Hughes was knocked back into the pit by another personal tragedy. All the hopefulness was knocked out of him. He refused, in his work for adults, to posit a resolution not validated by his own experience. He abandoned Crow and sought to by-pass him:

> In the little girl's angel gaze
> Crow lost every feather
> In the little boy's wondering eyes
> Crow's bones splintered
>
> In the little girl's passion
> Crow's bowels fell in the dust
> In the little boy's rosy cheeks
> Crow became an unrecognisable rag
>
> Crow got under the brambles, capitulated
> To nothingness eyes closed
> Let those infant feet pound through the Universe.

Crow's vision is assumed here to be fundamentally at odds with innocence. It is assumed that he can never achieve threefold vision. But Crow refused to be killed off so easily. He lay dormant for a few years waiting for his future to come clear in Hughes' imagination.

The style or non-style of *Crow* was another new departure. At the end of his 1970 interview, Ekbert Faas asked Hughes why he had 'abandoned such formal devices as rhyme, metre and stanza'. Hughes conceded that:

formal patterning of the actual movement of verse somehow includes a mathematical and musically deeper world than free verse can easily hope to enter. … But it only works … if the writer has a perfectly pure grasp of his real feeling … and the very sound of metre calls up the ghosts of the past and it is difficult to sing one's own tune against that choir. It is easier to speak a language that raises no ghosts. (*UU* 208)

What he did not say, and may not yet have become conscious of in theory – though it is clear enough in his practice, as Nick Bishop has shown – is that the mathematical and musical accomplishments of formal verse might actually prevent the poet's language becoming 'totally alive and pure', and deny him access to the deepest levels of his own psyche. He went on:

> The first idea of *Crow* was really an idea of a style. In folktales the prince going on the adventure comes to the stable full of beautiful horses and he needs a horse for the next stage and the king's daughter advises him to take none of the beautiful horses that he'll be offered but to choose the dirty, scabby little foal. I throw out the eagles and choose the Crow. The idea was originally just to write his songs, the songs that a Crow would sing. In other words, songs with no music whatsoever, in a super-simple and a super-ugly language which would in a way shed everything except just what he wanted to say without any other consideration and that's the basis of the style of the whole thing.

But Hughes does not explain what, in the folk-tale, is the advantage of choosing 'the dirty, scabby little foal', the advantage of crows over eagles, or of 'super-ugly' language over the beautiful musical language of our poetic tradition. In a letter to me, Hughes expanded a little:

> I tried to shed everything that the average Pavlovian critic knows how to respond to. It was quite an effort to get there – as much of an effort to stay there – every day I had to find it again. My idea was to reduce my style to the simplest clear cell – then regrow a wholeness and richness organically from that point. I didn't get that far.

But again Hughes does not explain the need for this stylistic ascetism. For that explanation we must turn to his writings on the East European poets, who seemed to Hughes to have discovered a universal poetic language, independent of surface sound and texture and therefore translatable, an ABC of what counts. In his essay on Popa he wrote:

> No poetry could carry less luggage than his, or be freer of predisposition and preconception. No poetry is more difficult to outflank, yet it is in no sense defensive. His poems are trying to find out what does exist, and what the conditions really are. The movement of his verse is part of his method of investigating something fearfully apprehended, fearfully discovered, but he will not be frightened into awe. He never loses his deeply ingrained humour and irony: that is his way of hanging on to his human wholeness. And he never loses his intense absorption in what he is talking about, either. His words test their way forward, sensitive to their own errors, dramatically and intimately alive, like the antennae of some rock-shore creature feeling out the presence of the sea and the huge powers in it. This analogy is not so random. There is a primitive pre-creation atmosphere about his work, as if he were present where all the dynamisms and formulae were ready and charged, but nothing created – or only a few fragments. ... (There is an) air of trial and error exploration, of an improvised language, the attempt to get near something for which he is almost having to invent the words in a total disregard for poetry or the normal conventions of discourse. (*WP* 223, 226)

What first attracted Hughes to Pilinszky's poems was, he says, 'their air of simple, helpless accuracy'. Pilinszky described his own poetic language as 'a sort of linguistic poverty'. He takes 'the most naked and helpless of all confrontations' and asks 'what speech is adequate for this moment?' His vision is desolate, his language as close as he can get to silence. In his essay on Pilinszky Hughes writes: 'We come to this Truth only on the simplest terms: through what has been suffered, what is being suffered, and the objects that participate in the suffering' (*WP* 233). The more affirmative, the more radiant with meaning, a work is going to be, the more essential that its starting point is Nothing, the silence of Cordelia, so that it cannot be said that the affirmative meanings have been smuggled in with the loaded language, that anything has been left unquestioned, that the negatives have not been fully acknowledged. Pilinszky has taken the route Hughes started out on in *Crow*. His images

> reveal a place where every cultural support has been torn away, where the ultimate brutality of total war has become natural law, and where man has been reduced to the mere mechanism of his mutilated body. All words seem obsolete or inadequate. Yet out of this apparently final reality rise the poems whose language seems to redeem it, a language in which the symbols of the horror become the sacred symbols of a kind of worship.
>
> These symbols are not redeemed in an unworldly sense. They are redeemed, precariously, in some all-too-human sense, somewhere in the pulsing mammalian nervous system, by a feat of homely consecration: a provisional, last-ditch 'miracle' achieved by means which seem to be never other than 'poetic'. (233–4)

Hughes did not get that far in *Crow*.

Through the early seventies Hughes, possibly without at first knowing it, struggled with parallel versions of the same story – *Orghast, Prometheus on his Crag, Gaudete, Cave Birds, Adam and the Sacred Nine*. The heroes of all these stories – Pramanath, Prometheus, Lumb, the nameless protagonist of *Cave Birds*, and Adam – are all, to begin with, split or crucified by their inability to unify or reconcile their mortal and immortal natures. All have violated 'material nature, the Creatress, source of life and light'.

Blake's idea of contraries probably derived from his reading of the Smaragdine Tablet of Hermes Trismegistus: 'That which is above is like that which is beneath, and that which is beneath is like that which is above, to work the miracles of one thing.' This is the tablet Hughes had in mind in 'Fragment of an Ancient Tablet'. But its alchemical wisdom is fragmented because Crow cannot yet unify his

vision, cannot yet see above and below in any other terms than those
of such dualistic clichés, single-vision judgements, as 'good and evil',
'beautiful and ugly'. His sexual consciousness is as sick as Lear's in his
madness: 'But to the girdle do the Gods inherit, / Beneath is all the
fiend's.' The only way in which this conflict can be transcended is 'by
creating a being which, like Prometheus, includes the elemental
opposites, and in whom the collision and pain become illumination'
(*Orghast at Persepolis* 132–3). This illumination is fourfold vision,
the recognition of the vulture not as monstrous obscenity, but as
helper and midwife, mother and bride.

Hughes is, of all contemporary writers in English, the one most
qualified by experience to feel and by intelligence to '*think* adequately about the behaviour that is at the annihilating edge' (R.D.
Laing, *The Politics of Experience*). *Prometheus on his Crag* begins at the
point of numbness which had characterized the later poems in
Wodwo and much of *Crow*. Crow had already contemplated a
Prometheus figure in 'The Contender':

> He lay crucified with all his strength
> On the earth
> Grinning towards the sun
> Through the tiny holes of his eyes
>
>   ...
>
> Grinning into the black
> Into the ringing nothing
> Through the bones of his teeth
> Sometimes with eyes closed
>
> In his senseless trial of strength.

Hughes, at that point in his life, had come close to rejecting nature
as a 'cortège of mourning and lament'. This left him in a limbo in
which the only alternative to suicide or despair seemed to be absur-
dist revolt, as advocated by Camus:

> The absurd man can only drain everything to the bitter end,
> and deplete himself. The absurd is his extreme tension which
> he maintains constantly by solitary effort, for he knows that in

that consciousness and in that day-to-day revolt he gives proof of his only truth which is defiance. (*The Myth of Sisyphus*)

But Hughes was not content to remain crucified on that rock. It was his study in 1971 of the fate of another Titan, in *Prometheus on his Crag*, which revealed to him the possibility that the agony and depletion might actually release the flow of *mana*.

The early poems in the sequence are made out of sheer pain, like pearls forming round the locus of pain, the ever-reopened wound at the centre, and out of sheer hatred of the apparently crazed god and his agent the vulture. Gradually he comes to understand that his only resource is consciousness, and that consciousness will serve him only if he can use it to come to understand and accept the god and the vulture.

Speaking of the etchings of Leonard Baskin, particularly his many versions of the hanged man, Hughes refers to the mythological motif 'that the wound, if it is to be healed, needs laid in it the blade that made it' (*WP* 95). Such healing is, Hughes claims, 'redemption incarnate' which 'is purchased by suffering':

> Like those Indian gods who play deaf to the mortifications and ordeals and cries of the suppliant, till they can't stand it any longer – the stones of their heaven begin to sweat, their thrones begin to tremble – whereupon they descend and grant everything. And the suppliant becomes Holy, and a Healer. (*WP* 93)

Like Lorca's *duende*, such *mana* is 'the goddess of the source of terrible life', perhaps of all blossoming and beauty:

> Blossoms
> Pushing from under blossoms -
> From the one wound's
> Depth of congealments and healing.   ('Photostomias')

We may speak of this healing and rebirth as a divine gift, but we may equally speak of it in biological terms, as demonstrating 'the biological inevitability of art, as the psychological component of the body's own system of immunity and self-repair' (98).

In the *Prometheus* sequence, the blade is the beak of the vulture, which gorges itself every day on Prometheus' liver. Prometheus knows that the vulture holds the key. It hangs 'Balancing the gift of life / And the cost of the gift'. Prometheus, the prototype of the human condition, also hangs weighing the cost, but for a long time can find nothing to set against it. It seems no less than the weight of the whole earth. The first clue comes when a lizard whispers to him 'Even as the vulture buried its head – / "Lucky, you are so lucky to be human!"'. The only advantage Prometheus has over the lizard is consciousness, which opens the possibility of understanding the situation, and thereby converting pain into payment. In poem 20 he permutates the possible meanings of the vulture, starting with all the mistaken meanings, such as Crow might have entertained: for example, that the vulture might be 'some lump of his mother'. But at last he comes to the realization that it was, after all, the helper 'Coming again to pick at the crucial knot / Of all his bonds'. In the final poem he correctly identifies the vulture as the midwife attending his own necessarily painful rebirth. That realization *is* his rebirth. And it lifts the weight of the world from him:

> And Prometheus eases free.
> He sways to his stature.
> And balances. And treads
>
> On the dusty peacock film where the world floats.

Eight thousand years ago the goddess was painted as vulture in the shrines of Catal Hüyük:

> For the vulture, feeding on carrion, does not so much 'bring' death as transform what is already dead back into life, beginning a new cycle by assimilating the end of the old one. In this way the goddess of death and the goddess of birth are inseparable. (Baring and Cashford 87–8)

Prometheus is released from his torment in the final poem, but remains detached from the world. The development of Hughes' vision from the crucifixion of Prometheus to the resurrection of

Adam spanned the years 1971–6. Shortly after his return from Persia, Hughes set out to extend *Five Autumn Songs* (1968) into a set of poems covering all four seasons. It was an unambitious work aimed at older children, but it served to ground his vision once more in the substantial, phenomenal world. While his eyes had been focused on the Needle of Elbruz or the furthest stars, he had neglected the mundane miracles under his feet.

One would have thought that there was little new to say about the countryside and the seasons. And indeed Hughes is only showing us what we see every year but take for granted. He writes like the only one of us who is really awake:

> Over the whole land
> Spring thunders down in brilliant silence.
>
> ('Spring Nature Notes')

Every April is our real birthday, when the world bombards us with gifts:

> And the trees
> Stagger, they stronger
> Brace their boles and biceps under
> The load of gift. …
> And rabbits are bobbing everywhere, and a thrush
> Rings coolly in a far corner. A shiver of green
> Strokes the darkening slope as the land
> Begins her labour.   ('April Birthday')

Season Songs is not at all sentimental or escapist. Death is ever-present. A fledgling swift suffers 'the inevitable balsa death'. Foxes and stags are hunted to death. A pheasant hangs from a hook with its head in a bag. A cranefly is going through with its slow death – the poet a watching giant who 'knows she cannot be helped in any way'. But death, for all the deep compassion it evokes, does not cancel vitality.

Perhaps this renewed vision was not unconnected to the fact that Hughes had now remarried. Also, on his return from Persia Hughes went into partnership with his father-in-law, Jack Orchard, at Moortown farm on the edge of Dartmoor, rearing cattle and sheep. That he should have married a farmer's daughter and shortly afterwards become a farmer may have been a lucky accident or an attempt, conscious or unconscious, to correct the psychic imbalance which had driven him (in the terms he himself uses of Shakespeare) to suppress the right side of the brain. This dominance of the left side produces the feeling of living in a state of Prometheus-like alienation from real things. Nowhere is it more necessary to accept and adapt to the chaos of real things than on a farm. Hughes abandoned his aloofness from tangible reality, even from the blood and mud. As he learned the feel of farming, the hard disciplines of stewardship and husbandry, Moortown farm became for him, in Craig Robinson's words, 'a working laboratory of co-operation between man and nature' (Sagar, *Achievement* 262).

Farming left little time for anything else, but in order not to lose the marvellous experiences this kind of farming yielded – triumphs and disasters, births and deaths – he wrote them out quickly in rough verse each evening, as diary entries, intending to return to them eventually and turn them into real poems. Jack Orchard died suddenly early in 1976, the stock was sold, and Hughes was able to look again at his diaries. But he found that whatever he did to them lost, in freshness and immediacy and authenticity and particularity, more than it gained in shape and polish. He decided to leave them as they were. The result is a set of poems with a tighter grip on reality than any others I know, where even the miracles are made of mud and smells and jellies and heat.

Perhaps Hughes embarked on these poems as an attempt to cheer himself up after the limbo of *Prometheus*. In the event, the renewed contact with the natural world, its births and deaths and failures and harvests, simply looking at it and recording it, proved so revitalizing, so revelatory, that it was to help to transform his entire vision. All the poems are sacramental, some of them visionary, but they remain rooted in common everyday realities. They are poems of observation, but such is Hughes' knowledge of and feel for natural processes that the observed details are selected and rendered, effortlessly, in such a way that they reveal not appearances but inner workings and connections. After the isolation and paralysis of *Prometheus*, all is now colour and variety, bustle and change, as the earth swings through its cycles on the poles of birth and death.

Any honest record of farming, especially of livestock rearing, is bound to be a record largely of disasters, and the proportion of deaths in *Moortown* is even greater than in *Season Songs*. Some, such as 'February 17th', where Hughes describes in detail his decapitation of a half-born dead lamb, are likely to sicken the sensitive. But if we do not exact a full look at the worst, we falsify the whole and devalue the best. When a three-year-old nephew persistently asks 'Did it cry?', Hughes answers at last, 'Oh yes, it cried.' Death must be confronted, taken seriously. A lamb suffering from a disgusting and incurable disease must be shot.

Such endings make the survivals all the more precious and miraculous. 'Birth of Rainbow', for example, ends:

> We left her to it.
> Blobbed antiseptic on to the sodden blood-dangle
> Of his muddy birth-cord, and left her
> Inspecting the new smell. The whole South West
> Was black as nightfall.
> Trailing squall-smokes hung over the moor leaning
> And whitening towards us, then the world blurred
> And disappeared in forty-five degree hail
> And a gate-jerking blast. We got to cover.
> Left to God the calf and his mother.

In his marginalia on Wordsworth's poems Blake wrote: 'Natural Objects always did & now do Weaken deaden & obliterate imagination in Me.' He spurns the corporeal, vegetable world as having no more to do with him than 'the Dirt upon my feet' (*A Vision of the Last Judgment* 95). Coleridge agreed with him:

> The further I ascend from men and cattle, and the common birds of the woods and fields, the greater becomes in me the intensity of the feelings of life. Life seems to me there a universal spirit that neither has nor can have an opposite.

Hughes' experience was exactly the reverse. It was by descending again from the far limits of pain and consciousness (where only archetypal images serve) into woods and fields among men and cattle that he recovered his sense of the universal spirit of life. 'The field and its grass', which he had flung away in 'Song of Woe', Beckett's 'absurdity of pastures', is now recovered, with the practical responsibility, as a farmer, of tending the earth and its flora and fauna. His imagination flourished on this daily input of its proper food. As Robert Bly said in an interview:

> Imagination requires food, as a horse does, and contrary to many Jungian speculations, the food of the imagination is not archetypes, but the actual energy given off by old tree roots, mountains, rocks, glaciers, fields of barley, crows.

What happened to Hughes is recapitulated in *Adam and the Sacred Nine*. Adam lies inert in Eden. Great things are expected of him, but he feels helpless and exposed. His dreams of technological achievements and immortality are so incongruous with his bruised body 'too little lifted from mud' that they merely bewilder him. *Adam and the Sacred Nine* is, in a sense, a sequel to both *Prometheus on his Crag* and *Cave Birds*, each of which ends with the rebirth of the protagonist, but leaves him still to learn how to live in terms of his new ego-free self in the substantial world. Adam, 'wrapped in peach-skin and bruise', lies dreaming of that life without an opposite, 'the religion of the diamond body', oblivious of 'the song made of joy' which tries to sing him, the song of the body alive in this world of animated Nature. He is visited by nine birds, each of which has discovered how to be wholly itself in that world, and has become thereby sacred. And Hughes rises splendidly to the challenge of recreating that selfhood and sacredness in poetry.

Each bird offers Adam an image of how to live. The Falcon could not be more different from his weeping and shivering self, with its unfaltering gunmetal feathers, mountain-diving and world-hurling wing-knuckles, bullet-brow, grasping talons, tooled bill. Then the Skylark, living and dying in the service of its crest, cresting the earth, trying to crest the sun, with bird-joy. Then the Wild Duck getting up out of cold and dark and ooze, and spanking across water quacking Wake Wake to the world. Then comes the Swift wholeheartedly hurling itself against and beyond the limits. Then the Wren who lives only to be more and more Wren – Wren of Wrens! Then the Owl, who floats, the moving centre of everything, holding the balance of life and death, heaven and earth. Then the Dove, the perpetual victim, but rainbow-breasted among thorns. Then the Crow comes to Adam and whispers in his ear a waking, reject-nothing truth. Finally comes the Phoenix, which offers itself up again and again and laughs in the blaze. Each bird has found what Adam lacks, its own distinctive mode of living fully within the given conditions. But what in Adam can answer to them? It is not for Adam to imitate any of them. Why should he aspire to flight? He is defined precisely by his lack of wings. The earth is his home. He accepts his lowlier station with its own special communion. He stands, and it is the first meeting of the body of man with the body of the earth. The sole of his foot gently presses the warm world-rock, saying:

> I am no wing
> To tread emptiness.
> I was made
> For you.

These are the first and only words Adam speaks, and they embody the simplicity, humility and acceptance that Boehme had in mind when he said that men must attempt to recover 'the language of Adam'.

Thus it is fitting that the volume *Moortown*, which begins with cattle knee-deep in mud in the poor fields, should end with Adam's affirmation of his total dependence on Nature, a Nature whose only god is a god of mud, but with miracles enough. As Whitman wrote: 'The press of my foot to the earth springs a hundred affections' ('Song of Myself' 14). Instead of dreaming of technological dominion ('flying echelons of steel … advancement of bulldozers and cranes' – the dreams of Prometheus) or of everlasting life ('the religion of the diamond body'), Adam must now set out on his quest for what is actually given, the world, and his woman and his work in it. Lawrence wrote:

You cannot dig the ground with the spirit. … The very act of stooping and thrusting the heavy earth calls into play the dark sensual centres in a man, at last, that old Adam which is the eternal opposite of the spiritual or ideal being. Brute labour, the brute struggle with the beast and herd, must rouse into activity the primary centres, darken the mind, induce a state of animal mindlessness, and pivot a man in his own heavy-blooded isolation. (*Symbolic Meaning* 169)

Three months later Lawrence imagined his St Matthew as experiencing much the same dilemma as Hughes' Adam. The Saviour would have him live 'like a lark at heaven's gate singing', but he is suspicious of too much uplift in this life, and insists that as a living man he must maintain his contact with the vitalizing earth:

> So I will be lifted up, Saviour,
> But put me down again in time, Master,
> Before my heart stops beating, and I become what I am not.
> Put me down again on the earth, Jesus, on the brown soil
> Where flowers sprout in the acrid humus, and fade into humus
>   again.
> Where beasts drop their unlicked young, and pasture, and drop
>   their droppings
>   among the turf.
> Where the adder darts horizontal.
> Down on the damp, unceasing ground, where my feet belong
> And even my heart, Lord, forever, after all uplifting:
> The crumbling, damp, fresh land, life horizontal and ceaseless.
>   ('St Matthew')

Lawrence and Hughes are both in the tradition of Meister Eckhart, who claimed that 'humility' derived from 'humus'. Jung wrote: 'Every renewal of life needs the muddy as well as the clear. This was evidently perceived by the great relativist Meister Eckhart' (*Psychological Types* 244).

This humility clearly must have implications for style. Again it seemed to be almost a matter of accident (Parzival letting the reins lie loose on his horse's neck) that Hughes had not the time or energy after a day's farming to write fully fledged poems, only to make a few purely factual notes of the more interesting things that had happened:

> In making a note about anything, if I wish to look closely I find I can move closer and stay closer, if I phrase my observations about it in rough lines. So these improvised verses are nothing more than this: my own way of getting reasonably close to what is going on, and staying close, and of excluding everything else that might be pressing to interfere with the watching eye. In a sense, the method excludes the poetic process as well. (*Moortown Diary* x)

It largely excludes the selective, interpreting, abstracting, ambitious ego, and all our preconceptions about what constitutes the poetic. When Hughes later tried to process the notes into 'real poems', he found that he lost much more than he gained, lost the integrity of the original raw experience. (Lawrence admired Etruscan art because it was not 'cooked in the artistic consciousness'.) So he resisted the high temptation of the mind and the meddling intellect and left well alone.

The new humility requires also that Hughes should no longer 'relegate Nature to a function of human perception' (Scigaj, 1991 180). On the contrary, it is now recognized as the only reality, into which we are granted an occasional privileged glimpse:

> I could think the deer were waiting for me
> To remember the password and sign
>
> That the curtain had blown aside for a moment
> And there where the trees were no longer trees, nor the road a
>   road
>
> The deer had come for me.   ('Roe-deer')

On the farm miracles so clearly issued out of the dirt and the body's jellies. Farming is a far from romantic undertaking. Hughes' affirmations are fully paid for. He indulges in none of the distortions that make traditional Nature worship so vulnerable to the attacks of any clear-eyed realist such as Samuel Beckett. There is no denying that farming is as much to do with deaths and misbirths (astride a grave) as with happier miracles:

> The deepest fascination of stock rearing is this participation in the precarious birth of these tough and yet over-delicate beasts, and nursing them against what often seem to be the odds. (*Moortown Diary* 65)

In 'Ravens' Hughes will not deny even to the three-year-old child that the lamb that died being born cried. But what the ravens have done to its body – 'its insides, the various jellies and crimsons and transparencies / And threads and tissues pulled out' – does not cancel the miracle that this mess and spillage so nearly added up to a new life, and that the same strange substances did so only a few yards away, where a ewe investigates her new lamb 'while the tattered banners of her triumph swing and drip from her rear-end'.

What had so disgusted Beckett, 'the pastures red with uneaten sheep's placentas', what he had reduced to 'the whole bloody business', 'a turd', 'a cat's flux', what Eliot had reduced to 'dung and death', Hughes redeems – in the unfallen vision of *Moortown Diary*, *Season Songs* and *What is the Truth?* Even death has its atonement (the lamb's hacked-off head has 'all earth for a body'), and even the worm, even the dirt is god.

Hughes will not isolate the single death from its larger context:

> Though this one was lucky insofar
> As it made the attempt into a warm wind
> And its first day of death was blue and warm
> The magpies gone quiet with domestic happiness
> And skylarks not worrying about anything
> And the blackthorn budding confidently
> And the skyline of hills, after millions of hard years,
> Sitting soft. ('Ravens')

The value of nature in Hughes is not aesthetic. By the mid-seventies he had got well beyond the aversion to beauty as something irreversibly compromised. The larger beauty of his later work had nothing to do with the charming and the picturesque, or with the Wordsworthian pieties still trundled out by sentimental preservationists. Nature is of supreme value not in spite of, but, in a mysterious way, because of the elements of ugliness, pain and death:

> For that's the paradox of the poetry, as if poetry were a biological healing process. It seizes on what is depressing and destructive, and lifts it into a realm where it becomes healing and energizing. ... And to reach that final mood of release and elation is the whole driving force of writing at all. (Norwich Tape)

It is the absence of this final stage that distinguishes the work of Samuel Beckett from that of the East European poets:

> At bottom, their vision, like Beckett's, is of the struggle of animal cells and of the torments of spirit in a world reduced to that vision (of disaster), but theirs contains far more elements than his. It contains all the substance and feeling of ordinary life. And one can argue that it is a step or two beyond his in imaginative truth, in that whatever terrible things happen in their work happen within a containing passion – Job-like – for the elemental final beauty of the created world. (*WP* 221–2)

Imaginative truth-tellings demands that both the disaster and the beauty be fully presented. To select the benevolent, comforting aspects of Nature is to cast her in the role of the green mother. The green mother in *Cave Birds* is Nature in its Lucy Gray aspect, Blake's threefold vision, Beulah, 'a soft Moony Universe, feminine, lovely, / Pure, mild & Gentle' (*Vala* I 95–6), which appears to its inhabitants 'as the beloved infant in his mother's bosom round incircled' (*Milton* 30:11). She seeks with 'songs and loving blandishments' to wipe Enion's tears. But her beauty is delusive. Beulah may be valued as a retreat for temporary solace and refreshment. As a permanent residence it becomes a Lotus Land where the soul dies:

> Where the impressions of Despair & Hope for ever vegetate
> In flowers, in fruits, in fishes, birds & beasts & clouds & waters,

The land of doubts & shadows, sweet delusions, unform'd
   hopes.
They saw no more the terrible confusion of the wracking
   universe.
They heard not, saw not, felt not all the terrible confusion,
For in their orbed senses, within clos'd up, they wander'd at
   will.
And those upon the Couches view'd them, in the dreams of
   Beulah,
As they repos'd from the terrible wide universal harvest.

                                             (*Vala* IX lines 377–84)

In *Cave Birds* the green mother offers the hero a return to the womb,
not for rebirth but for perfect security, the everlasting holiday
promised by all the religions, without contraries or suffering or consciousness:

This earth is heaven's sweetness.

It is heaven's mother.
The grave is her breast
And her milk is endless life.
You shall see
How tenderly she has wiped her child's face clean

Of the bitumen of blood and the smoke of tears.

                                             ('A Green Mother')

In a wood the protagonist sees all the animals move 'in the glow of
fur which is their absolution in sanctity'. But they have never fallen.
Their 'state of steady bliss' (*Moortown Diary* 65) is not available to or
ultimately desirable for Man: 'And time was not present they never
stopped / Or left anything old or reached any new thing' ('As I Came,
I Saw a Wood'). The only religion the hero's deepest humanity sanc-
tions for him is communion with a world whose gods are perpetually
crucified and eaten and resurrected, and men move not in perpetual
sanctity, but in the bitumen of blood and smoke of tears. There and
only there is the ground of his striving towards an earned atonement.

His task, like Blake's Milton, is 'to redeem the Female Shade' which is his own emanation, his anima, mother, bride and vision.

Part II of *Orghast*, Hughes tells us, 'is the story of the tyrant Hold-fast in the Underworld, the decomposition of the fallen ego among the voices of its crimes, oversights and victims'. This could equally well be a summary of *Cave Birds*. It gradually emerges that the protagonist's crime has been to get into a wrong relationship with the female, culminating in mutilation and attempted murder. They are lost, dead, to each other. And since the female is not only wife and mother, but also Nature and psychic demon, this failure is both murderous and suicidal. No real living is possible until this damage has been repaired, but the remaking cannot begin until the criminal has been scoured of his Socratic rationality and egocentricity. The birds work on him like a team of alchemists, refining and refining, breaking down and reconstituting, until finally both he and his victim are able to take over and reconstitute each other. The image for this healing and atonement is, as in Blake, marriage. In earlier poems of the Crow period Hughes had been unable to get beyond the failed, destructive, cannibalistic marriages of 'Lovesong', 'The Lovepet', 'The Lamentable History of the Human Calf' and 'Actaeon'. Now, in 'His Legs Ran About' and 'Bride and Groom', he enters into fourfold vision.

The green mother offers a world without goblins. The overweening male ego is the criminal throughout the sequence. But the unselving process is not an end in itself. There can hardly be life without self. The process of individuation must begin again, hoping to avoid some of the mistakes. The alchemical marriage, or *coniunctio*, is not only a marriage of male and female but of all the polarized elements of the divided self. It is a marriage of heaven and hell. It must be the opposite of the submerging of one in the other, a perpetual creative struggle of contraries. The goblin is the offspring. The couple must not attempt to kill or tame or disown the goblin. They must acknowledge this thing of darkness and attempt to accommodate its energies so that it does not turn ugly and destructive. Without the goblin there would be nothing for the married couple to do but lie in perpetual inertia, in a religious daze.

The reassembling of the bits and pieces of disintegrated man which takes place in these poems is, of course, a version of the Osiris story. The process also redeems nature itself by, as it were, sewing it together, reintegrating it as a harmonious unity.

It is hard to decide which poems are the more wonderful, those written out of fourfold vision, or those that re-enact the painful process by which that vision is achieved and renewed. For the former we would go to *River*, for the latter to the Epilogue poems in *Gaudete*.

Here the Anglican clergyman Nicholas Lumb has undergone a terrifying ordeal in the underworld, which is the spirit world and the animal world, the world under the world, the depths of his own unconscious. The experience has destroyed his old split self and enabled him to be reborn of the goddess who is simultaneously reborn of him. Lumb is returned to the surface world by a loch in the west of Ireland. We can imagine him surviving only on the fringe of the modern world, for he returns as a holy idiot, stripped of everything but his new sacramental vision which enables him to perform small miracles such as whistling an otter from the loch and triggering a shattering vision of the creation in an Irish priest, and to write these little poems, some confused memories of his ordeal, some hymns to the goddess. Lumb corresponds exactly (as does the nameless hero of *Cave Birds*) to Hughes' description of the doubling and subsequent correction of the tragic hero in *Shakespeare and the Goddess of Complete Being*. Here Hughes tries to imagine what it might be like to make the apparently impossible choice and accept, even worship, the goddess in her totality, including her role as Queen of Hell – to accept life, that is, unconditionally, with all its inevitable cargo of pain and death.

These Epilogue poems contain as much pain as poems can, pain that is felt to be essential to the ultimate exultation, the release of *mana*. It is a 'horrible world' into which, nevertheless, the hero manages to let in again 'As if for the first time – / The untouched joy'.

This is how Hughes now sees the 'drama of organic life', no longer simply as a battle between vitality and death:

life itself is what terrifies living things and possesses them with their various forms of madness, and exhausts them with their struggles to control and contain it and to secure its subjective essence of joy. (*Shakespeare* 326)

These are poems about atonement, what it would be like to be, in Lawrence's terminology, reconnected with the cosmos, or in Hughes' to become once again 'participants in the business of living in this universe' (*WP* 29). The protagonist prays to be enlisted, alongside the loyal grass-blade, the sleek blackbird and the grim badger (jaw-strake shattered by the diggers' spade), as one of the goddess's warriors:

Let your home
Be my home. Your people
My people.

This total identification with the world of animal suffering is part of the atonement which follows his recognition of his own earlier criminality and his ruthless determination through *Crow*, *Cave Birds* and *Gaudete* to acknowledge his guilt unconditionally, to identify himself with the suffering of the victim, and to accept whatever punishment his own imagination finds fit. The victim appears in these poems as a female figure, bride, mother or goddess. But since the goddess is all Nature, the victim can equally well be presented as an animal; and such poems are equally grounded in autobiographical experience.

We have seen how Hughes' first relationship with the natural world was determined largely by his elder brother, Gerald, 'whose passion was shooting':

He wanted to be a big game hunter or a game warden in Africa – that was his dream. His compromise in West Yorkshire was to shoot over the hillsides and on the moor edge with a rifle. He would take me along. So my early memories of being three and four are of going off with him, being his retriever. I became completely preoccupied by his world of hunting. He was also a very imaginative fellow; he mythologized his hunting world as

North American Indian – paleolithic. And I lived in his dream.
(*Paris Review* 59)

Hughes, in that innocence which, unlike Blake's state of innocence,
was also ignorance, had no compunction about shedding the blood
of animals: 'He could not kill enough for me.' Man, he assumed, is a
hunter. In 'Two' the narrator, evoking the bliss of the two brothers
returning from a successful hunting expedition, seems not to notice
the negative implications of the imagery, that the snipe have been
'robbed of their jewels', the grouse ('glowing like embers') of their
fire. The stream speaks 'oracles of abundance', and the purpose of
that abundance is to provide limitless game for the god-like brothers.

The last such expedition the brothers made was the one to
Crimsworth Dene recorded in 'The Deadfall'. To the seven-year-old
Hughes it was 'the most magical place I had ever been in': 'All down
the valley, over the great spilling mounds of foxgloves, grey columns
of midges hung in the stillness.' A thrush's 'every note echoed
through the whole valley'. In the tent at night, 'listening to the stars,
and the huge, silent breathing of the valley, I felt happier than I had
ever been'. He is aware of no incongruity that in all this Eden abundance, the most precious and beautiful thing is 'my brother's gleam-
ing American rifle'. He is woken in the night by the strange figure of
what he takes to be a little old woman, who calls him (but not his
brother) to help with an emergency. He is needed to release a fox-cub
trapped by the deadfall. As soon as he has done so, the 'woman' van-
ishes. The deadfall has killed the parent fox: 'When I lifted its eyelid,
the eye looked at me, very bright and alive. I closed it gently and
stroked it quite shut.' He declines his brother's offer to cut off the tail
for him. As they bury the fox, he finds in the loose earth a tiny ivory
fox (which Hughes kept all his life). It seems that Hughes is here
being initiated into some special protective relationship with foxes,
which involves distancing him from his brother, the hunter.

In a 1995 interview Hughes blamed Sylvia Plath for forcing him
to give up hunting early in their marriage, and went on to make large
claims for fishing as an activity that can restore the lost paradise of
atonement with the natural world and with the primal roots of one's

own psyche. He would have to leave the country, he said, if fishing were ever banned. Nevertheless, his poems and stories about hunting tell a very different story. Whenever he moves into imaginative mode, his identification with the hunted animal is boosted to the point where it overrides his rational justifications of hunting. As early as 1963, in 'A Moon Man-Hunt', Hughes attacked the 'noble rural vermin, the gentry' by reversing roles on the moon and giving the red jackets, horses and hounds to the foxes while the squire hopelessly runs. The hunters 'pretend it is all a good game and nothing to do with death and its introductory tears'. They tear the wretch to pieces. In 'Foxhunt', first published in 1977, the hunt is described as 'a machine with only two products: / Dog-shit and dead foxes', and the poem's sympathies are entirely with the fox:

> Will he run
> Till his muscles suddenly turn to iron,
> Till blood froths his mouth as his lungs tatter,
> Till his feet are raw blood-sticks and his tail
> Trails thin as a rat's?

In a newspaper article in 1997 Hughes wrote in favour of not banning hunting with hounds, but did not then have anything to say in favour of hunting except that the future might be even bleaker for deer and foxes without it. Even in prose his attitude was clearly ambiguous, since at the same time he wrote to me:

> Yes, the Hunt! That horse culture! When a man/woman gets up on a horse in his/her hunting kit he/she becomes something quite awful, as a rule. It has something to do with the nervous fear of what your horse might do if you relax your despotic control of its every move. But also to do with (a) being mounted & therefore 2/3 big powerful animal (b) being in a uniform (out of your normal self) with a rigid funny hat (the hat crucial to attitude – as cavalry and commanding officers have always known) and (c) suddenly being in the role of King William's barons. Decent folk become instantly dreadful. I've been in some scenes! Also, I've known for some years what a hunted

deer goes through physically. And a hunted fox. And a fish being caught, for that matter. For years I've kept having an idea that I daren't quite formulate: why aren't wild animals simply given the legal status of 'fellow citizens'?

When, after an estrangement of 18 years, the two brothers met again in Devon, and Gerald wanted 'a taste of English sport', they borrowed 'an old, rusty, single-barrelled' gun, and tried to recapture the joys of the hunt, with Hughes, as of old, in the subservient role: 'I am your dog.' 'A Solstice' falls into three distinct parts. The opening is dream-like, magical, idyllic, as befits the attempt to recapture the time in childhood when the hunting expeditions of the two brothers seemed in memory to have taken place in such an Edenic world. But the long middle part of the poem, the hunt itself, acquires a sinister tone as the gun seems to take over the two men for its own mechanical and bloody purposes, reducing them to 'two suits of cold armour', empty of human sensitivity and moral choice, hypnotized by the unstoppable logic of the hunt. The first shot only wounds the fox. 'I come close / As if I might be of help'.

> Blood beneath him is spoiling
> The magnificent sooted russet
> Of his overcoat. ...
> It is doing the impossible deliberately
> To set the gun-muzzle deliberately at his chest
> And funnel that sky-bursting bang
> Through a sudden blue pit in his fur
> Into the earth beneath him.

The shot affects Hughes like 'a cracking blow on the head', an image of the rude awakening from the dream. The desecration of the fox's coat is clearly related to an incident in the contemporary story *The Threshold*, where the narrator, about to be attacked by a tiger, but 'feeling a delicious surge of admiration and love for this dazzling beast', cannot bring himself to use the cleaver in his hand for fear of damaging the tiger's skin 'which I wanted above all to preserve intact'.

Hughes is no longer the boy untroubled by conscience and consciousness. He is now a man aware of the sacred purity and nobility of a fox, of a responsibility towards foxes of all creatures as his particular totemic beasts, of the fox as representing the most true, the innermost and most vulnerable part of himself, of an encounter with a wild fox as a particular epiphany, which the brothers have now profaned, not only killing the fox, but chopping off the tail and bundling the remains of this beautiful and 'phenomenal' creature into a hole 'like picnic rubbish'. He awakes from his trance too late, having been betrayed into the shameful and pointless destruction of a sacred life. The final section matches in tone the 'ultimate bitterness' in the smile of the dying fox. At the end it is no longer 'we' striding elated through a vividly coloured, sparkling, pristine landscape, but 'you' and 'I' walking through 'dank woodland', worlds apart.

Written at about the same time, 1978, 'The Head' is like a phantasmagoric nightmare version of the same story, with two brothers on a hunting trip. Again there is an abundance, a miraculous abundance of game. But this time it seems the brothers will not be satisfied until they have wiped out the whole animal creation. On the first night their camp-fire is surrounded by 'a close-up circle of magnificent foxes that lay with their noses on their paws watching him in deep concentration'. Next morning the massacre begins. It is made all the more obscene by the fact that the animals make no attempt to escape, but offer themselves like sacrifices, and by the fact that the corpses are skinned and then left in bleeding heaps. The narrator begins to be sickened, his sleep disturbed by even worse horrors than the enormities of the day. He tells his brother he never wants to 'see another animal drop':

> My whole being was saturated with animal wounds and animal pain and animal death. And the thought of killing one more animal wrenched me with agony like a hand grasping a raw burn.

The brother is disgusted with him, and insists on continuing the slaughter alone. That night the narrator dreams that his brother is 'tried and sentenced and executed' by wolves. Later, as in 'The Deadfall', he is visited by 'the shawled figure of a woman'. She bows low before the skinned victims 'as if before an altar'. She shrieks and laments over each body she finds. Then she takes his rifle from the tent and glides with it into the river. Next morning he finds the almost devoured remains of his brother.

The drift of these three works from the same period, 'Two', 'A Solstice' and 'The Head', is clear enough. Through them the brother figure gradually ceases to be the real-life brother and becomes an alter ego. Hughes, that is, uses the traditional two brothers motif to dramatize the split within himself between the two extremes of his own nature – the aggressively masculine, hubristic, insanely rational self, appropriating Nature ruthlessly to its degrading purposes, and the more feminine self, open to feeling and spirit, to what Hughes calls in his essay on Henry Williamson 'the pathos of actuality in the natural world'. (It is no coincidence that one of Williamson's books is called *The Fox Under My Cloak*.) Hughes is again attempting to correct a psychic imbalance, to heal an unnatural split, in exactly the spirit of Wolfram's *Parzival*, which he quotes as an epigraph to *Gaudete*:

> And I mourn for this, for they were the two sons of one man. One could say that 'they' were fighting in this way, if one wished to speak of two. These two, however, were one, for 'my brother and I' is one body, like good man and good wife. Contending here from loyalty of heart, one flesh, one blood, was doing itself much harm.

In *Gaudete*, where Lumb is similarly divided, the 'real' Lumb feels that he can only cleanse himself and appease the goddess, the Lady of the animals, by hunting down and extirpating the self who is capable of being a huntsman on his high horse. Unlike Crow, he is in no doubt where to look for the black beast. The one he hunts and will rend to pieces, whose blood he will dab on the cheek of the goddess, 'is under my cloak' (*Gaudete* 185).

The ending of 'The Head' is problematical. The skinned and severed head of the brother is alive, and follows the narrator with vindictive shrieks. Later it turns into a sort of owl, finally into a slender girl, whom, though she never speaks, he takes home and marries. It may be that the pain of the brother eventually releases his animal self, what connects him with the whole animal creation he had formerly repudiated, as if he could exist like a severed head, then finally releases his repudiated and victimized feminine self, which is a perfect body but without the power of speech. Only after this transformation does it become possible for the estranged brothers to be reconciled. The half of the self that is externalized as the brother undergoes transformations well grounded in the mystical tradition, where:

> beheading signifies 'removing carnal consciousness, replacing it with spiritual consciousness'. In general, beheading means to be reborn with a new, other consciousness. This meaning is constantly refreshed and re-enforced by recurring as a common, archetypal event in ordinary dream life. (*Shakespeare* 395–6)

The first phase of that rebirth, as in *Cave Birds*, is as an owl-flower; the final phase as the goddess herself restored to the naked maidenhood of the unfallen world (as the monstrous ogress would have turned into a slim naked girl, his intended bride, on the far side of the river, had Crow ever got there).

In *Remains of Elmet* Hughes turned to look at what had actually been done to his home and people in the Calder Valley. He cannot regret that the moors, into which so many lives were ploughed like manure, are now breaking loose from the harness of men.

It is not only the chimneys, chapels and dry-stone walls of the Calder Valley which must collapse before there can be any new building. The image of stone returning to the earth is one of many images in Hughes for the restoration to Nature of her own, the healing and rededication of the holy elements before Man can approach them again with clean hands, with respect and humility, and for purposes more natural, sane and worthily human than the enslavement of body and spirit that has characterized Protestantism and industrialism in England.

Many of the poems are bleak. The *duende* of the Calder Valley is a spirit of disaster and mourning. You can hear it in the 'dark sounds' of the moors – 'the peculiar sad desolate spirit that cries in telegraph wires on moor roads, in the dry and so similar voices of grouse and sheep, and the moist voices of curlews' ('The Rock'). But in spite of this, 'the mood of moorland is exultant'. Many of the finest poems in *Remains of Elmet* celebrate the exhilaration which is the recognition that out of these uncompromising and unpromising materials, this graveyard, this vacancy of scruffy hills and stagnant pools and bone-chilling winds, life is continually renewing itself and making miracles. The whole scene, like a mother,

> Lifts a cry
> Right to the source of it all.
> A solitary cry.
>
> She has made a curlew.   ('Long Screams')

Such mothers are not, in our sense, maternal. They have no concern to make life easy for plants or animals, let alone humans. The miracle is that 'out of a mica sterility' comes the harebell's blueness, the heather's nectar.

An indicator of the distance Hughes has now travelled from the world of blood is the extensive use he makes in *Remains of Elmet* of light. Imagery of light is common throughout Hughes, but in his earlier work light is often merely the polar opposite of blood, what you are left with when you have got rid of blood by getting rid of substance, as in 'I said goodbye to earth': 'I arrived at light / Where I was shadowless'. Light without shadow is not only bloodless, it is cold, empty, uncreative, associated with the moon rather than the sun.

Since imagination means wholeness, dualism is the disease it exists to cure. The poet can have no use for the word 'supernatural', not because he disbelieves in spirit, but because, seeing nature whole at last, he sees that everything commonly called supernatural is part of nature, the very essence of nature. All Hughes' work of the seventies was an effort to resolve that dualism of blood and light, to become capable of seeing that light which is nature replete with spirit, the radiance of spirit, creative energy, within all creation, streaming continually from it. In *Gaudete* such vision is granted only to a priest in a moment of exceptional visionary receptiveness:

> He seemed to be flying into an endless, blazing sunrise, and he described the first coming of Creation, as it rose from the abyss, an infinite creature of miracles, made of miracles and teeming miracles. And he went on, describing this creature, giving it more and more dazzlingly-shining eyes, and more and more glorious limbs, and heaping it with greater and more extraordinary beauties, till his heart was pounding and he was pacing the room talking about God himself, and the tears pouring from his eyes fell shattering and glittering down the front of his cassock.

In *Remains of Elmet* every dawn was such a blazing sunrise (at least for those who were out before 'the sun climbed into its wet sack / For the day's work') as the cocks kindled the valley with their crows – 'bubble-glistenings flung up and bursting to light':

> Till the whole valley brimmed with cockcrows,
> A magical soft mixture boiling over,
> Spilling and sparkling into other valleys.

Remains of Elmet is entirely about the crime against nature, which here takes the form of the enslavement of a people conscripted into the mills, the chapels, the trenches, conscripted also into the human attempt to conscript in turn the mothers, the sustaining elements of earth, air, fire and water, to degraded, spiritless purposes. Like Blake Hughes seeks to renew the fallen light. The poems and photographs which are set in the valley bottom are harsh and gloomy – mills, chimneys and bridges reflected in the dull canal. What light there is seems trapped by the surrounding darkness, as the human spirit was trapped in the mills and chapels:

> The fallen sun
> Is in the hands of water. ('It Is All')

Water, too, is fallen, conscripted into gulleys, drained of all promise of fertility in the 'worn-out water of women' and the 'lost rivers of men'.

But on the high moors the elements seem to revel and gleam in their freedom. Ann Skea writes:

> The contrast is seen, too, in the accompanying photographs, and is most marked if the photograph following 'It Is All' is included in the comparison. In the picture opposite this poem, light glows softly from alley paving stones, but it is surrounded by darkness, trapped in the polluted water of the clog-worn gully, and blocked by the blackness into which the path leads. Similarly, the photographs on page 24 show a disk of light reflected in dark turbid water, looking very like a sun trapped beneath the water's surface. In contrast with these, the picture above 'High Sea-Light' shows a stony causey glowing with a light which becomes soft and pearly where it robes the gentle curves of the open moors beyond. We see a pathway of light leading to the freedom of the lit moors; a path by which to escape into the 'lark-rapture silence'. Light and soul, which are trapped in the valley, are, here, released from human con-straints and can work with the other elemental energies to revive the damaged earth. (176)

The same wind that had so threatened the embattled ego in 'Wind' now blows great holes in the sky opening it to the huge light of spirit; it frees the hills from their harness of walls. The Methodists had built their four-square chapels in an attempt to imprison spirit and keep out Nature, even a single cricket. Nature is now reclaiming them: 'Chapels, chimneys, vanish in the brightening':

> The light, opening younger, fresher wings
> Holds this land up again like an offering
>
> Heavy with the dream of a people.   ('The Trance of Light')

However, the people are so cowed after generations of enslavement that they seem unable to awake from their dream, unable to accept the offering. In 'Open to Huge Light' the hills are lit with a visionary brightness, but:

Startled people look up
With sheeps' heads
Then go on eating.

There is a wonderful painting of this poem by Norman Adams. In the centre of the painting the text of the poem glows like a rainbow with all the colours of a rose window. Around the border ill-defined people and cattle plod in a ring, heads down, earth-bound, in a purgatory of muddy greens and browns, blind to the spectacle of coloured light being offered to them if they could only look up. The happiest men are those at play, the exposed, pitifully buffeted men trying to play football on the highest ridge for miles.

And the valleys blued unthinkable
Under depth of Atlantic depression -

But the wingers leapt, they bicycled in air
And the goalie flew horizontal   ('Football at Slack')

It is a comic poem, but the comedy arises partly from the incongruity of the fact that the men are so determined to enjoy their all-too-brief respite, so focused on a football that they seem totally unaware that their only spectator is a wild god leaning through a fiery hole in heaven:

And once again a golden holocaust
Lifted the cloud's edge, to watch them.

Only the children, it seems, ever rebelled against the 'submarine twilight' of the valley, and tried to let in some light. On his way to school Hughes passed every day a huge derelict mill, where 'vandal plumes of willow-herb' tried to survive under the five hundred green skylights. It seemed to him like a sacked tomb:

Lifelines poured into wagepackets
Had leaked a warm horror, like Pompeii,
Into that worn-out, silent dust.

But there was something he could do. With a heroic vandalism like that of the plumed willow-herb he set himself, over a period, to break all five hundred skylights with five hundred stones, and he achieved his purpose:

One by one
Five hundred sunbeams fell on the horns of the flowers.

The comedy of 'Football at Slack' is part of the feeling of release from that intolerable 'weight of Atlantic depression' which had characterized the earlier poems about the Yorkshire Pennines. The style, out from under that pressure, plays like the wind. So far has Hughes now travelled since 'The Hawk in the Rain' that Scigaj can speak of 'the ethereal lightness of his poetic line' in *Remains of Elmet*.

Scigaj has noted the accumulation of images of light in *River*:

> Most often Hughes portrays the spiritual component of the river's animistic energy through light imagery. Light imagery coalesces with river water regularly to imbue riverscapes with a numinous aura, a sense of the sacredness of the hydrological cycle. Cock minnows gathering in a pool at Easter work together solemnly in the 'lit water', an image Hughes expands at the poem's conclusion to convey brightness from the Source blessing their labour 'In the wheel of light – / Ghostly rinsings / A struggle of spirits' (23). On the island of Skye an encounter with a salmon leaves the fisherman with a sense of being momentarily absorbed into the spirit world after miles of hiking towards the river's source while staring at the pool tail's 'superabundance of spirit' (31). Under water, the mystical sea-trout 'Hang in a near emptiness of light' (40); the West Dart River 'spills from the Milky Way, pronged with light' (39); and the river's 'Unending' sustenance, a wine distilled from the harvest it helped to fertilize, is squeezed from hills packed 'Tight with golden light' (45). An abundance of visual and auditory similes and metaphors revive in the reader a sense of participation in an ecosystem that fulfills much more than one's craving for facts and analysis. (*Ted Hughes* 136–7)

Nature here is not clothed in celestial light, has no need of any borrowed glory. It is wholly constituted of earthly light. All life is matter radiant with spirit. 'In the marriage of these two is a bliss of making and unmaking, all matter spiritualized, all spirit materialized, in the divine harmony of Light' (Smith 93).

For all his admiration of Eliot, light symbolizes for Hughes now the polar opposite of light in the *Four Quartets*, where it symbolizes timelessness, a 'zero summer' without fructifying warmth, with 'no earth smell / Or smell of living thing', 'not in the scheme of generation'. Eliot seeks in the stillness of the Chinese jar what Keats sought in the Grecian urn; but Keats decided that 'all breathing human passion' was too great a price to pay for the urn's ultimately 'desolate' silence. In 'To Autumn' he reaffirmed his allegiance to the 'scheme of generation', the music of time passing. Similarly Yeats tried and failed to get off the wheel of 'those dying generations', and reaffirmed his allegiance to the real summer of 'salmon-falls' and 'mackerel-crowded seas', to the 'fecund ditch' where all the ladders start. Eliot's effort was to burn off the reader's last attachments to 'the life of significant soil': Hughes' effort was to root himself and his readers back in the tragic and blissful processes of earth and water.

Hughes' vision is very close to the vision Nietzsche calls Dionysian:

> The word '*Dionysian*' expresses ... an ecstatic saying of yea to the collective character of existence, as that which remains the same, and equally mighty and blissful throughout all change; the great pantheistic sympathy with pleasure and pain, which declares even the most terrible and questionable qualities of existence good, and sanctifies them; the eternal will to procreation, to fruitfulness, and to recurrence; the feeling of unity in regard to the necessity of creating and annihilating. (*Will to Power* § 1050)

In accordance with this spirit of acceptance, Hughes looks again at the previously unacceptable face of the goddess, the bloody face of the predator, and declares it good. Nature is indeed perfecting her killers; but if it were only that, the prey species would collapse and the perfect killers would soon have nothing left to kill. Nature must simultaneously perfect the survival skills of the prey. Neither species could have evolved without the other. They bring each other to perfection.

The 'religious daze, the state of steady bliss' which Hughes observed in new-born calves, can also be seen in the dying:

> The spider clamps the bluefly – whose death panic
> Becomes sudden soulful absorption.
>
> A stoat throbs at the nape of the lumped rabbit
> Who watches the skylines fixedly.   (*Gaudete* 177)

Predation is a form of holy communion:

> And already the White Hare crouches at the sacrifice,
> Already the Fawn stumbles to offer itself up
> And the Wolf-Cub weeps to be chosen.   ('Eagle')

'Tiger-psalm' was originally conceived as a dialogue between Socrates and Buddha. Gradually Buddha's side of the argument resolved itself into a tiger and Socrates' into the principle of machine-guns, 'as if the whole abstraction of Socrates' discourse must inevitably, given enough time and enough applied intelligence, result in machine guns'. It is an argument between single vision and four-fold vision. The tiger, unlike the machine-gunners, is carrying out a perfectly rational, restrained and sacred activity:

> The tiger
> Kills expertly, with anaesthetic hand.
> ...
> The tiger
> Kills frugally, after close inspection of the map.
> ...
> The tiger
> Kills like a fall of cliff, one-sinewed with the earth,
> Himalayas under eyelid, Ganges under fur -
>
> Does not kill.
>
> Does not kill. The tiger blesses with a fang.

The tiger does not kill but opens a path
Neither of Life nor of Death.

In his report on visions seen by 35 subjects after taking the hallu-
cinogenic drug harmaline in Chile, Claudio Naranjo tells us that
seven of them saw big cats, usually tigers, though there are no big cats
in Chile and no tigers in the New World. One woman had a tiger
guide throughout her journey. Another actually became a tiger:

> I walked, though, feeling the same freedom I had experienced
> as a bird and a fish, freedom of movement, flexibility, grace. I
> moved as a tiger in the jungle, joyously, feeling the ground
> under my feet, feeling my power; my chest grew larger. I then
> approached an animal, any animal. I only saw its neck, and
> then experienced what a tiger feels when looking at its prey.
> (Harner 185)

Naranjo comments: 'This may be enough to show how the tiger by
no means stands for mere hostility, but for a fluid synthesis of aggres-
sion and grace and a full acceptance of the life-impulse beyond moral
judgment.' A vision of such a synthesis occurs frequently in the oral
poetry of 'primitive' peoples. Here is a Yoruba poem called 'Leopard':

> Gentle hunter
> His tail plays on the ground
> While he crushes the skull.

> Beautiful death
> Who puts on a spotted robe
> When he goes to his victim.

> Playful killer
> Whose loving embrace
> Splits the antelope's heart.   (Finnegan 163)

Half Naranjo's subjects had ecstatic feelings of a religious nature:
'The sea was in myself. There was a continuity of the external with
the internal. ... The sand and the plants were myself or something of
mine. The idea of God was in everything' (Harner 188). But this
atonement must always be preceded by a descent into destruction:

The complex of images discussed first as portraying the polarity of being and becoming, freedom and necessity, spirit and matter, only set up the stage for the human drama. This involves the battle of opposites and eventually their reconciliation or fusion, after giving way to death and destruction, be this by fire, tigers, drowning, or devouring snakes. The beauty of fluid fire, the graceful tiger, or the subtle and wise reptile, these seem most expressive for the synthetic experience of accepting life as a whole, or, better, accepting existence as a whole, life and death included; evil included too, though from a given spiritual perspective it is not experienced as evil any more. Needless to say, the process is essentially religious, and it could even be suspected that every myth presents us one particular aspect of the same experience. (189–90)

This, certainly, is the controlling myth of Hughes' whole career. Only thus can Tennyson's agonized question be answered. God and Nature are not at strife, and to let the tiger die is to let God die.

In *River* Hughes is no longer writing about a community, but about private communings with nature in a rural setting. The epiphany which was qualified in *Remains of Elmet* because it seemed to be over the heads of the people, or to flood in only to fill the vacuum left by the withdrawal of people, is now evoked continuously. Hughes agrees with Eliot that the river is a god. But Eliot's river, 'with its cargo of dead Negroes, cows and chicken coops', is purely destructive, sweeping everything as wastage into the sea. Hughes' river is source not sink, it 'will go on issuing from heaven / In dumbness issuing spirit brightness / Through its broken mouth'. It 'will wash itself of all deaths' ('River'). It is as though water were 'flesh of light', the first incarnation of spirit, raw creative energy, *zoe*, the very body of the goddess at her most erotic, perpetually offering herself to land and sky, driving her denizens into erotic bliss. This is why Hughes sees the pollution of rivers, the killing of rivers, not only as economic madness, squandering nature's bounty, but as blasphemy.

On Hughes' expeditions to such pristine salmon and trout rivers as the Dean in British Columbia few fish, only those needed for food, would be killed. The fanatic 'steelheaders' (the steelhead are the most powerful and glamorous of sea-trout) with whom he fished 'would never dream of killing one of these creatures' (*Three Books* 186). They were relaunched to resume their epic journey. The purpose in catching them at all was not as trophies, tokens of the superiority of the hunter to wild nature – quite the contrary. The purpose was to try 'to hook ourselves into it', to be electrified, revivified by the 'giddy orgasm of the river' ('The Bear').

Hughes' fullest description of the actual moment of hooking a salmon, of 'the fascination of flowing water and living things coming up out of it – to grab at you and be grabbed' (*Wild Steelhead and Salmon* 52), is in 'Milesian Encounter on the Sligachan':

Eerie how you know when it's coming –
So I felt it now, my blood
Prickling and thickening, altering
With an ushering-in of chills, a weird onset
As if mountains were pushing mountains higher
Behind me, to crowd over my shoulder -

Then the pool lifted a travelling bulge
And grabbed the tip of my heart-nerve, and crashed,

Trying to wrench it from me ...
                              – what was it gave me
Such a supernatural, beautiful fright

And let go, and sank disembodied
Into the eye-pupil darkness?

Only a little salmon.
                    Salmo salar
The loveliest, left-behind, most-longed-for ogress
Of the Paleolithic
Watched me through her time-warped judas-hole
In the ruinous castle of Skye

As I faded from the light of reality.

The ogress who so terrified Crow that he could only blindly hack at her, reveals herself as she would have revealed herself to Crow had he ever been able to cross the river.

To enter river, to join water, to hook a powerful fish, releases in Hughes the self he has always wanted to be, the self he knows to be his 'real' self, symbolized by fox and wolf. In his interview with Tom Pero he said:

> Any kind of fishing provides that connection with the whole living world. It gives you the opportunity of being totally immersed, turning back into yourself in a good way, a form of meditation, some form of communion with levels of yourself that are deeper than the ordinary self. (56)

He described fishing as a 'corridor back into the world that's made us as we are'. Every fishing trip, like every myth, is a journey in search of this primeval self reconnected to the 'divine influx':

> one inside me,
> A bodiless twin, some doppelgänger
> Disinherited other, unliving,
> Ever-living, a larva from prehistory,
> Whose journey this was, who now exulted
> Recognizing his home.   ('The Gulkana')

This larval self is what Blake would have called his 'emanation'. After each fishing trip, especially into the wilderness, Hughes would return less and less of himself to civilization, a mere 'spectre / Lifted my quivering coffee, in the aircraft'.

'Peering into that superabundance of spirit' which is a pure river, the human intruder is humbled, feels ghostly, loses all sense of his own centrality and omnipotence as a lord of language. The waters wash away his sense of identity, cause him to lose language and identity, 'be supplanted by mud and leaves and pebbles':

> As if creation were a wound
> As if this flow were all plasm healing

After such an experience, 'new and nameless', he can only

Let the world come back, like a white hospital
Busy with emergency words

Try to speak and nearly succeed
Heal into time and other people ('Go Fishing')

This poem is like a palimpsest. Behind it are shadowy vestiges of earlier experiences which were at the time in some way negative, now transformed. At the outset of Hughes' career, the supplanting, displacement, dissolution, dismemberment, described, enacted in this poem, would have been terrifying to contemplate, to be avoided at all costs, or suffered in the spirit of sacrificial victim. In 'Wind', for example, the wind wounds, wielding 'blade-light'; it threatens madness, the loosening of our grip on the world and the self. Now it is precisely that loosening which constitutes the healing of all the wounds of the world, the world to which we cling with a madman's grip. The 'new and nameless' creature Hughes becomes is a latter-day wodwo, no longer supposing itself to be the exact centre, no longer appropriating the most secret interiors of other creatures. Now to enter water is to be reunited with the source, washed clean of the stain of blood, readmitted to an unfallen world. No longer, like the man/crow/cockerel of *Cave Birds*, is the protagonist mangled by judgemental birds; only the light is mangled by wing-shadows. He crawls out of the water with new face and limbs, like the wet-fresh bodies assembled by the bride and groom. He returns to a world 'like a white hospital / Busy with emergency words', but returns healed and capable of healing, unlike the helpless visitor by the banked hospital bed in *Gaudete*, soon to be kissing the victim's cold temple in the morgue, then as if defunct himself 'in the glaring metropolis of cameras' (*Gaudete* 186).

Here, as Nicholas Bishop points out 'the personal pronoun is absolutely eliminated from the poem as the protagonist becomes "translucent" to the processes of both the entire surrounding riverscape and those of the explored inner world' (248). Here Hughes fulfils the hope for poetry expressed in 1952 by the French poet Francis Ponge:

When man becomes proud to be not just the site where ideas and feelings are produced, but also the crossroad where they divide and mingle, he will be ready to be saved. Hope therefore lies in a poetry through which the world so invades the spirit of man that he becomes almost speechless, and later reinvents a language. ('The Silent World is Our Only Homeland')

Pilinszky castigates that narcissistic art that 'places the stylistic certainty of appearances before the self-forgetful incarnating of the world' (Bishop 144). The language Hughes reinvents in *River* is bright, fresh and green, as if it has just shed a skin, sharp and tangy as snow-melt.

The language of all these poems is a rich weave of relationships. A poem may be ostensibly about a single creature, but that creature is defined by its relationships with other creatures, with weather and season and landscape. Since 'all things draw to the river' it is therefore the language of atonement.

In his note to 'Rain-charm for the Duchy' Hughes describes in detail the astonishing breeding behaviour of salmon. He concludes:

This is how salmon come to be such sensitive glands in the vast, dishevelled body of nature. Their moody behaviour, so unpredictable and mysterious, is attuned, with the urgency of survival, to every slightest hint of the weather – marvellous instruments, recording every moment-by-moment microchange as the moving air and shifting light manipulate the electronics of the water-molecules. (*Rain-charm* 52)

The life of the salmon is also the life of the living waters, which is also the life of earth and sky. The salmon is part of a flow which 'will not let up for a minute'.

One of Lumb's poems addressed the salmon:

While the high-breasted, the haloed world
Opens herself for you

While your strength
Can enjoy her, lifting you through her

While your spine shivers and leaps
In the spate of your spirit

Before it trickles thin and low
Inhabited only by small shadows

Court the lady of the hill
Press to her source, spend your plunder

For her – only for her –
O salmon of the ghostly sea.   (*Achievement* 309–10)

The bliss of unmaking is the theme of, for example, 'October Salmon'. The cock-salmon, worn out with his two-thousand-mile journey, earth's 'insatiable quest', despite the 'covenant of Polar Light', ends as a 'shroud in a gutter' – 'this chamber of horrors is also home'. Only the salmon's superhuman 'epic poise ... holds him so steady in his wounds, so loyal to his doom, so patient / In the machinery of heaven'. The spent salmon is the defeated, torn and sacrificed hero whose acquiescence is a form of worship. The salmon poems are all hymns to the goddess, tributes to the mythic heroism of the salmon, dying in the cause of the goddess. Their sacrifice is also a sacrament, the consummation of being reborn from their own eggs and sperm.

The bliss of making is the theme of 'Salmon Eggs':

Something else is going on in the river

More vital than death –
...
- these toilings of plasm -
The melt of mouthing silence, the charge of light
Dumb with immensity.
The river goes on
Sliding through its place, undergoing itself
In its wheel.

The wheel, karma, the 'cycles of recurrence', were formerly for Hughes, as for most religions, images of horror and absurdity. The pressure was to get off the intolerable wheel. Now it seems that that horror was a product of defective vision and of the hubristic attempt to redeem nature. Hughes now echoes Lawrence's risen Christ (in *The Escaped Cock*): 'From what, and to what, could this infinite whirl be saved?'

Like Shakespeare in *A Midsummer Night's Dream*, Hughes seeks to rescue the language of spirit and the sacred from transcendental religion. The early church arrogated to itself many of the most powerful symbols, festivals, rituals, of pagan religion. Hughes returns the sacred to its own:

> The river is in a resurrection fever.
> Now at Easter you find them
> Up in the pool's throat, and in the very jugular
> Where the stickle pulses under grasses –
>
> Cock minnows!
> They have abandoned contemplation and prayer in the pool's crypt.
>
> There they are, packed all together,
> In an inch of seething light.   ('Under the Hill of Centurions')

And if the only language now available to us to express sacredness is the language of Christian worship, then the church's monopoly of that language must be broken. Hughes' eucharist gives thanks for 'earth's tidings' and the 'blessed issue' of salmon eggs. He translates the river's annunciation as '*Only birth matters*'. The Great Mother's only obligation is fecundity.

In the early seventies, as we saw, Hughes strove to find poetic equivalents (overtly in *Cave Birds: An Alchemical Cave Drama*) for the Great Work of Alchemy:

> The 'Great Work' of Alchemy aimed to discover the nature of 'spirit' and to see face to face the 'body of light' that was the foundation of the human body as well as the 'matter' of the universe. The alchemical marriage between sun and moon, king and queen, spirit and soul (including body), expressed the

essential identity of spirit and nature, so healing the split that had developed in human consciousness between these two aspects of life. Whoever this secret revealed itself to had penetrated to the mystery of creation and knew there was no death, for he or she understood how life continuously regenerated itself; how the manifest emanated from the unmanifest and 'dissolved' again into the unmanifest. (Baring and Cashford 649–50)

This vision of the 'body of light' expressing the divine harmony of matter and spirit is evident in most of the poems in *River*, but perhaps most clearly in 'That Morning', the poem with which Hughes chose to end his 1982 *Selected Poems*. Here two awe-struck human beings are allowed to re-enter Paradise, not as trespassers or intruders or voyeurs, but as long-time exiles being welcomed home. The place, a remote valley in Alaska, and its creatures demanded a sacramental response. The sheer profusion of salmon was a sign and a blessing, the body a 'spirit beacon / Lit by the power of the salmon', as if this were no longer a fallen world:

Two gold bears came down and swam like men

Beside us. And dived like children.
And stood in deep water as on a throne
Eating pierced salmon off their talons.

So we found the end of our journey.

So we stood, alive in the river of light
Among the creatures of light, creatures of light.

It is no derogation of the sacredness of the salmon that they should be also food, for both man and bear. Campbell writes:

The affect of the successful adventure of the hero is the unlocking and release again of the flow of life into the body of the world. The miracle of this flow may be represented in physical terms as a circulation of food substance, dynamically as a streaming of energy, or spiritually as a manifestation of grace.

> Such varieties of image alternate easily, representing three
> degrees of condensation of the one life force. An abundant har-
> vest is the sign of God's grace; God's grace is the food of the
> soul; the lightning bolt is the harbinger of fertilizing rain, and
> at the same time the manifestation of the released energy of
> God. Grace, food substance, energy: these pour into the living
> world, and wherever they fail, life decomposes into death.
> (*Hero* 40)

So, in *River*, Hughes found the end of his poetic journey, from a
world made of blood to a world made of light.

These moments out of time are of course precarious. They can
never be taken for granted, still less fabricated. The effort must be
resumed next day, or that afternoon, to rediscover the lost world, but
from now on with the knowledge that it exists, the assurance of one
who has been there, in the full flow of grace.

The poems ensure that we, if we are not completely sealed, have
also been there. What shall we make of that knowledge? Even if the
covenant held, and man had the option of life 'among creatures of
light', would he choose the goddess for his bride and nature for his
home?

> The ego's extreme alternatives are either to reject her and
> attempt to live an independent, rational, secular life or to abne-
> gate the ego and embrace her love with 'total, unconditional
> love', which means to become a saint, a holy idiot, possessed by
> the Divine Love. ... Man will always choose the former, simply
> because once he is free of a natural, creaturely awareness of the
> divine indulgence which permits him to exist at all, he wants to
> live his own life, and he has never invented a society of saints
> that was tolerable. (*Shakespeare* 392–3)

Perhaps the best we can hope for is that our civilization will pass like
the others, seeming no more than the nightmare of a stranded
immortal who will eventually awake to a world cleansed of humans
– in Lawrence's words, 'just the long grass waving, and a hare sitting
up':

Hills with raised wings were standing on hills.
They rode the waves of light
That rocked the conch of whispers

And washed and washed at his eye.

                              Washed from his ear

All but the laughter of foxes.
                    ('A Chinese History of Colden Water')

APPENDIX
The Story of Crow

If poetry is an attempt to communicate at a deeper level than any other kind of language, it is bound to confront the reader with many problems, to demand many and subtle readjustments. The poet surely has a responsibility not to put any unnecessary obstacles in the path of the reader's understanding. Yet most poets do, not least Hughes, despite the concrete immediacy of his verse at one level. It is difficult for a poet to imagine what it is like not to know what he knows, not to have his general knowledge derived from his unique reading and experience, not to know the background and genesis of a specific poem, and its place in the context of all his other writings. Hughes has himself demonstrated, in his essay on Plath's 'Sheep in Fog', that it is impossible to understand that poem without access not only to a good deal of inside information, but also to all the manuscript drafts. Hughes has become increasingly aware of this problem of communication, of the need to make sure that readers have enough coordinates to orient themselves, and has actually provided notes to several of his most recent collections (in the case of *Rain-charm for the Duchy*, 14 pages of them). But the collection that most needed notes, or rather a complete narrative context, was *Crow*.

About 1967, Hughes' friend Leonard Baskin invited him to write a few little poems to accompany some engravings of crows. Hughes' mythic imagination immediately recognized the manifold mythic potentialities of the crow, as trickster, quest hero and embodiment of almost all the themes that were most urgent to Hughes at that time. The crow figures prominently (usually as trickster) in many mythologies, including the Red Indian and the Eskimo. Hughes was very attracted by the trickster:

> Beneath the Hero-Tale, like the satyr behind the Tragedy, is the
> Trickster Saga, a series of Tragicomedies. It is a series, and never

properly tragic, because Trickster, demon of phallic energy, bearing the spirit of the sperm, is repetitive and indestructible. No matter what fatal mistakes he makes, and what tragic flaws he indulges, he refuses to let sufferings or death detain him, but always circumvents them, and never despairs. Too full of opportunistic ideas for sexual *samadhi*, too unevolved for spiritual ecstasy, too deathless for tragic joy, he rattles along on biological glee. (*WP* 241)

Crow, once conceived, completely possessed Hughes, grew out of all proportion to his origins, and became the protagonist of *The Life and Songs of the Crow*, an 'epic folk-tale' in prose, studded with hundreds of poems, most of them the 'super-ugly' songs of Crow, or songs about him, some the songs of other birds and characters in the story. The tale drew not only on trickster mythology, but on the whole body of myth, folklore and literature with which Hughes had by the late sixties familiarized himself. Its basic shape was that of the traditional quest narrative, ending, like all quests, with the hero's emergence from the blackness of his crimes and sufferings into a raw wisdom, the healing of the split within him, the release of his own deepest humanity, all expressed in images of ego-death, rebirth and marriage.

Like all Hughes' protagonists – Prometheus, Adam, the nameless hero of *Cave Birds* and Nicholas Lumb in *Gaudete* Crow was to function to some extent as an alter ego for Hughes, recapitulating aspects of his own experience. In a work for children (such as *The Iron Man*) an up-beat ending could be manufactured, but in a fully adult work such an ending had to be validated in life, and events in Hughes' life in 1969 plunged him back into the pit. He felt he could not continue the story beyond the point he had reached, where Crow was just beginning the upward movement of the final third. He abandoned the larger project entirely (though years of work and boxes of manuscripts had gone into it) and merely salvaged in *Crow* (1970) some of the poems from the first two thirds, with no attempt to provide them with a context. In a 1970 radio interview Hughes said:

> The main story takes the Crow through a series of experiences which alter him in one way and another, take him to the bot-

tom and then take him to the top, and eventually the whole purpose of the thing is to try to turn him into a man, which, as it stands, the story nearly succeeds in doing, but I haven't completed it, and whether one could complete it I don't know.

Or maybe, he added, he might 'use all the material in some other way'.

Crow in fact refused to be killed off in 1969, and Hughes wrote many more Crow poems, some of which are incorporated in *Cave Birds*, but most of which are scattered in limited editions or obscure magazines or unpublished.

Hughes later regretted having published the poems in this manner:

> A more graphic idea of the context – of the traditional convention I set out to exploit, as far as I could, and of the essential line and level of the narrative, which might make some misreadings less likely – ought to have been part of those published fragments.   (Letter to *KS*)

He attempted to provide this belatedly by publishing several articles and interviews on aspects of *Crow*, and by summarizing large segments of the narrative whenever he introduced the poems in recordings and at readings. But all this reached very few readers, and misreadings are still common, not least by professional critics, some of whom have given the poems precisely the opposite interpretation required by the missing context.

In what follows I have attempted to reconstruct the whole story, keeping close to Hughes' own words, by amalgamating segments of the story from recordings, broadcasts, readings, essays and letters.

The story begins in Heaven. God is trying to sleep after the hard labour of creation, but He finds it impossible to sleep. As soon as He begins to doze, He has a terrible nightmare – always the same nightmare. A giant hand grabs Him by the throat and throttles Him. This hand lifts Him out of Heaven, shakes him beyond the last stars, ploughs the earth with his face, making new valleys and new mountain ranges, and throws him back into heaven in a cold sweat. At the same time, the hand seems to be laughing. Every time he falls asleep, this Hand arrives, and he knows in his dream that this hand is also a voice. And he can't understand how there can be anything in his creation (since he considers, being God, that he created everything) that can be so unknown to him, and so hostile. Who created this thing that has such power over His sleep?

So there are long episodes where he tries to get this nightmare to divulge its secret. When at last the voice speaks, it abuses God, and is full of mockery of His creation, especially the crown of His creation – mankind. How could God take pride in such a paltry, ugly, miserable, futile being? God becomes very angry and defends man as godlike and noble. But the voice becomes only more and more derisive.

While the debate is going on, Man, on earth, has sent up a representative to the Gate of Heaven, and this Representative has been knocking on the mighty marble gates, and God has been so preoccupied with the nightmare that he hasn't heard him. And so this little figure is sitting at the Gate of Heaven waiting for God to hear him. At that point in the argument, where God is saying 'You're quite wrong', that Man is really a superb success on the earth, the voice, as the last, absolute, triumphant point in his argument, says 'Listen to what he's saying.' And the figure says to God 'take life back'. Man has sent this little figure up to ask God to take life back, because men are fed up with it. God is enraged that Man has let him down, and in a voice of tremendous fury, He challenges the voice to do better. He gives the voice the freedom of the earth to go and produce something better than Man, given the materials and the whole set-up. And this is what the voice has been contriving to bring about. So with a howl of delight it plunges down into matter, and God turns Man round and pushes him back down into the world. God is very curious to see what this production by the voice will be.

The voice begins to ferment and gestate in matter, and the little thing begins to develop. A little nucleus of something-or-other, a little embryo begins. But before it can get born it has to go through all manner of adventures, and find its way to a womb, and then through the womb, and finally out of the womb and into the world.

First of all he's nothing at all. He's just a black lump. Eventually, as things go along and experience defines him and exercises him and enlightens him, he becomes something like a crow. Nobody knows quite how Crow was created, or how he appeared. There are several contradictory, apocryphal stories. 'Two Legends', 'Lineage' and 'A Kill' are some of them. Right at the womb-door he meets an examiner and has to pass an oral examination. Because of all the adventures he's been through, he's a very canny embryo now, so his answers are circumspect. The first question is 'Who owns these scrawny little feet?' He thinks he's going to be outflanked in some way. He thinks long thoughts, short thoughts, and he answers 'Death'.

Having been created, he's put through various adventures and disasters and trials and ordeals, a pin-table of casual experiences, and the effect of all these is to alter him not at all, then alter him a great deal, completely transform him, tear him to bits, put him together again, and produce him a little bit changed. He's a man to correct man, but of course he's not a man, he's a crow. And maybe his ambition is to become a man, which he never quite manages.

The world he appears into is a world where everything is happening simultaneously, so the beginning and the end are present, and all the episodes of history are present, as in all the different rooms of a gigantic hotel, and every single thing goes on happening for the first time forever.

God, having come down into the world to see how this creature is going to size up, first sees what a wretched, black, horrible little nothing it is. He befriends the strange, helpless little creature. He's rather indulgent towards it and tends to let it look on while he shows the marvels of the beginning. So God lets Crow watch the creation of man and woman. Eden is all going on, and God has the old Talmudic problem with Adam and Eve. The Talmudic legend is that when God created Adam and Eve, he took clays from the four corners of the earth, waters from the great rivers, so that Man shouldn't feel lost wherever he wandered on the earth, and he modelled these two beautiful people. But then he couldn't get the souls into them. The souls stay away out in the gulf for five hundred years howling and wailing because, being perfectly clairvoyant, they don't want the lives that they are going to have to live. And eventually he gets them in by music.

God lets Crow into these early experiments as a sort of mascot. Then (in 'A Childish Prank') Crow sees a short cut, a very obvious short cut it seems now, which has great consequences in the story later on. God forgives him for that. In 'Crow's First Lesson' he gives Crow another chance, again with serious consequences. God, who was initially indulgent, becomes worried, because he sees that this is an alert little beast, so he begins to try to frustrate him.

Crow is simply a pupil of God's in the early world, just a little childish hanger-on to the events of the creation. Crow interferes at every point, of course, because God, having created the world, has created it slightly wrong, and Crow's efforts over-correct it. This particular God, of course, is the man-created, broken down, corrupt despot of a ramshackle religion, who bears about the same relationship to the Creator as, say, ordinary English does to reality. He accompanies Crow through the world, in many guises, mis-teaching, deluding, tempting, opposing and at every point trying to discourage or destroy him. To begin with Crow is full of flawless courage, but then he becomes, through what happens to him, more complicated. All God does to him simply toughens him up, wises him up.

Most of the story is prose. The poems are here and there along the narrative. The original idea was simply to get the Crow's songs, not so much the stories about him – the things he sang and the songs that various things sang back at him. As he goes along he holds dialogues with everything he meets: rocks and trees and rivers and so on. Every plant, stone, creature, has its own version of any event. Everything sings its own song about itself.

Crow wanders over the earth staring at creation. He begins to learn strange lessons about the creation and about himself. The hopeful sign is that he recognizes pain – or rather 'travail'. He does not recognize it so much as become conscious of it by projecting it, because he too is in pain, though he doesn't know it. Everything in himself that he refuses to acknowledge is in pain. And pain calls to pain. Mystified, he detects this. He experiences the whole exchange, yet observes it as a non-participant. In other words, he is still infantile –

he evades the reality in himself. Or, for some reason or other, he cannot yet recognize it, so does not take responsibility for it, and so
remains infantile.

As he learns more, he thinks more. He begins to wonder where he
came from, who created him. Crow sees wonders, horrors, follies. He
learns a thing or two about them. Occasionally, fury gets the better
of him, and he decides to solve the mystery by force.

In these ways, little by little, he learns who he is. But the more he
learns about himself, the clearer and closer the real problems come. As
he goes along he finds himself involved repeatedly with various female
figures, and this coincides with a growing curiosity about his own
make-up. A certain question begins to trouble him more and more,
fundamental and simple: 'Who made me?' This curiosity turns into a
search, and becomes a serious quest for whoever made him, a quest to
locate and release his own creator, God's nameless prisoner, whom he
encounters repeatedly, but always in some unrecognizable form.

He journeys on, always looking for his creator, following every
clue. He begins to question everything he meets for clues to his creator, and he follows these clues and they inevitably and repeatedly
lead him to some sort of female being. His misfortune is that he
always bungles the encounter. Again and again, this search brings
him to some being that he hopes will be his creator, but it always
turns out to be something else. At least it seems to Crow every time
that this being is not his creator. He never understands that this is
what he is actually looking for. He's expecting a male being. It's
female, but not beautiful or obviously female. It's seemingly monstrous and enigmatic. He misinterprets it. He tries to destroy it ('A
Horrible Religious Error'). He mismanages his opportunity to find
whatever it might be that this thing holds for him. So it's a disaster,
and he has to go right back and start again. So his whole life is one
succession of adventures with female beings.

Often wearied by his search and his travails, he feels low. Ordinary
human reflexes puzzle him, like laughter. Sometimes he just wonders
about himself and his quest. The power of thoughts, he realizes, is
very strange, very real. The power of words, too, is very great, he
finds, but not quite great enough.

So he goes along, always looking for his creator, getting help wherever he can, trying to make use of everything, but not always with very much success. He sees many strange things, and tries to understand them. The world he sees is definitely a very strange place, a painful place, sometimes a very dark place. He sees that if he is going to survive, he needs supernatural strength. And yet he has to survive. The world is suddenly dangerous, but Crow struggles to cope. He sees that God's creation is a commendable effort, but it's constantly falling apart. God himself seems weary of it. Crow sees the creation needs help. On every side, things go wrong, great and small. He makes songs about it all.

He becomes more learned too, and involved in all the cultures, intrigued by all the possibilities and the interesting tales. He encounters all sorts of cultural monuments, and begins to realize that the whole business of religion and so on is very much a game for everybody, and that really it's a matter of rearranging the elements in the plot. One religion arranges it this way, another religion arranges it that way, similar elements, or even the same elements. He sees that in fact anybody can do it, and that most arrangements are greatly mistaken. He can see that there is after all a very simple explanation for the obvious elements in the religion of this particular God that he's encountered. So he simply rearranges them ('Apple Tragedy').

In his travels, he has heard many stories, many variants of stories, and he watches the dramas Man puts on the stage. He sees that some have more truth than others. As he gets older, more aware, more able to deal with what happens, he begins to invent his own variants and his own drama but it's very crude. He never gets much beyond the bare outline. He produces plays and stories, but can never get more than two characters into them, and always the same two, a man and a woman. Early on he encounters the literature of Oedipus. He reads Sophocles and Seneca and Freud, and decides they all got it wrong, so he makes his version ('Song for a Phallus'). 'Notes for a Little Play' is one of his efforts, a simple outline just like a stage direction. Sometimes he makes observations about the characters in his plays ('Fragment of an Ancient Tablet'); occasionally, he simply recounts a note

for a dramatic scene ('Crow Paints Himself into a Chinese Mural').
Perhaps it came to him in a dream.

One problem Crow can see is the universal business of Death. He
decides to tackle Death ('Crow Sickened'). He makes a head-on
attempt to grasp the truth of things. 'Maybe', he thinks, 'maybe it
was Truth who created me.' At last, in 'Truth Kills Everybody', he's
located what he thinks is the truth, in the shape of Proteus, a sea-god
who can change into any shape. The hero who wants to speak to Proteus has to grab him and hang on to him, and not be frightened by
whatever he turns himself into, until he finally turns back into himself. Crow knows that he has to come to terms with reality somehow.
He understands at last that he has to accept the way things are, the
nothingness in which everything began, the fire of the sun in which
everything will end. The 'violence' of this poem, therefore, is limited
to a purely psychological and even barely conscious event. Either
Crow gives up or he breaks through to what he wants and is exploded
by it – his culpable ego-machinery is exploded. That he explodes is
positive. It is not an image of 'violence' but an image of breakthrough. If he had withdrawn, he would have remained fixed in his
error. That he pushes to the point where he is annihilated means that
now nothing remains for him but what has exploded him – his inner
link with his creator, a thing of spirit-fire ('he that loses his life shall
find it' etc.). This is Crow's greatest step forward. But he regresses,
and has to make it again and again, before his gain is finally consoli-
dated in his union with his bride.

Eventually Crow meets the ghost of an Eskimo hunter, who adopts
him and becomes his mentor. As a medium might have a Red Indian
guide, he has an Eskimo guide. Because he's failing on the way, the
Eskimo supports him, and shows him how to muster his energies and
spirits. He does this by teaching him little stories and songs. The
Eskimo convention is that your good spirits live in various songs and
when you learn one of these songs you get that particular spirit.
When you give the song away you lose it. So the Eskimo's giving him
these spirits. The more of these songs Crow possesses, the better
armed he is against all the trials that beset him. Each song contains a
helpful spirit, a power. One of these magical songs is called 'Little-

blood'. One's a little fable in the shape of a song: 'How Water Began to Play'.

This guide promises to lead him finally to his creator. Crow comes to a river which he must cross to get to the Happy Land where he believes his bride awaits him. Sitting beside the river is a hag, an ogress, a great monstrous assemblage of all the horrific parts of all the female beings that he's encountered on the way. She demands that he carry her across the river. She's huge, so he has no choice. So he gets her up on his shoulders, piggy-back, and wades into the river. Suddenly she begins to get heavier and heavier, until her weight drives him down into the gravel. When the water is level with his chin, she stops growing heavier and asks him a question. It is a question about all the female figures he's encountered on his journey, about the relationship between male and female, about love. But it is also a dilemma question, that is a question without any final answer, or with several contradictory answers. Nevertheless, the great hag demands not only that he answer the question, but that he sing the answer. But he is only a crow, so he sings a primitive one-note croak. He tries to answer, but most of his answer is sadly wrong. So he has to keep starting again, correcting his tack. Wherever his answer approaches the truth, the ogress becomes lighter, and when he goes wrong she becomes heavier. So he just has to home in on the fragment of rightness in his answers, like a negative feedback machine. So every line that he sings is a new start, a new answer. At last he gets her back to her original weight, then he steps out of the hole and sets off again across the river. But soon her weight increases again and he cannot move until he has answered another question. This happens seven times. With each question Crow learns from his earlier mistakes, and makes fewer.

The questions change. They begin at the negative extreme and end at the positive. The first question expects the darkest answer: 'Who paid most, him or her?' Crow's answer is 'Lovesong'. The third question is 'Was it animal, or was it a bird?' Crow's answer is 'The Lovepet'. The last, and seventh, question, when they are close to the far side of the river, expects a joyful answer. The question is 'Who gave most, him or her?'. Crow's answer is 'Bride and groom lie hidden for three days'. At this point the hag leaps from his back. She has become a beautiful, lithe, naked maiden, who runs towards an oak-wood with Crow in pursuit.

SELECT BIBLIOGRAPHY

A full description of all Hughes' books, contributions to books and periodicals, translations of his work, broadcasts, and recordings, books and articles about him up to the end of 1995 can be found in *Ted Hughes: A Bibliography*, by K. Sagar and S. Tabor, Mansell, 1998.

Books by Ted Hughes

Unless otherwise stated, all titles are published by Faber and Faber, London, and Harper and Row, New York

The Hawk in the Rain (1957)
Lupercal (1960)
Meet My Folks! (1961; US edn Bobbs-Merrill, 1973)
How the Whale Became (1963; US edn Atheneum, 1964)
The Earth-Owl and Other Moon People (1963)
Nessie the Mannerless Monster (1964; US edn Bobbs-Merrill, 1974)
Recklings (Turret Press, 1966)
Wodwo (1967)
Poetry in the Making (1967; US edn *Poetry Is*, Doubleday, 1970)
The Iron Man (1968; US edn *The Iron Giant*)
Seneca's Oedipus (1969; US edn Doubleday, 1972)
The Coming of the Kings (1970; US edn *The Tiger's Bones*, Viking, 1974)
    Only the US edn contains 'Orpheus'.
Crow (1970; US edn 1971)
    Seven poems were added at the sixth printing (1972). 'The Lovepet' appears only in the US edn, but is in *New Selected Poems* (1995) .
Poems: Ruth Fainlight, Ted Hughes, Alan Sillitoe (Rainbow Press, 1971)
    Contains six important *Crow* poems, five of which ('Genesis of Evil', 'Crow's Song About England', 'Crow's Courtship', 'Crow's Song About God' and 'Crow the Just') have never been collected in a trade edn. The

181

sixth, 'Crow Rambles', is in *Moortown* as 'Life is Trying to be Life'.

Prometheus on his Crag (Rainbow Press, 1973)

Contains three poems not in *Moortown*.

Season Songs (US edn Viking, 1975; Faber, 1976, 1985)

The English edn omitted 'The Defenders' and added 'March Morning Unlike Others', 'Icecrust and Snowflake', 'Apple Dumps', 'A Cranefly in September' and 'Two Horses'.

The, 1985 edn omitted 'The Stag' and 'Two Horses' and added 'He Gets up in Dark Dawn', 'A Swallow', 'Evening Thrush', 'A Dove', 'Barley', 'Pets' and 'Starlings Have Come'.

Moon-Whales (US edn Viking, 1976; Faber, 1988)

The English edn omits six poems.

Gaudete (1977)

Cave Birds (1978; US edn Viking, 1979)

Moon-Bells (Chatto, 1978)

A Solstice (Sceptre Press, 1978)

Orts (Rainbow Press, 1978)

Only 14 of these 63 poems are in *Moortown*.

The Threshold (Steam Press, 1979)

Adam and the Sacred Nine (Rainbow Press, 1979)

Contains five poems not in *Moortown*: 'Awake!', 'All This Time His Cry', 'He Had Retreated', Light', 'Bud-tipped Twig'.

Remains of Elmet (1979)

Contains 21 poems not in *Elmet* or *Three Books*.

Moortown (1979)

Under the North Star (1981; US edn Viking)

River (1983)

Contains 12 poems not in *Three Books*.

What is the Truth? (1984; also as vol. 2 of the *Collected Animal Poems*, 1995)

Flowers and Insects (US edn Knopf, 1986)

Ffangs the Vampire Bat and the Kiss of Truth (1986)

Moortown Diary (1989)

Tales of the Early World (1988; US edn Farrar Strauss and Giroux (FSG), 1991)

Wolfwatching (1989; US edn FSG, 1991)

Shakespeare and the Goddess of Complete Being (1992; US edn FSG, 1992)

Rain-Charm for the Duchy and Other Laureate Poems (1992)

The Iron Woman (1993; US edn Dial Books,1995)

Three Books: Remains of Elmet, Cave Birds, River (1993)

The *Remains* section omits 21 poems and adds four.
The River section omits 12 and adds 13.
Winter Pollen (1994; US edn Picador, 1995)
    Contains most of Hughes' important essays and reviews.
New Selected Poems (1995)
The Dreamfighter (1995)
Difficulties of a Bridegroom (1995; US edn Picador)
    Contains most of Hughes' short stories.
Wedekind's Spring Awakening (1995)
Collected Animal Poems: The Iron Wolf, What is the Truth?, A March Calf, The
    Thought Fox (1995)
Lorca's Blood Wedding (1996)
Tales from Ovid (1997; US edn FSG)
Birthday Letters (1998; US edn FSG)
Racine's Phedre (1998)
The Oresteia of Aeschylus (1999; US edn FSG)
The Alcestis of Euripedes (1999; US edn FSG)

Books, Periodicals and Tapes with Important Uncollected Contributions by Hughes.

'Context', in *London Magazine*, February 1962.
The Poet Speaks (XVI): Ted Hughes Talks to Peter Orr (British Council, 1963)
    A duplicated document.
'The Rock', in *Writers on Themselves* (BBC, 1964).
'Myth and Education', in *Children's Literature in Education* (1970). ('Myth
    and Education I').
    This is different from the essay of the same title in *Winter Pollen* and else-
    where.
The Art of Sylvia Plath, ed. Charles Newman (Faber, 1970).
    Contains Hughes' 'The Chronological Order of Sylvia Plath's Poems'.
Orghast at Persepolis, by A.C.H. Smith (Eyre Methuen, 1972).
    Contains outlines of *Orghast* by Ted Hughes.
Worlds, ed. Geoffrey Summerfield (Penguin, 1974).
    Contains 'The Rock'.
Ted Hughes and R.S. Thomas (Norwich Tapes, 1978).
Johnny Panic and the Bible of Dreams, by Sylvia Plath (Faber, 1977).
    Contains Hughes' foreword.

Ted Hughes: The Unaccommodated Universe, by Ekbert Faas (Black Sparrow Press, 1980).
> Contains two major interviews and several prose pieces not in *Winter Pollen*.

The Reef, by Keith Sagar (Proem Pamphlets, 1980)
> Contains introduction by Hughes on simplicity in poetry.

The Way to Write, by J. Fairfax and J. Moat (Elm Tree Books, 1981).
> Contains foreword by Hughes.

The Achievement of Ted Hughes, ed Keith Sagar (Manchester University Press, 1983).
> Contains 30 uncollected poems.

William Golding: The Man and his Books, ed. John Carey (Faber, 1986).
> Contains Hughes' essay 'Baboons and Neanderthals: A Rereading of *The Inheritors*'.

The Paris Review, 134, Spring 1995.
> Hughes interviewed by Drue Heinz.

The Guardian, 5 July 1997.
> Contains Hughes' article on hunting: 'The Hart of the Mystery'.

The Daily Telegraph, 31 October 1998.
> Hughes interviewed by Eilat Negev.

Wild Steelhead and Salmon, Winter 1999.
> Hughes interviewed by Tom Pero. Extract reprinted in *The Guardian*, 9 January1999.

Critical Studies

Bentley, Paul, *The Poetry of Ted Hughes: Language, Illusion and Beyond* (Longman, 1998).

Bishop, Nicholas, *Re-making Poetry: Ted Hughes and a New Critical Psychology* (Harvester Wheatsheaf, 1991).

Dyson, A.E., ed., *Three Contemporary Poets: Thom Gunn, Ted Hughes and R.S. Thomas* (Macmillan, 1990).

Faas, Ekbert, *Ted Hughes: The Unaccommodated Universe* (Black Sparrow Press, 1980).

Gammage, Nick, ed., *The Epic Poise: A Celebration of Ted Hughes* (Faber and Faber, 1999).

Gifford, Terry, and Roberts, Neil, *Ted Hughes: A Critical Study* (Faber and Faber, 1981).

Hirschberg, Stuart, *Myth in the Poetry of Ted Hughes* (Barnes and Noble, 1981).

Moulin, Joanny, *Ted Hughes: La Langue Rémunerée* (L'Harmattan, Paris 1999).

—— ed. *Livre Ted Hughes: New Selected Poems* (Editions du Temps, Paris 1999).

Robinson, Craig, *Ted Hughes as Shepherd of Being* (Macmillan, 1989).

Sagar, Keith, *The Art of Ted Hughes* (Cambridge University Press, 1975; extended edn 1978).

—— *Ted Hughes* (Profile Books, 1981).

—— ed., *The Achievement of Ted Hughes* (Manchester University Press, 1983).

—— ed., *The Challenge of Ted Hughes* (Macmillan, 1994).

Scigaj, Leonard M., *The Poetry of Ted Hughes* (University of Iowa Press, 1986).

—— *Ted Hughes* (Twayne, 1991).

—— ed., *Critical Essays on Ted Hughes* (G.K. Hall, 1992).

Skea, Ann, *Ted Hughes: The Poetic Quest* (University of New England Press, Australia, 1994).

Stella, Maria, *L'Inno e L'Enigma: Sagio su Ted Hughes* (Bibliotheca Ianua, Rome, 1988).

Uroff, Margaret, *Sylvia Plath and Ted Hughes* (University of Illinois Press, 1979).

Walder, Dennis, *Ted Hughes* (Open University Press, 1987).

West, Thomas, *Ted Hughes* (Methuen, 1985).

Other Books Cited

Attar, Farid Ud-din, *The Conference of the Birds* (Penguin, 1984).

Bachelard, Gaston, *Water and Dreams* (Dallas, 1983).

Baring, Anne, and Jules Cashford, *The Myth of the Goddess* (Viking, 1991).

Beer, John, *Blake's Visionary Universe* (Manchester University Press, 1969).

Blake, William, *Complete Writings*, ed. Geoffrey Keynes (Oxford University Press, 1971).

Bly, Robert, Interview in Roger Housden, *Fire in the Heart* (Element, 1990).

Brown, Norman O., *Life Against Death* (Wesleyan University Press, 1970).

Campbell, Joseph, *The Hero with a Thousand Faces* (Princeton University

Press, 1972).

—— *The Masks of God* (*Primitive Mythology, Occidental Mythology, Oriental Mythology, Creative Mythology*) (Souvenir Press, 1973–4).

—— *Myths to Live By* (Souvenir Press, 1973).

Camus, Albert, *The Myth of Sisyphus* (Hamish Hamilton, 1955).

Carey, John, ed., *William Golding: The Man and his Books* (Faber and Faber, 1986).

Carlyle, Thomas, 'Characteristics' in *The Norton Anthology of English Literature*, 4th edn, vol. 2, (1979).

Castaneda, Carlos, *Tales of Power* (Hodder and Stoughton, 1974; Penguin, 1976).

Conquest, Robert, ed. *New Lines* (Macmillan, 1956).

Finnegan, Ruth, ed. *The Penguin Book of Oral Poetry* (Penguin, 1978).

Frazer, J.G., *The Golden Bough*, abridged edn (Macmillan, 1957).

Graves, Robert, *The White Goddess* (Faber, 1961).

Harner, Michael J., *Hallucinogens and Shamanism* (Oxford University Press, 1973).

Havel, Vaclav, *Living in Truth* (Faber, 1987).

Jung, C.G., *Aion* (*Collected Works* vol. 9 ii) (Routledge and Kegan Paul, 1959).

—— *Psychological Types* (Bollingen, 1974).

—— *The Spirit of Man* (*Collected Works* vol. 15) (Routledge and Kegan Paul, 1966).

Kerényi, C., *The Gods of the Greeks* (Thames and Hudson, 1951).

—— *Prometheus* (Pantheon, 1963).

Laing, R.D., *The Politics of Experience* (Penguin, 1967).

Lawrence, D.H., *Apocalypse*, ed. Mara Kalnins (Cambridge University Press, 1980).

—— *Complete Short Novels*, ed. Keith Sagar and Melissa Partridge (Penguin, 1982).

—— *Phoenix* (Penguin, 1978).

—— *The Rainbow*, ed. John Worthen (Penguin, 1981).

—— *Study of Thomas Hardy*, ed. Bruce Steele (Cambridge University Press, 1985).

—— *The Symbolic Meaning*, ed. Armin Arnold (Centaur Press, 1962).

Levi-Strauss, Claude, *Structural Anthropology*, (Penguin, 1963).

Lorca, Federico Garcia, 'The Theory and Function of the Duende', in *Lorca*, ed. J.L. Gili (Penguin, 1960).

Lowell, Robert, Foreword to *Ariel*, by Sylvia Plath (Harper and Row, 1966).

Matthiessen, F.O., *The Achievement of T.S. Eliot* (Oxford University Press, Galaxy edn, 1959).

Nietzsche, Friedrich, *The Birth of Tragedy* (Anchor, 1956).

—— *A Nietzsche Reader*, ed. R.J. Hollindale (Penguin, 1977).

Plath, Sylvia, *Collected Poems*, ed. Ted Hughes (Faber, 1981).

—— *Johnny Panic and the Bible of Dreams*, ed. Ted Hughes (Faber 1977).

—— *The Journals of Sylvia Plath*, ed. Ted Hughes and Frances McCullough (Dial, 1982).

—— *Letters Home*, ed. Aurelia Schober Plath (Harper, 1975).

Ponge, 'The Silent World is Our Only Homeland', in Beth Archer, *The Voice of Things* (McGraw-Hill, 1974).

Redgrove, Peter, *The Black Goddess* (Bloomsbury, 1987).

—— *The Moon Disposes: Poems, 1954–1987* (Secker and Warburg, 1987).

Stein, Walter, ed. *Peace on Earth: The Way Ahead* (Sheed and Ward, 1966).

Stevenson, A., *Bitter Fame* (Viking, 1989).

Thomas, Dylan, *Collected Letters*, ed. P. Ferris (Macmillan, 1985).

Von Eschenbach, Wolfram, *Parzival* (Vintage Books, 1961).

INDEX OF WORKS BY TED HUGHES

GENERAL INDEX